A
Poet's
Rage

Understanding Shakespeare through authorship studies

Edited by William Boyle

Forever Press

Somerville, Massachusetts

Published by

Forever Press
PO Box 263
Somerville MA 02143

ISBN 978-0-9835027-5-3

©2013
New England Shakespeare Oxford Library

First printing, August 2013

The cover image is Thomas Moran's
The Angry Sea (1911). Cover design by Forever Press.

Table of Contents

·

Contributors

Charles Beauclerk: A writer, lecturer and graduate of Hertford College, Oxford, he is a descendant of Edward de Vere. He founded the De Vere Society in Great Britain and was its president for 25 years. He has delivered papers at numerous authorship conferences since 1991, and in the early 1990s travelled extensively in the US and Canada delivering hundreds of lectures on the Shakespeare authorship question. He is the author of *Nell Gwyn: Mistress to a King, Shakespeare's Lost Kingdom: the true story of Shakespeare and Elizabeth* and *Piano Man: A Life of John Ogdon.*

Charles Boyle: An actor, director, author and playwright who is a graduate of Lesley University in Cambridge (MA). His work has appeared on stage in New York, Boston and Chicago. He has been involved in the Shakespeare authorship question since 1980, served on the Board of Trustees of the Shakespeare Oxford Society for many years, and has presented papers at both Oxfordian and Shakespeare Association of America conferences. His book *Another Hamlet* is a fictionalized account of British actor Leslie Howard's Oxfordian sympathies.

William Boyle: A librarian who is a graduate of Lake Forest College and SUNY-Albany. He has been involved in the Shakespeare authorship debate for more than 30 years. In the 1990s he founded and managed some of the earliest websites on the authorship question, organized several authorship conferences, and edited the newsletters for two Oxfordian societies from 1995-2005. Since 2005 Boyle manages Shakespeare Online Authorship Resources (SOAR), a database of Shakespeare authorship related materials, and edits and publishes authorship-related books through the Forever Press.

William Plumer Fowler (1900-1993): A lawyer and recognized poet (he composed 141 sonnets in his lifetime), and a graduate of Dartmouth College and the Harvard Law School. A life-long "student-scholar" of the works of the poet-dramatist William Shakespeare, Fowler was for 12 years, prior to 1984, president of The Shakespeare Club of Boston. In 1986 he published his master work on the Oxfordian thesis, *Shakespeare Revealed in Oxford's Letters.*

James Daniel Gaynor: A senior Math and Chemistry major at the University of Portland in Portland, Oregon. He is serving his fifth year as an intern at the Shakespeare Authorship Research Centre at Concordia University under the direction of Professor Daniel Wright. He has been a presenter at various conferences, including the Shakespeare Authorship Studies Conference, and his scientific work has been published by the Royal Society of Chemistry in Great Britain.

Alex McNeil: Holds a BA from Yale and a J.D., *cum laude*, from Boston College, and served as the Court Administrator of the Massachusetts Appeals Court for 37 years. He has been involved in the Oxfordian theory of the Shakespeare authorship question for more than 20 years, is one of the founding members of the Shakespeare Fellowship and editor of their newsletter *Shakespeare Matters*. He also authored a reference book on television, *Total Television*, which went through four editions from 1980 to 1996.

Hank Whittemore: A former journalist and the author of nine nonfiction books including *The Super Cops* and *CNN: the Inside Story*. A graduate of Notre Dame, he has been a radio news director, a professional actor, an Emmy Award-winning documentary writer and a contributor of many articles to PARADE and other magazines. In 1998, after a decade of research, he had an insight that led in 2005 to *The Monument*, a radical explanation of the meaning and purpose of *Shakespeares Sonnets*. Since then he has performed a 90-minute one-man show entitled *Shakespeare's Treason*, based on the Monument theory, while continuing his Oxfordian research and writing.

Daniel L. Wright: Holds a BA and an MA from Valparaiso University, an M.Div from the Lutheran School of Theology at Chicago, and a PhD in English from Ball State University. He is Professor of English Literature and Director of the Shakespeare Authorship Research Centre at Concordia University in Portland, Oregon. He also founded and directs the annual Shakespeare Authorship Studies Conference at Concordia, now in its 18th year. Professor Wright has published numerous articles and reviews in both Stratfordian and Oxfordian publications and in such mainstream publications as *Harper's, Renaissance and Reformation, The Sixteenth Century Journal, The Southern Literary Journal, The Journal of Evolutionary Psychology,* et al. His 1993 book, *The Anglican Shakespeare: Elizabethan Orthodoxy in the Great Histories*, was based upon his doctoral dissertation.

Introduction

Understanding Shakespeare

*"When a man's verses cannot be understood, nor a man's
good wit seconded with the forward child, understanding,
it strikes a man more dead than a great reckoning
in a little room."* —Touchstone, *As You Like It (III.iii)*

*"Every rule of objectivity requires that an author first
be understood as he understood himself; without
that, the work is nothing but what we make of it."*
—Alan Bloom with Harry V. Jaffa, *Shakespeare's Politics.*

The idea for this book first came about in the winter of
2013, after engaging in yet another round-robin battle on a
discussion board over the Prince Tudor theory, a
movement inside the Oxfordian movement in the
Shakespeare authorship debate. This theory has been around
almost as long as the Oxfordian movement itself, and it generates
as much heated debate as any battle between Stratfordians and
anti-Stratfordians. [see Appendix A for some background about
the theory] The fallout from the 2011 Hollywood movie
Anonymous (which incorporated some aspects of the theory), plus
the current state of the debate in 2013—with yet more books
coming out from all sides, including the Shakespeare Birthplace
Trust in Stratford with their *Shakespeare Beyond Doubt*—is all
around us. For those of us who have been around for a while it is,
really, just some more of the "same old, same old." It's been this
way for 150 years and counting. All one needs to carry on is a
very thick skin and tons of patience.

The purpose of this book is to demonstrate that the existence
of both the Prince Tudor theory and the Oxfordian theory (and, for
that matter, of all theories about the Shakespeare authorship) is
really one and the same, which is to understand Shakespeare's

verse. It is as simple as that—to understand. But, worthy as that goal is, in the end one still must have some correct answers in place in order to achieve it—the correct author, the correct time and place in which he lived and wrote, and finally, the correct story about what he was up to in his life and in his writing. If any of these answers are incorrect, then one will come up short of fully understanding his verse. And, contrary to what some may think, a lot of the best evidence we have to that end is in the author's body of work—his verse—truly his last will and testament.

The articles selected to appear in this volume do, I believe, meet all these requirements. Not everyone agrees, and certainly within the Oxfordian movement not everyone agrees. There is a deep division among Oxfordians over this theory, literally a schism. Feelings run high, and the stakes are high.

These articles have all been written over the last twenty-five years and for the most part are ones that I myself have either written or edited for Oxfordian publications, and/or worked on in collaboration with the authors. This selection is not meant to be representative of all that has been written over these years, nor to present a point-counterpoint debate about each aspect of the authorship issue, or even of the Prince Tudor theory. The purpose here is to demonstrate how the explanatory power of any theory can itself indicate that that theory may be on the right track. For those within the Oxfordian movement who have promoted this theory as being the best answer to how and why the authorship mystery came to be in the first place, this explanatory power is one of the theory's strongest points.

First, to understand what is meant by the Prince Tudor theory, let me borrow some words from my contribution to this collection (Chapter 7, "Unveiling the Sonnets"), written to explain how the Sonnets are intimately connected to their author and how understanding who the author was and what he was doing can then "unveil" the sonnets themselves, and the whole hidden story that drives the authorship debate:

> The notion of the royal allusions [in the Sonnets] being real was introduced into the Oxfordian movement in the 1930s by B. M. Ward and Percy Allen. Their theory was that the Poet / Fair Youth relationship was not one of an older lover and a younger lover but rather one of father and son—and that the son was a prince, seen by

the father as the rightful heir to Elizabeth (the Dark Lady).

This theory—generally referred to among contemporary Oxfordians as the "Prince Tudor" theory—has divided the Oxfordian movement ever since it was first proposed, not least because there seems to be no independent historical evidence for it, but also because it seems, to many, so outrageously "over the top," or "hopelessly romantic," or — worst of all—conspiratorial.

This theory of the Sonnets was aptly summed up by Charlton Ogburn, Jr.:

> We are left with a compelling question raised by the Sonnets. It is a question that is inescapable and one that traditional scholarship is resolved upon escaping at all costs ... How is it that the Poet of the Sonnets can—as he unmistakably does—address the fair youth as an adoring and deeply concerned father would address his son and as a subject would his liege-lord? (75)

The "royal" theory has been the source of much contention among Oxfordians over the past seventy years. The exact details of who may have slept with whom to create such a scenario we will leave to another day, but the import of demonstrating the "royal" theory, if it can be demonstrated, is crucial to the resolution of the Shakespeare Mystery, as this is the one issue that divides Oxfordian scholars more than any other contested issue within the Oxfordian community.

When we consider whether the Prince Tudor theory is "outrageous," we should keep in mind that Oxford himself (writing as Shakespeare four centuries ago) had the same thought. The lines in Sonnet 17 that are the source of this collection's title play with this concept:

> So should my papers, yellowed with their age,
> Be scorned, like old men of less truth than tongue,
> And your true rights be termed *a poet's rage*
> And stretched meter of an antique song. (9-12)

The real problem with postulating such a theory as being at the center of the authorship mystery has not been so much that the theory itself is outrageous, but rather that the "outrageous" events have already occurred—centuries ago—and a theory today trying to unravel that centuries-old mystery cannot help but be "outrageous" itself in trying to explain what was going on four centuries ago.

iii

So, if we can get beyond the outrage, the question then becomes whether the Prince Tudor theory does or does not inform our understanding of the Shakespeare works. The contributors to this collection would all say, "Yes, it does." In these essays one will find several distinct threads that illustrate this understanding. First, detailed examinations of the four major sets of poems that Shakespeare left us are prominent throughout—*Venus and Adonis*, *The Rape of Lucrece*, *Phoenix and Turtle*, and the *Sonnets*. This should not be surprising, because poetry is, after all, the most personal of writing, and most would agree it is more based on the real thoughts and feelings of the poet rather than drawing on or imitating source material.

The second most prominent feature of the collection is a view of several plays (*As You Like It, Troilus and Cressida, King John, The Tempest, Hamlet*), and how the author is present in each of them—illustrating how significant the author himself is as a "source" for his plays. This notion of there being an authorial presence in all the plays—as well as an authorial purpose—is quite controversial in all Shakespeare circles (Stratfordian and anti-Stratfordian), but it is a key, we believe, to understanding what is going on in all the plays.

Finally, we get to the most intriguing thing that all twelve essays in this collection have in common, and that is the authorship debate itself, both as the original author experienced it (and was shaped by it) four centuries ago, and as Oxfordians are experiencing it today. It is a continuing saga over what is true and what isn't and how in the world does anyone figure that out. How can one be true to oneself and to the truth (then and now) when lies are the coin of the realm (then and now)?

This last point is really the essence of what the authorship debate is all about: a search for the truth of what really happened four centuries ago, and the truth about the author's own story in that distant time. How close can we get to the true story, and will that true story inform our understanding of what he wrote?

It is, after all, Oxford's *story* that made him Shakespeare. And from the Prince Tudor point of view that story is that he was an *internally exiled* peer of the realm—a prince denied his birthright, made to forfeit his name, condemned to anonymity and oblivion, unseated and denied by his own family, cast into the darkness of banishment and enforced silence.

What the Stratfordians don't get, however (and, for that matter, many anti-Stratfordians don't get either) is that all the evidence about Shakespeare's education, skills, life in the theatre—even facts about his love life, his sex life and his marriages—all that still leave us short of understanding why he wrote what he wrote. Surely there is more to the Shakespeare story than making a buck (as some Stratfordians would have it) or showing off to the court that he's better than Philip Sidney (as some Oxfordians would have it). No, the Shakespeare story must have been more than how smart he was, or how skilled, or how well-traveled, etc. All these basic attributes of life experience, education and worldliness certainly give any candidate for Shakespeare the technical *capacity* to become Shakespeare, but those attributes are still not the *essence* of Shakespeare.

The view of Oxford as Shakespeare as shared by the contributors to this book is that he always dissembled. While his contemporaries (from Lyly and Marlowe, to Middleton, Dekker, or Jonson, to name but a few) could all stay above the surface (using their own names), a hidden Shakespeare had to dive into the darkest waters of concealment. Why? And why would the only power in England that mattered—the State—care what HE (Oxford as Shakespeare) might have to say? The real authorship mystery, accordingly, is not the fact of the mask "Shake-speare"— it is *why* the mask?

"Give a man a mask, and he will tell you the truth," Oscar Wilde revealingly once said. It is Shakespeare's truth, as much as Shakespeare the man, which we are seeking to discover here. The Prince Tudor theory shows us—as the contributors to this book are persuaded—that the answer to that question "Why?" revolves around the fate of Elizabethan England, the succession to the Crown, and the author's own strong interest in that fate, even to the point of his apparently having more than just an interest, but perhaps even an actual stake, in the outcome.

The truth of Oxford's story is, finally, the truth of England's history—and our own.

William Boyle
Editor

Foreword

Why be Shakespeare?

James Daniel Gaynor

"You can know the name of a bird in all the languages of the world, but when you're finished, you'll know absolutely nothing whatever about the bird ... So let's look at the bird and see what it's doing—that's what counts. I learned very early the difference between knowing the name of something and knowing something."
— Richard Feynman, physicist

Writers invariably have something vital and personal to say. They have zeal and purpose. Is there anywhere a writer, whether a novelist, playwright, poet, essayist, etc, who writes unmoved by that which chiefly shapes his life, or focuses on things other than his most personal anxieties, knowledge and concerns?

During my high school years I was taught by my teachers that Shakespeare, though a merchant in a backwater and all-but-bookless, largely-Catholic town, became—almost overnight—a Renaissance and Humanist poet to shame all courtier poets, the chief wordsmith of the English language and the creator of works of the most refined artistry. We were taught that this occurred because he wanted to make some quick cash in the public theatre. This story, though, had never seemed to me very plausible. After all, that is not how any of us creatively develop our particular skills or geniuses.

Our lives become narratives that can be read in our achievements. Our accomplishments are stamped with the themes of our passions and the years spent in the formative domains of our expertise. I suspect, for example, that no one could read the most recent paper of mine published by the Royal Society of Chemistry and come away with any conclusion other than that I was a research scientist intensely interested in nanotechnology and its scientific promise. I wouldn't credit someone's declaration, after such an exposure, that I was a deep-sea fisherman, or a rodeo clown, or a robber baron. The simple fact is that what one does in one's life is what one is.

In the same way, it became clear to me that, whatever else Shakespeare was, he was not a man consumed by a love of money, even though the traditional story of his life suggests a scheming businessman. No, the poems and plays of Shakespeare reveal a man of generous aristocratic temper, deeply read in music, art, the law, and the languages of ancient Rome and Greece. His works are suffused in the disciplines of Renaissance learning. And clearly he was a man passionately concerned—apparently in the most personal way—with the future of the kingdom and the threat of its impending dissolution, due to the recklessness of a vain and aging queen who, by her inaction, was abdicating her primary duty as Monarch to settle the matter of who should succeed her.

In my studies of Shakespeare as an undergraduate at Concordia University I learned how the civil wars that had torn England asunder in the fourteenth and fifteenth centuries, (until the coming of the Tudors) provide the basic historical context for most of Shakespeare's chronicle plays. And further, in looking beneath the bloody surface of these plays to see what the author was doing in them, I've discovered the essence of what makes Shakespeare the true "shaker of the spear"—a real writer with a real agenda, a trumpeter of political alarm, a disrupter of complacency, and a would-be inspiration to action against the moral bankruptcy of a failed state.

So, once Edward de Vere, 17th Earl of Oxford, was presented to me as this author "Shake-speare," I knew I had found just such a person, a writer possessed, in a deeply personal way, with intense and personal distress about the most dangerous and volatile political issues of his day—issues about which few, without a literary shield, dared to write.

As I learned more about Oxford more things became clear. In surveying the final decades of the 16th century one can see that Oxford was indeed one man before 1593 (with a long, well-documented biography, a sort of proto-Hamlet), and then, with the publications of *Venus and Adonis* and *The Rape of Lucrece* in 1593 and 1594, he literally became another. He burst upon the scene (seemingly from nowhere) in 1593, a particularly perilous time in English history. It was as if he had—like a late sixteenth-century Clark Kent—popped into a literary phone booth as one man only to emerge as another. He christened himself as *"Shakespeare"* (his new "invention") and forever thereafter tied his name to the man to whom he would dedicate all that he ever would dedicate—Henry Wriothesley, the 3rd Earl of Southampton, whom he declared in the *Sonnets* to be not only his "lord" but his "Sovereign."

Of all the dangerous political issues about which Shakespeare now wrote, he did so most keenly and obsessively about the terrifying prospect of an aborted succession—a dynastic plunge into an abyss. Absent Queen Elizabeth's provision of an heir, England was going to fall (shades of *Hamlet*) into the hands of an alien power, and we can then see that this political danger most likely forced him to use a pseudonym, and that then—in a cruel, ironic twist of fate—these same dangers forced the pseudonym to live on forever while the true author was erased from history.

This Oxfordian point of view, represented by the writers of the essays that follow in this book, is what made me truly realize that Shakespeare was indeed—like all great men I have learned about—the embodiment of his own often-tortured sensibilities and tempest-tossed time. He was real. Writers, if they matter, reveal the underside of their times; they open otherwise-closeted aspects of their often-tortured souls and illuminate the secrets of their cultures. How could Shakespeare, the *greatest* of humanity's writers, not do the same? Are we truly expected to believe that this man was simply a money-grubbing purveyor of politically sterile entertainments, that he had nothing to say about the future of his native land and who should next wear the Crown, just at the very time when the national anxiety over the irresolution of those all-important questions was at its height?

Sometimes, in the frenzy to focus on the question of who Shakespeare was, we forget that the real question about Shakespeare is *why he had to be*. The authorship questioner's task is, primarily, not so much searching for a name, but rather searching for the Shakespeare *story*—the story of what one man was actually doing with his life all those years ago, and of how and *why* he became the timeless, iconic "Soul of the Age." The attempt to answer this all important question is what—in my mind at least—makes the whole authorship quest so compelling. After all, it is one thing to know that Shakespeare was Oxford, but it is quite another to know *why* Oxford was Shakespeare.

James Gaynor is an undergraduate student of Chemistry at the University of Portland and the assistant to Professor Daniel Wright, Professor of English and Director of the Shakespeare Authorship Research Centre at Concordia University in Portland, Oregon. He is currently serving his fifth year as a SARC intern. In 2013 he had the distinct honor to be published, as an undergraduate student, in the internationally read Royal Society of Chemistry publication Journal of Materials Chemistry B.

Chapter 1

Lessons from a Seminar

Charles Boyle

This article was first published in the Shakespeare Oxford Newsletter
*(Summer 1996). The unidentified eminent Stratfordian professor
with whom Boyle speaks is Prof. David Bevington,
then the President of the SAA.*

This Los Angeles World Congress [1996] is the fourth Shakespeare Association of America conference I have attended. As a member I have delivered seminar papers at the previous two. Last year's was on the role of the courtier fool Touchstone in *As You Like It*. Later I learned that members of my seminar had met beforehand and agreed among themselves to ignore anything I said.

My seminar topics this year revolved around the 16th century theatre world. My paper described a production of *Twelfth Night* from an Elizabethan point of view, seeing it as a political satire of the Court, with the Queen as Olivia and Sir Christopher Hatton sketched in the character of Malvolio.

I interpreted some of the more obscure jests along these lines, looking for the original laugh. In the process I suggested the Fool, like Hamlet, was the central character (though often dismissed as if peripheral, which only captures half his meaning). Perhaps he had been modeled on Oxford? That was as far as I went.

I didn't bring up authorship directly but I did emphasize the play's political and personal reality. But with Stratfordians you generally find that not only won't they talk about the author as

1

real, they won't talk about what he was writing about as real either.

The paper I was assigned for special review also concerned the Fool in *Twelfth Night*. It suggested that the Fool was not so much the creation of Shakespeare as it was the witty actor who must have played him, Robert Armin. In this gregarious and likeable paper I saw everything that infuriated me about Stratfordianism. Of course I understood his problem. Robert Armin is a more real and interesting person to him than the author.

But still, the casual assassination permitted the "one opinion is as good as another" courtesy, which allows them to whittle away at this poor author, making him ever more insignificant and irrelevant to his own genius. And who can explain "genius" anyway? Why try? In seminar after seminar I've sat through endless, circling talk that never made a point that had the courage of conviction.

So when I was called upon to respond to this other paper I was angry. I didn't act angry but anger was driving me. I knew I couldn't discuss authorship directly. Experience has taught me that if you do everyone groans and throws up their collective hands.

So I went on and on about reality without coming to my real point until an eminent Stratfordian professor in the audience started yelling that I was "boring, boring, boring!" and talking to scholars like they were fools and that I should just shut up!

I protested I had only one more thing to add anyway, which was true enough, but pointless. The chair of the seminar asked me to stop and, half out of spite, I never said another word.

Yet I went over and over the uproar for two days afterwards, trying to figure some tactful way to have made my major point— human identity matters—without giving offense. But each strategy I devised felt like defeat.

Later at one of the conference functions I was speaking with another eminent Stratfordian professor. We acknowledged a personal liking for each other and a mutual regard for our love of Shakespeare.

He mentioned the awful reports he had heard of my seminar.

I told him I truly regretted what had happened. He shook his head sadly and told me I had burned a lot of bridges there. I was genuinely taken aback. Bridges? I was unaware I had any bridges. Except for him, mum's been the word to me. I mentioned the plan last year to ignore me. He seemed to be aware of it and nodded with grave concern.

So what was to be done? We agreed the Authorship Question mattered and that indeed there was a tangible truth involved. Some real individual actually sat down and wrote these lines. In the simple question of who he was one of us was right and the other wrong. I remembered a question put to Norrie Epstein, author of *The Friendly Shakespeare,* at the 1993 Boston Shakespeare Oxford Society Conference. She had expressed ambivalence about the traditional attribution but also a deep personal and professional respect for the orthodox professors who had been her friends and mentors. She would not attack their conclusions.

Someone finally asked her what piece of evidence would ever convince the Stratfordian establishment they were wrong. She answered that she didn't think there was any evidence that could convince them. It wasn't a matter of evidence but of faith. They Believed. Case closed. You were better off trying to talk the Pope out of the Virgin Birth. I asked my friend if he thought what she said was true. He smiled and nodded in a serious but friendly manner. Yes, he said, probably it was. He particularly liked the religious metaphor. We were like two churches. His candor made a strong impact. Suddenly I realized I didn't want to spend the rest of my life arguing with Stratfordians.

Most of what I know about Shakespeare I learned from Stratfordians. They've done some of the best work and still do. It's just that lacking a real author in the flesh and blood sense—who ever gave a tinker's damn about the Stratford man?—they have no unifying authorial voice to test their theories against.

Authorship itself has become just another theory. Which isn't right. I'm a reality, you're a reality. Let Shakespeare be a reality too. Stratfordians are intelligent and informed. But this case represents a kind of blindness they've been talked into by their priesthood. Why make yourself crazy banging your head against it? At this point I'd rather learn more about Shakespeare's motives, about the life of Oxford and the true history of Tudor England, the age that set the stage for the world we live in now.

No, I don't want to argue anymore (though I know I will). I would rather talk Shakespeare with the professors and Oxford with those who haven't fallen in love with Shakespeare yet. It would even be fun to build a movement so prosperous and powerful it made the Oxford story famous throughout the world—and then let the world decide.

Chapter 2

Writing History

Facts are facts, but interpretation is all

This article was first published in the Shakespeare Oxford Newsletter
*(Winter 1997). It was published as by "The Editors," who in a
later issue of the newsletter were identified as: William Boyle,
Charles Burford, [Beauclerk], and Charles Boyle.*

In covering the Minneapolis Conference [1996], the last issue of the Newsletter reported on the "Prince Tudor" controversy [see Appendix A for an explanation of this theory and its role in the authorship debate], an ongoing debate within the Society between proponents and detractors of the proposition that the 3rd Earl of Southampton was the royal son of Elizabeth and Oxford. Since then, all Society members have received a copy of Gary Goldstein's Autumn 1996 issue of *The Elizabethan Review*, in which Diana Price, in an article entitled "Rough Winds do Shake," attempts to deal the death-blow to the controversial theory. At first glance, she might seem to have succeeded.

The debate has also been a recent feature of the Oxfordian internet discussion group "Phaeton," where the argument has begun to revolve around definitions of evidence—what is, what isn't, and who judges the difference. The present discussion was sparked principally by the following claim made by Price in her "Rough Winds" article:

...the Tudor Rose theory is one of many conjectural interpretations of the Shakespeare canon, and interpretive evidence does not carry the same weight as documentary evidence.

Chief among those Phaetonites who have taken exception to this claim are Mark Anderson and Roger Stritmatter, whose work on Oxford's Geneva Bible has involved them in a similar debate with Stratfordians over what constitutes legitimate evidence. It is Price's faith in the infallibility of documentary evidence and its superiority over so-called interpretive evidence that has persuaded Anderson and Stritmatter that her article is based upon a false premise.

"Let's not forget," wrote Anderson, "that by these standards the Oxfordian theory loses much, if not all, of its persuasive force. Looney did not solve the authorship problem by means of 'documentary evidence.' He looked at the works and asked what they tell us about the author and the life he lived. And it was that investigation and not an examination of the documentary evidence that led Whitman to conclude that, 'one of the wolfish earls or some born descendant and knower might seem to be the true author of these amazing works.'"

In other words, Looney did something considered unscholarly by Stratfordians: he used the works of Shakespeare as evidence— evidence which, as "fiction," cannot be considered "documentary." Thus, the father of Oxfordianism himself made strong use of so-called interpretive evidence.

Roger Stritmatter followed up on this point by citing a passage from a section entitled "Interpretation in History" from historian Hayden-White's book *The Tropics of Discourse*:

Theorists of historiography generally agree that all historical narratives contain an irreducible and inexpugnable element of interpretation. The historian has to interpret his materials in order to construct the moving pattern of images in which the form of the historical process is to be mirrored. And this is because the historical record is both too full and too sparse. On the one hand, there are always more facts in the record than the historian can possibly include in his narrative representation of a given segment of the historical process. And so the historian must "interpret" his data by excluding certain facts from his account as irrelevant to his narrative purpose.

On the other hand, in his efforts to reconstruct 'what happened' in any given period of history, the historian inevitably must include in his narrative an account of some event or complex of events for which the facts that would permit a plausible explanation of its occurrence are lacking. And this means that the historian must 'interpret' his materials by filling in the gaps in his information on inferential or speculative grounds. A historical narrative is thus necessarily a mixture of adequately and inadequately explained events, a congeries of established and inferred facts, at once a representation that is an interpretation that passes for an explanation of the whole process mirrored in the narrative.

In short, what this rather Polonian narrative means is that interpretation is an unavoidable part of the process of writing history. There is really no such thing as interpretive evidence, as all reported facts and opinions have to be interpreted by the historian. Even the "official record" is still only somebody's individual interpretation of what happened at a given time, and is further "distorted" when filtered through the historian's lens.

As Oxfordians struggle to develop a concise and coherent theory of the hows and whys of the authorship problem, they must be prepared to make responsible speculation a part of their overall theory. Indeed, it should be remembered that the very existence of the authorship controversy is the result of an interpretive process, and were it the case that "documented facts" alone hold validity, the Stratford story would prove unassailable.

Over the last two centuries many have noticed how significantly the works of Shakespeare seem both to contradict and at the same time supplement the official, documentary account of the times. For the Shakespeare canon itself is a richly revealing documentary record that deserves to be considered as a key piece of evidence in elucidating the story of the times. Whether one calls it documentary or interpretive evidence is irrelevant given Hayden-White's axiom that all evidence used for historical purposes is *ipso facto* interpretive.

7

Because Stratfordians maintain such a blinkered reverence for "documented facts," they end up with a bizarre array of unrelated and uninterpretable events, which not only leave a jumble of unanswered questions in their wake, but which fail to yield a coherent picture of Elizabethan society and politics. However hard they try to join up the dots, they can never produce a meaningful creature. It's hardly surprising, then, that they insist on the inadmissibility of the Shakespeare canon as evidence, for if one thing above all gives the lie to the two-dimensional Cecilo-Stratfordian worldview, in which politics and literature are separate planets, it's "the abstracts and brief chronicles of the time."

The way Stratfordians deal with Francis Meres illustrates the point very well. In his *Palladis Tamia*, Meres makes it crystal clear that Shakespeare and Oxford are two different men, for they are both mentioned in the same list of those who have excelled at comedy. Stratfordians are eager and happy to take him at his word. But in doing this, they must leave a whole host of very basic and important questions unanswered, such as who is Francis Meres, what is the meaning of *Palladis Tamia*, why was it published in 1598, and why is the passage about Shakespeare so obviously a cuckoo in the nest? If, on the other hand, these questions are properly considered, the conclusion is inescapable that here is a document whose meaning lives between the lines (and thus demands to be interpreted), and which is part of the overall effort to conceal Oxford's authorship of the Shakespeare canon. In such a world, politics and literature are inseparable.

Although the historian of the Elizabethan age has at his disposal an apparent wealth of surviving documents from the period, he is also confronted by a conspicuous absence of some key documents. Historian Hugh Ross Williamson, in research notes appended to his 1959 book *The Crown and the Conspirators*, made several observations that are germane to our discussion of evidence. Here are a couple of particularly relevant ones:

No one who has studied the Domestic State Papers can doubt that all of them went through Cecil's hands as soon as he became Elizabeth's Secretary of State on Mary's death and that he weeded them out with great thoroughness. (p. 216).

While this observation refers to Queen Mary's reign, it is surely equally true of her sister Elizabeth's reign. Here too the Cecils, father and son, were careful to leave behind a thoroughly sanitized documentary record for future historians to ponder. Williamson goes on to note the importance of ambassadorial reports in filling gaps in the official record. In considering Queen Mary's relationship with Elizabeth, Williamson stresses the importance of dealing with the issue of Elizabeth's supposed bastardy (i.e., that she was the daughter of Anne Boleyn and Mark Smeaton, not of Anne and Henry VIII). He writes that

… the first requisite for understanding Mary's attitude to Elizabeth is to know whether she thought of her as a sister or not. And in this (which is quite distinct from the question of whether her belief was or was not in accord with the facts) there is no room for any genuine doubt. Mary believed that Elizabeth was not her father's daughter. (p. 218).

These are two critically important observations for those living in the house of mirrors known as the authorship debate. They assist us in understanding that it's often impossible to draw a meaningful distinction between what is belief and what is fact, and that one can't rely for the truth on a documentary record that has been deliberately sanitized. For there can be little doubt that over the 40 years that he was Elizabeth's chief counselor, Lord Burghley plucked many a document from the state archives, leaving behind a very personal, not to say willful, version of the truth. It's also likely that the most significant document to escape such a fate was the Shakespeare canon, much as the grand possessors and grand censors might have wished otherwise.

The works of Shakespeare are, then, as much a historical and political document, as they are a literary one. If we fail to appreciate this, we run the risk of creating a new quasi-

Stratfordian orthodoxy with Oxford substituted for Shakespeare, but with all the other political icons such as the Virgin Queen left intact. We will thus have failed in our duty to interpret the works, and the authorship question will be reduced to an act of legerdemain; a cheap trick instead of a philosophical quest. In such a scenario "Oxford is Shakespeare" becomes a meaningless statement, for it implies nothing beyond the all too familiar cover-story.

The Prince Tudor theory is itself a metaphor for the whole authorship question. Here again, the Shakespeare canon constitutes important evidence and helps us in our interpretation of the "historical record," which states that the Virgin Queen was indeed a virgin queen as unequivocally as it states that Shakespeare was the Stratford actor.

In her article "Rough Winds do Shake," Diana Price unwittingly demonstrates the pitfalls of taking the documentary-evidence-is-supreme high ground. They are most evident in her handling of the so-called crown signature[1] and her failure to deal with the political fallout of Oxford's death on June 24, 1604.[2]

Price dismisses the crown signature with the observation that the squiggles and dots above the center of the signature represent an earl's coronet while the horizontal line and seven dashes indicate the number seventeen. Thus Oxford was announcing to the world what everyone already knew, i.e. that he was the 17th Earl of Oxford. (The sort of behavior one would expect from a parvenu.) Because the fact that Oxford stopped using the crown signature when the Queen died in 1603 is irrelevant to Price's purpose—which is to scupper the Prince Tudor theory—she fails to mention it at all. In ignoring such an important piece of information, Price does what all the Stratfordians are forced to do: she creates a minefield of unexplained coincidences. This is the big danger of not attempting a theory to which all the facts can be accommodated.

Price creates even more coincidences around June 24, 1604, by opting to ignore the significance of James I's panic that day in rounding up Southampton and his followers (many of them survivors of the Essex rebellion). Nor does she find it significant that James I and Robert Cecil subsequently attempted to erase this event from history by leaving it blank in the official record. These things just happen to have happened.

In fact it is only through ambassadorial reports that we know about James's actions on this occasion, which confirms Hugh Ross Williamson's assertion that such reports are vital in piecing together the history of the time. Ironically, Diana Price makes very pregnant use of French ambassador Fenelon's reports in her attack upon the Prince Tudor theory. Clearly, some pieces of evidence are more convenient than others, while for some Oxfordians questioning the Virgin Queen's virginity is "an icon too far."

Interestingly, there is a debate today over an American icon that has some instructive parallels to the Shakespeare story. Documentary filmmaker Ken Burns (*The Civil War*, *Baseball*) has produced a 3-hour biography of Thomas Jefferson, which has drawn praise from professionals and laymen alike for its clear, uncompromising view of this contradictory figure of American history.

Although not an academic historian, in order to make his film Burns made use of all the documentary records of the time as well as the written histories and all the other available stories and anecdotes that contribute to the complex process known as "history."

In an article in the *Boston Globe* (Feb. 16 [1997]), several quotes from Burns about how he dealt with the historical record in this case resonate with echoes of the authorship battle and our various "fact versus fiction" disagreements. The article's author, Renee Graham, reviews the current state of Jeffersonian biography, in which revisionists trash him as a "slave owner" who is therefore "useless," while the old school continues to revere him as the author of the Declaration of Independence, and therefore as "god."

"It takes a discriminating eye," writes Graham, "to discern the many parts of Jefferson. Indeed historians on both sides of this fervent debate have played fast and loose with the facts, highlighting or discarding whatever details might further their particular stance."

One of the decisions Burns made was to include all the controversial and contradictory aspects of Jefferson's life, such as the matter of his supposed relationship with one of his slaves, Sally Hemmings, on whom he is said to have fathered several children. Burns took the view that it would have been irresponsible to ignore the Hemmings story, for although there is no direct documentary evidence to verify it, there is a good deal of anecdotal and circumstantial evidence.

In talking about the contradictions inherent in Jefferson's life, Burns was quoted as saying: "This guy could sit there and distill the essence of the Enlightenment into one remarkable sentence, and yet surrounding him are more than 200 human beings he never saw fit to free ... Jefferson is a convenient cipher because he is the author of our national creed. In many ways, he's the author of who we are."

It's a familiar phenomenon for students of the authorship question: the more of an icon someone becomes in his or her national culture, the greater seems to be the collective urge to turn that icon on a personal, human level into a cipher. It's happened to Shakspere-as-Shakespeare, and now there are those who wish to submit Oxford-as-Shakespeare to the same process. Burns concluding comment in the article was: "I make stories about our family drama; these are all our family members, and we don't get rid of our family members. But it's just as important to tell the truth."

While a documentary about an 18th-century American might seem out of place in our story about a 16th-century Englishman, it is clear that they are bound by a common thread. History is as much interpretation and story-telling as it is a laundry list of documented facts, and it is too early in the authorship debate for anyone to insist on a single interpretation of the facts in order to banish certain theories from further consideration.

In his book *The Shakespeare Controversy*, Warren Hope points out that when the true story of the authorship is known a curious inversion will take place: cranks will become respected authorities and respected authorities will become mere cranks. He could have gone further and said that history will become fiction, and fiction will become history.

As Mark Anderson suggested in his Phaeton posts, we all have to be willing to confront this complex problem of fact and fiction, evidence and interpretation; otherwise, it might be in order to keep repeating the following mantra, rather like Dorothy before she returned to Kansas (or like some Oxfordians with one foot still planted in Stratford town): "It's just a meaningless play, it's just a meaningless play, it's just a meaningless play..."

Endnotes

[1] The "Crown Signature" that Oxford used throughout his life has become an important element in the authorship debate, especially among those who promote the "Prince Tudor" version of the Oxfordian theory. Oxford began using this signature in his late teens (1569), and used it on every known document that he signed up until the death of Queen Elizabeth in 1603. He used a varied form of it in one final April 24th, 1603 letter to Robert Cecil on the eve of the Queen's funeral (the signature was "E. Oxenford" rather than "Edward Oxenford"), and then totally abandoned it two weeks later in a May 1603 letter to King James.

In Diana Price's 1996 article taking on the "Prince Tudor" theory one of the pieces of evidence she tries to debunk is the "Crown Signature," which she claims to have done by stating that top of the signature looks more like an earl's coronet than a crown, and that the seven hash marks at the bottom are not the number 7 (as in—maybe—Edward the Seventh?), but rather are meant to be understood as 10 + 7, meaning the 17th Earl of Oxford. But Price leaves out the fact that Oxford stopped using the signature upon the Queen's death in 1603, the one crucial fact that forms the basis for considering that the signature is significant and may be a signal of some sort about Oxford's relationship

13

with the Queen.

[2] Another crucial piece of evidence in the "Prince Tudor" version of the Oxfordian theory is the fact that on June 24th, 1604 (the day Edward de Vere died), Southampton and other survivors of the Essex Rebellion were rounded up by the government and held overnight, then released the next day. We know about this event since two different ambassadors wrote back to their home offices (French and Venetian) about it. They did so because they considered (rightly) that this was a significant event. Yet there is no official record anywhere in the Public Records Office or among the Cecil papers at Hatfield about this episode and the possible connection of the two events. (The event is discussed in G.P.V. Akrigg's *Shakespeare and the Earl of Southampton* on pages 140-141.)

That these two events occurred on the same day would seem to indicate that there is something special about the relationship between Oxford (i.e., Shakespeare) and Southampton (Shakespeare's dedicatee in *V&A* and *Lucrece*, and most likely the Fair Youth in the *Sonnets*). And the government clearly tried to cover it up by "disappearing" it from the record. This is an important lesson in how history is written, and how crucial facts can simply be hidden if the powers that be want it that way. Without the ambassadors' letters we would have no knowledge at all that this significant event had occurred. For Price to leave this fact out of her article on the "Prince Tudor" theory is quite telling, and an important lesson about how authorship history is written.

Chapter 3

The Author Invents Himself: Fernando Pessoa

Alex McNeil

This essay was originally published in Shakespeare Matters *(Winter 2003) under the title, "What's in a 'Nym?: pseudonyms, heteronyms and the case of Fernando Pessoa."*

If there's one thing Oxfordians can agree on, it's that Edward de Vere used an alias as a professional writer. His most famous alias, of course, was William Shakespeare. It's highly likely that he used other aliases as well during his career (I suppose he'd probably cringe at the use of the word "career").

We may disagree about whether "William Shakespeare" was a name made up by de Vere, or whether de Vere's imagination was somehow sparked after meeting a man from Stratford-on-Avon with a remarkably similar name. In any event, the name "William Shakespeare," as used by de Vere, can be termed a pseudonym, literally a "false name" (from the Greek *pseudes*, false and *onoma*, name). The use of pseudonyms, especially by those in the arts, is common. It may be worthwhile to catalog some of the reasons why persons use pseudonyms; perhaps the exercise will help us gain some insight on de Vere's reason or reasons for doing so. The list below is by no means inclusive, and in some cases the categories I've used may overlap with one another. Here's my highly arbitrary list of the Top Ten Reasons Why Artists Use Pseudonyms:

1) The real name may be too hard to spell, pronounce or remember. Performers are especially likely to choose a pseudonym, or even change their names legally, for this reason. Let's face it—Doris Day is easier to remember than Doris Kappelhoff, and Chad Everett has a nicer ring to it than Raymond Cramton.

2) The real name may be "too ethnic." The artist may want to appear as domestically mainstream as possible. Thus, in films Ramon Estevez becomes Martin Sheen, Raquel Tejada becomes Raquel Welch, and in literature Teodor Josef Konrad Korzeniowski becomes Joseph Conrad by retaining and anglicizing his middle names.

3) The artist may want to use the pseudonym to "make a statement." Whoever wrote the "Martin Mar-prelate" tracts (and there is reason to suspect Oxford here) chose that name for obvious reasons. In modern times, would the Sex Pistols have been the Sex Pistols without Johnny Rotten (nee John Lydon) and Sid Vicious (nee John Simon Ritchie)?

4) The artist may be making a joke. Edward Gorey used several anagrams of his name, thereby coming up with Dreary Wodge, Dogear Wryde, and Garrod Weedy.

5) The artist may be saluting a personal hero. Bob Zimmerman chose the name Bob Dylan because of his infatuation with Welsh poet Dylan Thomas.

6) Perhaps there are gender issues. Mary Ann Evans is far better known as George Eliot. Edward Stratemeyer considered the genders of his readers when he chose two pseudonyms—Franklin W. Dixon for the Hardy Boys stories and Carolyn Keene for the Nancy Drew mysteries. His daughter, Harriet Stratemeyer Adams, continued the pseudonyms when she took over after her father's death.

7) Two or more persons may be collaborating. Amandine

Dupin Dudevant collaborated with Jules Sandeau on her first two novels, which were published under the name of Jules Sand; when she wrote on her own, it was a short step to the new pseudonym of George Sand. More recently, the spicy novel *Naked Came the Stranger* was among the top ten most popular fiction works of 1969. Although it bore the name "Penelope Ashe" on the cover, it was actually the effort of a group of journalists, mostly from *Newsday,* each of whom took a turn writing a chapter.

8) The artist may be embarrassed to have his or her name associated with the work, usually because the work has been altered by others. Sci fi author Harlan Ellison (who used at least 25 pseudonyms) created a syndicated television series, *Starlost,* in 1973; he was so disappointed with the finished product that he had his name removed from the credits, substituting the moniker Cordwainer Bird instead.[1]

Another modern example is the name "Alan Smithee," coined by the Directors Guild of America in 1967 for use by a film director who can demonstrate to the Guild's satisfaction that a to-be-released motion picture is catastrophically inferior to the director's version. Over the past 35 years "Alan Smithee" has directed quite a few dramas, comedies and adventure films, all of them terrible. In one of showbiz's great ironies, Arthur Hiller (former DGA president) directed the 1997 comedy, "An Alan Smithee Film: *Burn Hollywood Burn!"* You guessed it—Hiller was so offended by the final cut that he successfully petitioned the Guild to remove his name and to give Alan Smithee yet another directing credit.

9) Legal or contractual reasons may prevent the artist from using his or her real name. John Wilson's teaching contract prohibited him from publishing fiction under his own name, so he put out his first novel using his two middle names— Anthony Burgess.[2]

A more shameful example comes from America's "Red Scare" in the late 1940s and early 1950s, when a number of actors, writers and directors were accused of being

Communists; those who refused to "name names" were "blacklisted," effectively prohibited from working in their respective professions. For actors and directors, who of course had to appear in person on the set, the blacklist was totally effective.[3]

Blacklisted writers, however, could employ a variety of methods to remain in their craft. Some used pseudonyms, some collaborated with another writer (who would get the sole on-screen credit but would presumably share the paycheck), some worked anonymously (e.g., rewriting a script submitted by a first writer, who would get sole credit), and some used "front men"—real persons who held themselves out as the ostensible authors of material written by the blacklisted writers.[4]

10) The writer may be writing outside of his or her milieu. When writing poetry, anthropologist Ruth Benedict used the name Anne Singleton; Ezra Pound wrote art criticism as B. H. Dias. Other examples exist.[5]

No doubt there are other reasons for the use of pseudonyms, but the ten listed above must be the most common. How many apply to de Vere / "Shakespeare"? It's hard to say. A few reasons can be ruled out easily; Oxford wasn't concerned that his own name was too hard to spell, or was too "ethnic," nor was he concerned with gender issues. We do not know of anyone named "William" or "Shakespeare" who was a personal hero to Oxford. Likewise, it's impossible to conceive that Oxford viewed the Shakespeare pseudonym as a joke. But there are aspects of the remaining five reasons that hold appeal in varying degrees for Oxfordians:

1) Oxford chose the Shakespeare pseudonym to make a statement. This view was championed by Charlton Ogburn, Jr., who maintained in brief that Oxford chose the name because of its pregnant symbolism: the image of Pallas

Athena, patron goddess of Athens, birthplace of the theatre, brandishing a spear, coupled with the image of the playwright wielding his pen as a sword. The existence of a real person with a strikingly similar name was coincidental, having nothing to do with the coining of the pseudonym.

2) A collaboration. Some Oxfordians see Oxford as the patron of a number of young Elizabethan writers, including Lyly, Lodge, Nashe, Kyd, and Marlowe. Perhaps Oxford functioned somewhat like a head writer on a contemporary TV show, inspiring and supervising his underlings, and polishing their efforts. They see evidence of multiple hands in a number of plays in the Canon, and consider "William Shakespeare" to be a pen name chosen for this largely collaborative effort.

3) The other three reasons (embarrassment, legal reasons, and writing outside one's milieu) can best be discussed together, as none fits exactly and elements of each are present in the case. In this scenario, social mores, rather than strictly legal reasons, prohibited Oxford from publishing under his own name.

In Elizabethan times, it was almost unthinkable for a member of the nobility to publish plays (or almost any piece of fiction) bearing his name; such an association would bring shame on his entire family. Thus, the "embarrassment" factor is present here, too, although the author is not embarrassed by the inferior quality of the finished work, but rather is embarrassed to be known as the author of anything in that genre. In that sense, the third factor—writing outside one's milieu—is also present, for in Elizabeth's day it was all right for a nobleman to write an English translation of another work, or even to write poetry as long as it circulated privately and was not published.

In this scenario, William Shakspere of Stratford is the analog of a front man, a real person who can deal with printers and who can appear as the true author if a need should arise. (One assumes that Shakspere lacked the pangs of guilt that led twentieth century front man Seymour Kern to back out. See footnote 4.)

There is another form of pseudonym, employed more rarely than the above ten, which brings us to the remarkable case of the Portuguese poet, Fernando Pessoa (1888-1935). Pessoa wrote under his own name, but also used many pseudonyms throughout his life (some estimates run as high as 75). He is best known for

Fernando Pessoa

three: Alberto Caeiro, Ricardo Reis, and Alvaro de Campos. Pessoa took pains to explain that these alter egos were not simply pseudonyms, but—to use Pessoa's term—heteronyms.

"A pseudonymic work," he explained in a 1928 article, "is, except for the name with which it is signed, the work of an author writing as himself; a heteronymic work is by an author writing outside his own personality: it is the work of a complete individuality made up by him, just as the utterances of some character would be."[6]

Caeiro, Reis and Campos were poets, each with his own distinctive style. Caeiro, "the Master," embraced "pastoral and philosophical themes." Reis and Campos were disciples of Caeiro, but Reis wrote "exquisitely formal verses" while Campos was "a ranting experimentalist."[7] As Pessoa himself explained, in a preface to a never-issued compilation of his heteronymic works, Caeiro rediscovered paganism, Reis "intensified" it "and made it artistically orthodox," while Campos, "basing himself on another part of Caeiro's work, developed an entirely different system, founded exclusively on sensations.[8]

Reis and Campos also wrote prose, and occasionally disagreed with each other on how to interpret "the Master," Caeiro's, works.

In a letter to magazine editor Adolfo Casais Monteiro in 1935, Pessoa offered an explanation of the genesis of the three heteronyms:

> . . . It one day occurred to me to play a joke on [fellow poet Mario] Sa-Carneiro—to invent a rather complicated bucolic poet whom I would present in some guise of reality that I've since forgotten. I spent a few days trying in vain to envision this poet. One day when I'd finally given up—it was March 8, 1914—I walked over to a high chest of drawers, took a piece of paper, and began to write standing up, as I do whenever I can. And I wrote thirty-some poems at once, in a kind of ecstasy I'm unable to describe. It was the triumphal day of my life, and I can never have another one like it. I began with a title, 'The Keeper of Sheep.' This was followed by the appearance in me of someone whom I instantly named Alberto Caeiro.
>
> Excuse the absurdity of this statement: my master had appeared in me. That was what I immediately felt, and so strong was the feeling that, as soon as those thirty-odd poems were written, I grabbed a fresh sheet of paper and wrote, again all at once, the six poems that constitute 'Slanting Rain,' by Fernando Pessoa. All at once and with total concentration. . . . It was the return of Fernando Pessoa as Alberto Caeiro to Fernando Pessoa himself. Or rather, it was the reaction of Fernando Pessoa against his nonexistence as Alberto Caeiro.
>
> Once Alberto Caeiro had appeared, I instinctively and subconsciously tried to find disciples for him. From Caeiro's false paganism I extracted the latent Ricardo Reis, at last discovering his name and adjusting him to his true self, for now I actually saw him. And then a new individual, quite the opposite of Ricardo Reis, suddenly and impetuously came to me. In an unbroken stream, without interruptions or corrections, the ode whose name is 'Triumphal Ode,' by the man whose name is none other than Alvaro de Campos, issued from my typewriter."[9]

Pessoa invented biographies and physical descriptions of his main heteronyms. Caeiro was born in Lisbon in 1889 and committed suicide in 1915; Reis was born in 1887 in Oporto, became a physician, and moved to Brazil in 1919; Campos was born in 1890, studied to be a naval engineer in Glasgow, and met

Caeiro by chance while visiting Lisbon.[10]

Pessoa even claimed to have met Campos. Although Pessoa readily admitted creating his heteronyms, he refused to concede that they didn't actually exist. As he noted in the preface to the never-issued collection of his heteronymic works,

> The author of these books cannot affirm that all these different and well-defined personalities who have incorporeally passed through his soul don't exist, for he does not know what it means to exist, nor whether Hamlet or Shakespeare is more real, or truly real.[11]

It is interesting that Pessoa mentioned "Shakespeare" in this context. Pessoa's own life resembled Oxford's in several ways. Both men lost their fathers at an early age—Pessoa was five when his father died. Indeed, Pessoa later reported that the first of his heteronyms appeared shortly afterward, "a certain Chevalier de Pas, when I was six years of age, from whom I wrote letters to myself, and whose figure, not completely vague, still dominates that part of my affection confined to longing."[12]

Both Oxford and Pessoa were fluent in several languages. Though he was born in Portugal, Pessoa lived in Durban, South Africa (or Natal, as the British colony was then known), from age seven to seventeen, as his mother had married a Portuguese diplomat who was stationed there. In Durban he attended an English school and began to write poetry in English. He also became fluent in French, and would write prose and poetry in all three languages. Both men were exceptionally well read and were interested in many subjects.

Pessoa not only wrote poems (including 35 sonnets in English), plays (most of them unfinished), and short stories, but also epigrams, translations, political tracts, and essays on subjects as diverse as alchemy, Rosicrucianism, and Mahatma Gandhi. One of his heteronyms, Bernardo Soares, "defended prose as the highest art form."[13] Both men also befriended and encouraged other young writers.[14]

Only a small portion of Pessoa's copious literary output was published during his lifetime. After his death (from cirrhosis of the liver) in 1935, his literary executors found a steamer trunk full of papers—some 25,000 documents, in English, French and Portuguese, some finished, many not.[15] His complete works have yet to be published.

Among the many writers whose works Pessoa had read, and among the many topics about which he wrote, was Shakespeare. If Pessoa was aware of the authorship controversy, he did not address it, at least in those of his writings which have so far been published.[16] One translator notes that he "left many passages for a projected essay on Shakespeare "[17] Of those that have surfaced, several are fascinating because of their insight into the creative process.

Unquestionably, Pessoa appreciated Shakespeare's greatness. In a 1930 essay titled "The Levels of Lyric Poetry," Pessoa identified four levels of consciousness expressed by the lyric poet. Those at the first level (the "most common" and "least estimable") expressed their emotions, but did so in a "monotonic" way, expressing a relatively small number of emotions. Those at the second level were "more intellectual or imaginative or even simply more cultured," and were not "monotonic." Pessoa did not identify any specific poets as level one or level two. At the third level "the poet, more intellectual still, begins to depersonalize, not just because he feels, but because he thinks he feels—feels states of the soul that he really does not possess, simply because he understands them. We are on the threshold of dramatic poetry in its innermost essence."

As exemplars of this level, Pessoa named Tennyson (specifically, "Ulysses" and "The Lady of Shalott") and Browning's so-called "dramatic poems." At the fourth ("much rarer") level, "the poet, more intellectual still but equally imaginative, fully undergoes depersonalization. He not only feels but lives the states of soul that he does not possess directly." At this supreme level Pessoa placed Shakespeare and also Browning. "Now, not even the style defines the unity of the man; only what is intellectual in the style denotes it. Thus in Shakespeare, in whom the unexpected prominence of phrase, the subtlety and complexity of expression, are the only things that make the speech of Hamlet approximate to that of King Lear, of Falstaff, of Lady Macbeth."[18]

Elsewhere, Pessoa again recognized Shakespeare's genius, but qualified his adulation because of his concern for the writer's state of mind:

> He had, in a degree never surpassed, the intuition of character and the broad-hearted comprehension of humanity; he had, in a degree never surpassed, the arts of diction and of expression. But he lacked one thing: balance, sanity, discipline. The fact that he entered into states of mind as far apart as the abstract spirituality of Ariel and the coarse humanity of Falstaff did to some extent create a balance in his unbalance. But at bottom he is not sane or balanced.[19]

In the same essay Pessoa asserted that Shakespeare's lack of sanity and balance made his plays and poems "from the pure artistic standpoint, the greatest failure that the world has ever looked on." More specifically, he attributed that failure to "the fundamental defects of the Christian attitude towards life."[20]

Pessoa's longest discourse on Shakespeare was probably written in 1928. In it he offers remarkable observations about the man who was Shakespeare. Because Pessoa apparently accepted the Stratford man as the poet/playwright, not all of his insights are accurate as far as Oxfordians are concerned, but many seem to fit what we know of Oxford to an uncanny degree. First, Pessoa characterized Shakespeare, like all great lyric poets, as "hysteric," i.e., given to outbursts of emotion. He deduced that Shakespeare was "a hysteric" in his youth and early adulthood, "a hystero-neurasthenic" in manhood, and "a hystero-neurasthenic in a lesser degree" toward the end of his life.[21] Pessoa does not define "hystero-neurasthenic," but presumably he means one whose emotional condition brings about feelings of debility, fatigue and inadequacy. Pessoa continues:

> Great as his tragedies are, none of them is greater than the tragedy of his own life. The gods gave him all great gifts but one: the one they gave not was the power to use those gifts greatly. He stands forth as the greatest example of genius, pure genius, genius immortal and unavailing. His creative power was shattered into a

thousand fragments by the stress and oppression of [such things.] It is but the shreds of itself. Disjecta membra, said Carlyle, are what we have of any poet, or of any man. Of no poet or man is this truer than of Shakespeare.

He stands before us, melancholy, witty, at times half insane, never losing his hold on the objective world, ever knowing what he wants, dreaming ever higher purposes and impossible greatnesses, and waking ever to mean ends and low triumphs. This, this was his great experience of life; for there is no great experience of life that is not, finally, the calm experience of disillusion.[22]

Pessoa believed that Shakespeare's two long narrative poems were "highly imperfect as narrative wholes, and that is the beginning of his secret."[23] He was certain that Shakespeare was unappreciated during his lifetime, mainly because he was ahead of his time, or, as Pessoa put it, "above his age."[24] Shakespeare's awareness of his unappreciation, coupled with appreciation shown to lesser writers and Shakespeare's "knowing himself (for this he must have done) the greatest genius of his age," must have shaken or destroyed his vanity and brought about depression. And yet, Pessoa concludes, Shakespeare was able to rise above depression by continuing to write, and in so doing Pessoa sees Shakespeare grappling with the spectre of insanity:

Depression leads to inaction: the writing of plays is, however, action. It may have been born of three things: (1) the need to write them—the practical need, we mean; (2) the recuperative power of a temperament not organically (only) depressed, reacting in the intervals of depression against depression itself; (3) the stress of extreme suffering—not depression, but suffering—acting like a lash on a cowering sadness, driving it into expression as into a lair, into objectivity as into an outlet from self, for, as Goethe said, 'Action consoles of all.'

. . . The need to write these plays shows in the intensity and bitterness of the phrases that voice depression—not quiet, half-peaceful, and somewhat indifferent, as in *The Tempest*, but restless, somber, dully forceful. Nothing depresses more than the necessity to act when there is no desire to act. The recuperative power of the temperament, the great boon to Shakespeare's hysteria, shows in the fact that there is no lowering, but a heightening, of his genius. The part of that due to natural growth need not and cannot be denied.

But the overcuriousness of expression, the overintelligence that sometimes dulls the edge of dramatic intuition (as in Laertes' phrases before mad Ophelia) cannot be explained on that line, because these are not peculiarities [in the] growth of genius but [are] more natural to its youth than to its virile age. They are patently the effort of the intellect to crush out emotion, to cover depression, to oust preoccupation of distress by preoccupation of thought. But the lash of outward mischance (no one can now say what, or how brought about, and to what degree by the man himself) is very evident in the constant choice of abnormal mental states for the basis of these tragedies. Only the dramatic mind wincing under the strain of outer evil thus projects itself instinctively into figures which must utter wholly the derangement that is partly its own.[25]

Has anyone come closer, in just two paragraphs, to getting inside the mind of the man who was Shakespeare? To be sure, much of what Pessoa saw in Shakespeare—or projected onto Shakespeare—was exhibited in Pessoa himself. Pessoa described himself as a "neurasthenic hysteric," questioned his own sanity, and certainly felt unappreciated. He was ahead of his time—only in recent years has his talent come to be recognized widely.[26]

What is significant is that this extraordinary insight into the mind of Shakespeare comes not from a critic, an academic or a historian, but from a person with remarkably similar creative impulses and talents. Even more significant is that this writer used self-created distinctive personalities—heteronyms—to channel his creative powers. For Pessoa to create fully, he had to lose himself fully within his heteronyms.

And just perhaps, so did Edward de Vere. Though we have seen that there were eminently pragmatic reasons for de Vere to use the Shakespeare pseudonym—to avoid shame and embarrassment while maintaining some control over the publication process—perhaps there were purely artistic reasons as well. Perhaps the existence of the Shakespeare pseudonym freed de Vere to be someone who was not himself. As Pessoa put it, "To feign is to know oneself."[27]

Endnotes

[1] Alex McNeil, *Total Television* (4th ed., Penguin, 1996), 788.

[2] Kevin Jackson, *Invisible Forms: Literary Curiosities* (Macmillan, 1999), 18.

[3] For example, Jeff Corey did not appear in a movie between 1951 and 1963, and became a well-respected acting teacher during the forced hiatus. Lionel Stander also had no film credits between 1951 and 1963; he moved to New York and became a successful stockbroker. Patrick McGilligan & Paul Buhle, *Tender Comrades: A Backstory of the Hollywood Blacklist* (St. Martin's Press, 1997), at 177-198, 607-625.

[4] See generally *Tender Comrades*, op.cit. For example, blacklisted writer John Berry recalled revising another writer's script, but leaving out the characters' names in the revision; the first writer merely added them back in to get the credit. Id. at 71. Writer Ernest Kinoy served as the "front" for blacklisted writer Millard Lampell while both wrote for the 1954 TV series *The Marriage*. Id. at 398. Blacklisted writer Robert Lees wrote scripts for *Lassie* using as a front a non-writer friend, Seymour Kern, and letting the front keep ten per cent of the fees. Kern backed out after a year because he "couldn't take being complimented by his family and friends for work he didn't do." Lees then coined a pseudonym, J. E. Selby. Id. at 436- 437.

[5] *Invisible Forms*, op. cit., 29-31.

[6] Id. at 41-42.

[7] Id. at 38.

[8] Richard Zenith (ed. & trans.), *The Selected Prose of Fernando Pessoa* (Grove Press, 2001), 3. A fourth heteronym, Antonio Mora, was a "philosophical follower" of Caeiro, though not a poet, and Pessoa foresaw a fifth (unnamed) heteronymic philosopher who would write "an apology for paganism based on entirely different arguments." Ibid.

[9] Id. at 256. A slightly different translation may be found in Edwin Honig (ed. & trans.), *Always Astonished: Selected Prose by Fernando Pessoa* (City Lights Books, 1988), 9-10. Some Pessoa scholars doubt Pessoa's account. See http://home.earthlink.net/kunos/Pessoa/interview.html, where translator Chris Daniels observes, "That's the myth he propagated. You have to take Pessoa's statements about the genesis of heteronymy with a grain of salt. He prevaricated a lot."

[10] Honig at 10-11, 23.

[11] Zenith at 2.

[12] Honig at 8.

[13] Zenith at xiv.

[14] Honig at v.

[15] Pessoa lamented that he hated to begin a new work, and, having begun, hated to finish it. Honig at vii.

[16] In an essay dated 1910, Pessoa refers to "the 'Shakespeare Problem,'" but does not explain further. In another writing he used the term "anti-Stratfordians," but the context does not seem concerned with the authorship question. See Honig at 4 & 46.

[17] Zenith at 335-336.

[18] Honig at 65-66.

[19] Zenith at 215.

[20] Ibid.

[21] He also believed that Shakespeare was of frail constitution and deficient vitality, but not unhealthy. Honig at 56.

[22] Ibid.

[23] Id. at 57.

[24] Id. at 59.

[25] Id. at 62-63.

[26] Though Pessoa is hardly a household name in English speaking countries, he is idolized in Portugal. Harold Bloom cites him as "one of the twenty-six authors essential to the Western canon." Jackson, op. cit. at 41.

[27] Honig at 124.

Chapter 4:

Is Touchstone vs. William in *As You Like It* the First Authorship Story?

This essay was originally published in
Shakespeare Matters. *(Spring 2003)*

*"Come Sweet Audrey. We Must Be Married,
Or We Must Live in Bawdry."*

Shakespeare's *As You Like It* should be of particular interest to Oxfordians, if for no other reason than Act V, Scene 1—the encounter in the forest between the fool Touchstone and the local bumpkin William, Touchstone's rival for the hand of the country wench Audrey. The scene appears to be a deliberate implant; had it been omitted, the play would not suffer. One must ask, then, what motivated the playwright—a skilled dramatist at the height of his career—to throw in such an apparently gratuitous scene?

I will suggest that the key to the answer lies not in the two male suitors, but in Audrey. The analysis may also shed light on the play's date (or, as seems more likely, dates) of composition. It should be noted here that the idea that this scene between Touchstone and William in *As You Like It* is actually an encounter between Oxford and Shakspere is not original. It was explored as

29

early as 1952 by Dorothy and Charlton Ogburn in *This Star of England* and was further developed by Oxfordian Charles Boyle in an unpublished 1995 conference paper.

This article will examine the idea in more detail. Some background, including an overview of mainstream criticism, may be helpful. Although *As You Like It* did not appear in print until the First Folio in 1623, the first external evidence of its existence is traced to 1600, when that title, together with three other plays, is entered in the Stationers Register "to be stayed."[1]

Stratfordians generally have little trouble dating its composition to 1599, though many agree that the play shows signs of revision. That year may be "confidently accepted," says George Lyman Kittredge, because of the fact that the play is not among those listed by Meres in 1598, and because it contains an allusion to Marlowe's *Hero and Leander*, a work not published until 1598. Kittredge also cites Jaques's famous "All the world's a stage" speech (II,vii.) as further evidence of composition in 1599, linking it to the opening of the Globe Theatre that year.[2]

Kittredge himself thought that the 1599 effort was a revision of an earlier work.[3] A.L. Rowse believed that the play had been written earlier "for private performance," while John Dover Wilson offered an ingenious theory that it had been first written in the summer of 1593 and was heavily revised in 1600.[4] Some Stratfordians offer more fanciful notions, particularly when speculating on the play's title. One asserts that "Shakespeare laughed out the title one day after reading what he had written,"[5] while another conjectures that "a Globe manager- actor sent a note over to Will at Blackfriars asking for a name . . . . Will was busy that week . . . . So he just scrawled, in effect, 'no preference' across it and sent the tricksy slave back."[6]

As to the source of the play, Stratfordians are unanimous in identifying Thomas Lodge's novel, *Rosalynde: Euphues Golden Legacie*, first published in 1590.[7] Lodge, in turn, seems to have been inspired by an anonymous fourteenth century poem, *The Coke's Tale of Gamelyn*, though the latter story was not printed until 1721.[8]

The basic plot of Lodge's novel is almost identical to the central story of *As You Like It*—the daughter of a banished French king (Rosalynde) falls in love with a young man (Rosader) she sees in a wrestling match; she and her cousin (Alinda) are banished by the usurping king, and, disguised as Ganymede and Aliena, they flee to the Forest of Ardennes; there they encounter Rosader, who has fled there himself to escape the wrath of his evil older brother (Saladyne); a romance develops between Rosalynde and Rosader; Saladyne is later exiled to the forest by the usurping king, where he reforms and falls in love with Alinda; finally, news arrives that the usurping king has been overthrown, and Rosader is named the rightful heir.[9]

While Shakespeare retained the central story of *Rosalynde* in fashioning *As You Like It*, he made several changes. Among the most obvious are the names of the characters. Although Rosalynde keeps her name (now spelled Rosalind), and the two females' forest aliases are retained, the other main characters' names are changed—younger brother Rosader becomes Orlando, older brother Saladyne becomes Oliver, and Rosalind's cousin Alinda is now Celia; a minor character, the old shepherd Corydon, is now Corin. Curiously, even the forest itself undergoes a slight transformation, from the very French Forest of Ardennes to the apparently English Forest of Arden.[10]

More importantly, Shakespeare added two main characters—Jaques and Touchstone—and several minor ones, including Audrey and William. As one critic observes, "these additional characters add nothing at all to the story—if you were to tell it, you would leave them out. They show us that story was not Shakespeare's concern in this play; its soul is not to be looked for there."[11] To others, the addition of characters "vivifies the play."[12]

A fair sampling of Stratfordian opinion discloses that the play is considered one of Shakespeare's best comedies, showing the author's "characteristic excellence. . . and [his] distinctive virtues as a writer of comedy have their fullest scope."[13] Swinden calls it "the most perfect" of the comedies, Gardner "the most refined and exquisite," and Ward cites its "most extraordinary elusive subtlety."[14]

There is also general agreement that dramatic, or comic, action is almost nonexistent in the play; instead, the focus is on dialogue and the developing relationships between and among the characters. "[T]he manner of the play, when once it settles down in the forest, is to let two people drift together, talk a little, and part, to be followed by two more. Sometimes a pair will be watched by others, who will sometimes comment on what they see. . . . This may all sound rather static, but such is the ease and rapidity with which pairs and groups break up, re-form and succeed one another on the stage that there is a sense of fluid movement."[15]

To another Stratfordian, "Talk is the very medium of *As You Like It*. Action is absent, and language is abundantly rich, allegorical at least of the foliage of the forest where it occurs. The characters spend much of their time talking, simply talking."[16] Within such a format, the author satirizes the concepts of pastoral life and pastoral romance, and further explores themes of preservation and order, time and timelessness, all within a forest which is "no conventional arcadia."[17]

These interpretations, it must be conceded, are sound, especially if the play is analyzed as a work of the late 1590s largely derived from a then-popular book. Their soundness is reinforced if extensive thought is not given to why Shakespeare made the changes that he did to Lodge's novel. An Oxfordian interpretation will not supplant this set of interpretations, but will supplement it.[18] As to the time of composition of the play, Oxfordian Eva Turner Clark points us to a period shortly after November 1581, when Queen Elizabeth pledged to wed her longtime French suitor, the Duke of Alençon.[19] As Clark sees things, Alençon is the prototype of Orlando (even down to his "little beard," III.ii.)[20]; his secretary de Bex is that of the minor (and similarly named) character Le Beu; his envoy Simier is that of Orlando's servant Adam[21]; and Alençon's brother, King Henry III of France, is that of Orlando's brother Oliver.

If Alençon is Orlando, then to Clark it follows that Elizabeth herself must be Rosalind; support for that may be found not only in the relationship between the two characters, including the mock marriage between Orlando and Rosalind when she is disguised as Ganimed (which Clark takes to be a direct allusion to Elizabeth's 1581 public declaration of intent to marry), but also in such details as Rosalind's gift of a chain to Orlando (which Clark interprets as an allusion to Elizabeth's gift of one of her garters to a French emissary, who in turn gave it to Alençon).

And in the melancholy Jaques, Clark sees that Oxford grafted something of himself, including the highly personal references to Jaques as an exiled courtier, and a traveler who has sold his "own lands to see other men's" (IV,i.24). Although Clark does not speak of revision of the play, she suggests that the scene between Touchstone and William (V,i) was inserted in 1589, as was the character of Sir Oliver Mar-text.

If Clark's principal composition date is correct, then what does that do to the relationship between *As You Like It* and Lodge's *Rosalynde*? Obviously, the play could not have been based on the novel. On the other hand, the similarities between the two works are too striking for them to have been written entirely independently of one another.[22] Could it be that *Rosalynde* was derived from an early version of *As You Like It*? Charlton Ogburn thought so,[23] and there is evidence to support this view. Although Lodge's *Rosalynde* was published in 1590, the book was written (according to Lodge's dedication) "to beguile the time" on a voyage with a Captain Clarke to the islands of Terceras and the Canaries. Kittredge believes the voyage to have been "about 1588,"[24] but a biographer of Lodge has uncovered a record of a voyage to the Canaries by a Captain Clarke in 1585.[25]

Furthermore, the euphuistic style of *Rosalynde* would suggest a date of 1585 rather than 1590, because the euphuistic "rage" was launched in the late 1570s and had already begun to fade by 1590. If, then, Lodge's novel is derived from a pre-1585 version of *As You Like It*, the play must not have contained characters such as Jaques and Touchstone, for Lodge would not have excised figures of such importance in reworking the story. Thus, it is plausible that very substantial revisions were made to the play during the late 1580s, and, as we shall see, further revisions came even later.

Let us now turn to the play to look for specific evidence of revision. [Much of the following is taken from Kristian Smidt's *Unconformities in Shakespeare's Later Comedies*, a very perceptive work by a Stratfordian analyst.] A glance at the list of characters suggests something is amiss, for there are two characters named Jaques and two named Oliver. Any dramatist would avoid this clumsy, and potentially confusing, situation, especially if he were creating the work during one span of time. In the play as it has come down to us, the "first" Jaques is the middle brother of Oliver and Orlando, a minor character; he is mentioned by name at the beginning of the play (I,i.5), but does not make an entrance until the end (V,iv.158).

The "second" Jaques is the melancholy Jaques, a major character who appears throughout the play beginning at II,v. Coincidentally, he too is mentioned by name (II,i.26) some time before his entrance. Based on a close reading of the text, Smidt offers a very sensible explanation of the "unconformity" of the two Jaques. The first Jaques is mentioned by name only once, in Orlando's opening dialogue with Adam, as Orlando explains his dire situation to his old servant.

Two dozen lines later, Orlando's brother Oliver appears, and much of the same information is repeated during the brothers' quarrel. "It would be a reasonable guess to suppose that Shakespeare first wrote that opening passage as we have it, then thought it was a clumsy expository device to have Orlando explain things to Adam which the old man must have well known, and wrote a quarreling scene with Oliver to replace it. In so doing he would have discarded Orlando's mention of his second brother . . . and left himself free to use the name of Jaques for another character."[26]

It should also be noted that when the "first" Jaques finally appears in the play, the stage direction refers to him merely as "second brother," that the character introduces himself as "the second Son" (V.iv.160), and that no one else refers to him by name. This further indicates that, in the final version of the play, the second brother was not intended to share a name with another character.[27]

The second paired character name is Oliver, who as a main character is the evil older brother, and as a minor one is the forest vicar, Sir Oliver Mar-text. Oliver Mar-text appears briefly in only one scene (III,iii, with only three speeches) and is referred to once later. The first name may be a reference to Oliver Pigge, a Puritan minister about whom a song was licensed in 1584.[28] Oxfordians and Stratfordians agree that "Mar-text" is an allusion to the Martin Mar-prelate controversy—a series of pamphlets "promoting the Puritan cause and attacking the Episcopacy, signed Martin Marprelate"—which began in late 1588 and reached its height a few months later.[29]

Thus, the second Oliver character cannot have existed before 1589, and it is likely that the duplication of name was intentional in this case. Smidt notes several more "unconformities," all of which again point to a revision or a reworking: whether the usurping duke or the banished duke is named Frederick; whether the duke's banishment was recent or distant; and whether Rosalind is taller than Celia. She further notes that these inconsistencies usually arise when there is a change from prose to blank verse, and concludes, "it looks like Shakespeare began writing the play in prose and when he got to the point of emotional ignition, so to speak, thought that verse would be in keeping with the importance of the occasion and the dignity of the characters."[30]

To an Oxfordian, that "emotional ignition" occurred when the author decided to depict himself. In a play which centers around pairings, it is not surprising that he did so by putting himself into a pair of characters—the melancholy Jaques and the wise fool Touchstone. It is not necessary to discuss in depth the numerous parallels between Oxford and this pair; both are exiled courtiers, one of whom (as noted above) is a traveler who has "sold [his] own lands to see other men's." As one Stratfordian perceptively notes, Jaques dwells on three main themes throughout the play— "the fool and his role; his own right to speak to the world; [and]

that world itself as a mere stage of stage players."[31] All of those themes, of course, are central to Oxford, and appear over and over again in the dramatic works. Touchstone, in the eyes of another critic, "is a man of intelligence and insight, under no illusions about the Court—or Arden, for that matter."[32]

Together, the pair acts much like the chorus of ancient drama.[33] For our purposes, it may be helpful to view Jaques as Oxford the observer, and Touchstone as Oxford the expresser. Imbued with melancholy—a melancholy which he actually enjoys (see II,v.9-19)[34]—Jaques is first described to us as weeping at the plight of a wounded deer. His very name is a play on words: the name is not pronounced "Jacques," but rather "jakes," Elizabethan slang for a privy.[35] Throughout the play he remains cynical; in his most famous speech (II,vii.), chronicling the seven ages of man, he dwells on the drawbacks and infirmities attendant on each of the seven periods. At the end of the play, as the other main characters march off in their ordered pairs, he is the only one not to be paired off, and the only major character who will not return to the court.

Of course, the one character with whom Jaques should be paired is the one brings him joy: Touchstone. Jaques's only real moment of happiness is when he muses rhapsodically on his first encounter with Touchstone in the forest (II,vii.12-61) and wishes that he, too, were a fool. However, as the play develops, Touchstone appears to have found himself a mate—or has he? Touchstone is a fool, but he "plays no practical jokes, sets no traps, hides in no corners, gets no one drunk, brings no false tidings."[36]

His very name suggests that he tests things.[37] To Stratfordians, this sense of testing is narrow, existing only within the play itself. "'[H]e tests all that the world takes for gold, especially the gold of the golden world of pastoralism' . . . . Touchstone in his relationships advances a standard by which we are invited to measure the relationships in the play."[38] To Oxfordians the character name has a broader significance, suggesting that Touchstone (the author as the utterer) is who testing for truth.

We first encounter Touchstone at the court, where he jests with Rosalind and Celia. At the end of Act I, when the two ladies have been banished, Celia is confident that he can be persuaded to join them in exile. They simply desire his company; because Rosalind has already decided to disguise herself as a male in the forest, his presence is not needed to provide for their safety. Celia's confidence is well-placed; Touchstone happily accompanies them to, and within, the Forest of Arden. The trio arrives in the forest in Act II, scene iv, and shortly encounter the two shepherds, old Corin and young Silvius. We next see Touchstone in Act III, scene ii, when he matches wits with Corin, comparing life at court to the pastoral life.

Up to this point, Touchstone appears to be a fairly conventional fool, exchanging in witty banter and playing on words. His special qualities begin to develop in the next scene. In Act III, scene iii, Jaques and Touchstone appear together for the first time, and the fool is accompanied by a woman, the forest goatherd Audrey. Within a few lines we learn that Touchstone intends to marry Audrey as soon as possible. It is unusual for a Shakespearean fool to be depicted as fully male; most are styled as apparently sexless windbags.[39] Interestingly, there is no "backstory" about Audrey; we do not know where or how they met (presumably it was in the forest).

To Stratfordian critics, the Touchstone-Audrey match is a burlesque, a counterpoint to the pastoral romantic nature of the other three forest pairings; Touchstone is seen as impelled by sexual desire to wed—and bed—Audrey as quickly as can be arranged.[40] Audrey, with a scant dozen speeches in the entire play, is perceived by Stratfordians as "sluttish" and "graceless."[41] To at least one Stratfordian, the inclusion of Audrey was an unfortunate mistake by the author.[42]

However, if we examine the scene with Oxfordian eyes, something altogether different suggests itself. First, the very name Audrey is significant. Although, as a proper name, its derivation is Anglo-Saxon,[43] Shakespeare may be suggesting a connection to the Latin verb *audire*—to hear—from which the familiar words "audience," "audit," and "auditory" are derived. Shakespeare's dramatic words were written, of course, but they were written to be heard by an audience.

This is the first clue that Audrey may not personify a human being. Next, it is apparent that she does not understand much of what Touchstone says; she is unfamiliar with "feature" and "poetical," for example, two words with which even an unsophisticated country wench would be acquainted. However, those words may have additional meaning in the scene. Touchstone's question to Audrey—"Doth my simple Feature content you?"—is usually taken to mean "Are you pleased with my ordinary looks," with a possible sexual suggestion as well ("Does my [uniquely male] feature make you happy").

But if Touchstone represents the author, "feature" could mean not the form of the physical body or face, but a creation made by Touchstone,[44] and "content" could mean not "to make happy," but rather "to comprise." The question then becomes a rhetorical one: "Are you comprised of my creation[s]?" Audrey, then, is not merely a country wench, but represents the author's dramatic works. If she personifies an inanimate object, she then would not "understand" the meanings of words. The scene continues.

After Audrey misunderstands the question ("Your Features, Lord warrant us; what Features?"), Touchstone responds with a play on words ("Goats" and "Gothes") while comparing his plight to that of "honest Ovid."[45] The remark cannot be intended for Audrey; if she does not know what "Feature" means, she certainly would not recognize the name of a Roman poet. Jaques then weighs in ("O Knowledge ill inhabited, worse than Jove in a thatch'd House"), reinforcing the reference to Ovid with one of his own.[46]

It is usually assumed that the speech is directed at Touchstone, but it is possible that the phrase "O knowledge ill inhabited" is intended to describe Audrey. Touchstone replies, "When a man's Verses cannot be understood . . . it strikes a man more dead than a great Reckoning in a little Room." Critical attention is generally lavished on the latter phrase, with the supposed allusion to the death of playwright Christopher Marlowe in a tavern quarrel in 1593; that supposition may be well founded, for there appear to be two other references to Marlowe's work in the play.[47]

But perhaps the author himself may have had his own "great Reckoning" concerning the publication of his works; and, if it had been made plain to him that someone else's name would be attached to their publication, he would have worried (and justifiably so) that his "Verses" would not then "be understood." Touchstone then turns to Audrey, and says, "truly, I would the Gods had made thee poetical." Characteristically, Audrey does not understand the word, and wonders, "Is it honest in Deed and Word: is it a true thing?" Touchstone explains that it is not, that "the truest Poetry is the most feigning." He reiterates his wish that Audrey were poetical, and laments that "thou swear'st to me thou art honest."

There are further references to "honest" and "honesty;" the two words occur seven times in the first three dozen lines of the scene.[48] Conventional criticism holds that "honest" and "honesty" as used here refer to chastity, but if Audrey is what we think, the words connote truth and truthfulness. Of all the qualities that a suitor might wish his intended bride to possess, being "poetical" would likely not rank high on the list. The author's repeated use of the word must be deliberate, however, and is understood as something more than wordplay if Touchstone and Audrey are seen as the author and the dramatic works. What he is saying is that the dramatic works are honest, that they depict the truth. And their very honesty is a likely impediment to the marriage.

In contrast, if the dramatic works were merely "poetical," they would (almost by definition) not be honest, and there would, perhaps, be no such impediment. At this point we should speak about marriage, the pair's intended destination. Of all the attributes of marriage—a physical and legal union, recognized by law and by God—the most significant in this context is that the bride will take the groom's name. In other words, the author's paramount hope (although unarticulated) is that the works will be published under his own name.

To be sure, Oxford must have realized that it would have been virtually impossible for his works to have been so published. As Diana Price and others have noted, in a class-bound society such as his it was unthinkable for a nobleman to publish an original work as his own; to have done so would have brought disgrace to the family name and to all of nobility. Publishing plays would have been an especially low blow. At the same time, Oxford must have felt the all-too-human pride of authorship, and part of him must have chafed at the necessity to hide behind another name. As the characters wait for the vicar to arrive, Audrey remarks that "I am not a Slut, though I thank the Gods I am foul." Interestingly, the words "foul" and "foulness" occur three times within a space of four lines. One cannot help thinking here that Audrey is describing herself not as plain-looking or unattractive—even if she were, why would she "thank the Gods" for it?—but rather that she is describing herself literally as "foul," meaning handwritten and hand-corrected.[49]

In due course the "Vicar of the next Village" arrives, ready to perform the ceremony. Curiously, he bears the name Sir Oliver Mar-text. This name is usually taken as an allusion to the Martin Mar-prelate controversy of 1588-1589, with a possible secondary allusion to the minister Oliver Pigge (see above) and a suggestion in "Martext" that the poor fellow will be unable to get the formalities right. Many critics see the vicar as a Puritan,[50] with one noting that his "very name suggests the real problems the church has always faced in country parishes."[51]

To an Oxfordian, however, the name Mar-text suggests not only the Martin Mar-prelate affair, but also the "real problems" the author was about to face if he went forward with his plans to "marry," or publish the works under his own name. The text would, if it were then published, have to be marred in order to obscure the truth.

Nevertheless, it appears that the marriage will take place. Jaques at first agrees to give the bride away, but then abruptly counsels Touchstone to postpone the wedding until he can find "a good Priest that can tell you what Marriage is." Touchstone agrees, and addresses Audrey: "Come, sweet Audrey / We must be married, or we must live in Bawdry." In other words, if they do not get married, they will still have a physical relationship, but

Touchstone, Audrey and William in the Forest of Arden.

Audrey will not belong to him legally and will not share his name.

Bearing in mind that Jaques, as well as Touchstone, represents Oxford, it may be suggested that the author had talked himself out of going ahead with publication at this early time. Here the play takes leave of Touchstone and Audrey for a while. But it seems clear that theirs is no ordinary relationship. Although many critics see the pair as driven by sexual impulse, I do not believe Audrey exhibits any sexual desire. One Stratfordian critic has gotten it right when he concludes that Audrey, whoever or whatever she is, "is an object to be possessed."[52]

With an aborted marriage ceremony as prelude, we now arrive at V.i, the truly extraordinary scene with Touchstone, Audrey and William. Nothing in the play has prepared us for it, and, as noted earlier, the play would not suffer if the scene were omitted. Why, then, did the author bother with this digression? Few Stratfordian critics have paid much attention to the scene;

indeed, many do not mention it at all in their analyses of the play.

Dover Wilson cites the comic effect of Touchstone "lording it as a courtier, a gentleman and a philosopher, over the simple rustics of Arden."[53] Swinden echoes that view, terming it another example of "bringing together different members of different groups for purposes of dispute and argument."[54] Ward sees the scene as another example of Touchstone's tendency to bully the locals.[55] Jenkins suggests that Touchstone "not only deprives the yokel William of his mistress, but steals his part in the play, making it in the process of infinitely greater significance."[56] Berry has looked at the scene a bit more deeply, observing that the "unfortunate William finds Touchstone in a terrible mood, and his cadenza on the means whereby William is to be destroyed effectively exposes William's pretentions to the hand of Audrey. It is a complete demolition of an inferior."[57]

To be sure, there is comic irony in the banishment of William from the forest by Touchstone, one of those banished to the forest. To an Oxfordian, however, the scene is far more significant. It opens with Touchstone and Audrey walking together through the forest; Audrey wistfully notes that she would have been happy to have had Mar-text marry them, but Touchstone responds that Sir Oliver (who had only three innocuous speeches) is "wicked" and "vile." He then turns their conversation to something more important to both of them, a rival for Audrey's hand whose existence is already known to him: "But Audrey, there is a Youth here in the Forest lays claim to you."

The words "lays claim" are significant, for they suggest a "claim" in the legal, not amorous, sense. This connotation is reinforced by Audrey's reply: "Ay, I know who 'tis: he hath no Interest in me in the World." The word "interest" again suggests a legal term, not a romantic one; this is reinforced a few lines later, when William, answering one of Touchstone's queries, agrees that he loves Audrey. William's love for her must have been known to Audrey, so when she tells Touchstone that William "hath no interest" in her, she is either lying or is using "interest" in a specific sense. We already know that she considers herself "honest," so we should conclude that she is not referring to a romantic "Interest," but rather to a legal one. William then makes his appearance.

The Stratfordian consensus is predictable—poor William is a "yokel," a "dumb yokel," and "a dolt" of "bumpkinish ways."[58] Let us pause to consider the name, something few Stratfordians seem to have done.[59] The William of *As You Like It* lives in the Forest of Arden, close to Stratford-on-Avon; of the several non-historical Williams in the plays, this one would appear to be the most personal to the Stratford man. It seems odd, though not inconceivable, that an author would loan his own first name to such an apparently unimportant, unsophisticated and unimpressive character.

But Oxfordians find it not odd at all; Ogburn observes that several of Shakespeare's non-historical Williams, including those who do not appear but are merely referred to, are cast in unflattering terms.[60] Such a consistent categorization of Wills and Williams suggests that the author had something definite in mind when using the name—to Oxfordians, of course, a deliberate reminder that the most famous "William" was not who he seemed to be. Noting William's entrance, Touchstone eagerly awaits the opportunity to belittle the country "Clown," noting (as much to the audience as to Audrey) that "we that have good Wits have much to answer for." The implication, of course, is that William does not have "good Wit," a point that will soon become obvious.

William is literally a man of few words; in his 11 speeches are a total of 44 words, only five of which are of more than one syllable (including his own name and that of Audrey). William has removed his hat as a sign of deference to Touchstone—the fool, in other words, is his social superior. Touchstone graciously bids William to put his hat back on and begins to question him. In short order we learn three things about the "Forest Youth": he is "five and twenty," his name is indeed William, and he was born in the Forest of Arden. Let us look more closely at each of these responses. That William is age 25 suggests that the scene was added in 1589 or 1590, when William Shakspere was exactly that age; it is also possible that the scene was added even later, but was intended to refer specifically to that period.

There are two reasons in support of the deliberate reference to 1589-1590: first, for comedic purposes the scene would work just as well, if not better, if poor William did not know exactly how old he was; therefore it must be significant that William in fact knows his age. Second, to Oxfordians there is ample evidence throughout the plays that when the author makes specific time references, he is doing so deliberately. A few examples, familiar to most Oxfordians, will suffice: the reference in *Romeo and Juliet* to an earthquake "eleven years" earlier suggests the Verona earthquake of 1570, thus a composition date of 1581[61]; the reference in *Cymbeline* to the abduction of Guiderius and Arviragus 20 years previously parallels Queen Elizabeth's "banishment" of the two sons of Edward Seymour and Lady Catherine Grey in 1561, again suggesting a composition date of 1581[62]; and in *The Famous Victories of Henry the Fift*, the robbery of the king's receivers by Prince Hal's followers is dated as May 20th in the fourteenth year of Henry IV's reign, while the real-life robbery at Gad's Hill of two of Oxford's former employees took place during May in the fourteenth year of Elizabeth's reign.[63]

After eliciting William's age, Touchstone inquires, "Is thy name William?" William replies, "William, Sir." Touchstone already knows this fact; Audrey has greeted William by name only six lines earlier. Thus, the reiteration of the name bit must be to set up Touchstone's response: "A fair Name." The pun on fair/Vere (pronounced ver) seems obvious—William is a name used by de Vere. William's acknowledgment that he was born in "the Forest here" further indicates a specific reference to William Shakspere, for the Forest of Arden is only a short distance from Stratford-on-Avon. Oxford himself was also associated with two places close by the Forest of Arden, Billesley Hall and Bilton Hall.[64]

The questioning continues. "Art rich?" "Faith Sir, so, so." Touchstone quibbles on "so-so." "Art thou wise?" "Ay Sir, I have a pretty Wit." Touchstone recalls the proverb of the fool and the wise man, then speaks of the "Heathen Philosopher" who would "open his Lips" when "he had a desire to eat a Grape." The latter reference is still not fully understood; some critics suggest that it is merely a comedic device to accompany William, who has begun to open his mouth in amazement. Back to the interrogation: "You love this Maid?" "I do, Sir." The significance of this exchange is noted above, indicating that Audrey's earlier use of the word "interest" is meant in a legal sense.

Next, Touchstone commands William, "Give me your Hand: art thou learned?" "No sir." According to the Oxford English Dictionary, in early usage the word "learned" did not connote erudition or "profound knowledge" of something, but rather meant "taught, instructed [or] educated." Thus, William seems to be admitting that he is unschooled or illiterate. That William Shakspere was illiterate comes as no surprise to Oxfordians; it is sobering, however, to have it pointed out by the true author.

Now the scene intensifies, as Touchstone prepares to dismiss William. Although most critics agree that Touchstone is having fun with the hapless fellow (perhaps with a touch of insensitivity), to an Oxfordian Touchstone appears to be losing his temper. He begins with a short lesson: "To have, is to have. For it is a Figure in Rhetoric, that Drink being powr'd out of a Cup into a Glass, by filling the one, doth empty the other."

The lesson is certainly an elementary one.[65] Ogburn has noted the "metaphor of the drink . . . as Shakspere is filled with credit for the plays, Oxford is emptied of it."[66] It should also be noted that the Folio spelling of "powr'd," often amended by modern editors to "pour'd," suggests a play on the words "power" and "pour." Were the author's dramatic works being ordered to appear under another's name? Touchstone continues with a line that "makes no sense in reference to anything else in the play"[67]—"For all your writers do consent, that ipse is he: now you are not ipse, for I am he." Obviously, the line bears scrutiny. First, it is the writers who "consent" (or "agree," as seems the intended gloss) "that ipse is he."

"Writers" could refer to the ancient Latin writers or to Latin grammarians, but it could also refer to the author's contemporaries, suggesting that Oxford's fellow writers knew that he was the true author of the works. Second, it is not quite accurate to say that "ipse is he." "Ipse" connotes something more than merely "he." It is "he himself," or "the emphatic he, the man himself, the very man."[68] Touchstone concludes the lesson by reminding William that he (William) is "not ipse, for I am he."

Recalling that Touchstone is holding William's hand, the speech is powerful—even if circumstances have necessitated that the works are to be transferred from Oxford's name to Shakspere's, Oxford's literary companions—and the Stratford man himself—all know the identity of the true author. The scene concludes shortly. Poor William does not understand the rhetorical lesson, replying "Which he, Sir?" This reinforces William's lack of schooling, for he does not recognize a common Latin pronoun.

Touchstone answers William's ignorant question: "He, Sir, that must marry this Woman." In context, "this Woman," or Audrey, has to represent the dramatic works, and the use of the word "must" is truly poignant, for we know that the "marriage" — the linking of the correct name to this woman—did not come to pass. At this point, as Touchstone continues, he begins to grow angry, ordering the "Clown" to "abandon . . . the Society . . . of this Female," translating his remarks simultaneously into simpler words that William can understand: "'leave' . . . the 'Company' of this 'Woman.'" If Touchstone has his way, William's failure to comply will be punishable by death: "I will bandy with thee in Faction, I will o'er-run thee with Policy[69]; I will kill thee a hundred and fifty ways, therefore tremble and depart."

Kittredge explains the first two phrases: To "bandy with thee in Faction" is to "engage in party strife with thee. To bandy is literally to knock to and fro, like a tennis ball. Faction was constantly used for 'political party' without the modern implication of disorder or sedition." To "o'er-run thee with Policy" is to "outstrip (overcome) thee by means of statecraft. Policy is used in the dignified sense and carries out the threat made in the preceding sense."[70]

That Touchstone is here using terms associated with

government is surprising; there is no need to resort to statecraft when dealing with a country bumpkin such as William. But if the scene means what we think it does, the choice of words is appropriate, suggesting that Oxford will resist efforts to have the works published under another name, and that he has allies at court who will assist him in his cause. Finally, given the author's frequent precision in use of numerical terms, we can only wonder why Touchstone threatens to kill William exactly "a hundred and fifty ways."

The scene ends. Even William has gotten the message. After a prompt from Audrey ("Do [depart], good William."), he offers a vapid "God rest you merry, Sir," and exits. He does not reappear in the play. Audrey, however, does reappear twice (in V,iii. & iv.), though she has only one more line. As V,iii. opens, Touchstone announces that they shall be married "tomorrow." Audrey responds happily: "I do desire it with all my Heart; and I hope it is no dishonest Desire to be a Woman of the World?" The usual interpretation of "Woman of the World" is a married woman[71]; the connotation here is that she will be known publicly as having taken the author's name. Audrey concludes her final speech recognizing two minor characters who have just entered: "Here come two of the banish'd Duke's Pages." It may be farfetched, but it is worth noting that the first recorded use of the word "page" as meaning the "leaf of a book, [or] manuscript" is in 1589![72]

Touchstone and Audrey resurface in the play's final scene (V,iv.), as one of the four couples who have gotten together and appear destined for marriage. Introducing himself to Duke Senior, Touchstone says, "I press in here, Sir, amongst the rest of the Country Copulatives to swear and to forswear, according as Marriage binds and Blood breaks." Although the word "copulative" carries a sexual connotation today, in Shakespeare's time its principal connotation was grammatical, as a word which served "to couple or connect" other words, or a "copulative" conjunction.[73]

Again, the word underscores the personification of the dramatic works as Audrey. Touchstone then describes Audrey to the Duke: "A poor Virgin, Sir, an ill-favour'd thing, Sir, but mine own, a poor Humour of mine, Sir, to take that that no man else will: rich Honesty dwells like a Miser, Sir, in a poor House, as your Pearl in your foul Oyster." Though the description could apply to a homely country lass, the recurrences of "honesty" and "foul" suggest an association with a written work.

The phrases "mine own," "a poor humour of mine," and "to take that that no man else will" all suggest ownership. Later in the scene, Hymen, the marriage god, appears and addresses each of the four couples in turn. To the first three (usually taken as Orlando and Rosalind, Oliver and Celia, and Phebe [who is standing with Silvius]), he offers positive greetings: "You and you no Cross shall part/You and you are Hart in Hart/You to his Love must accord/Or have a Woman to your Lord." But he offers a darker, though still appropriate, greeting to Touchstone and Audrey: "You and you, are sure together/As the Winter to foul Weather."[74]

Again, the word "foul" appears, presumably to describe Audrey; as for the comparison of Touchstone to "Winter," Oxfordians have long been aware that the French word for "winter" is "hivre," strongly suggesting a play on the name "E. Vere." At last, Jaques (who has elected not to return to court, after learning upon the unexpected arrival of the "second brother" that the usurping duke was converted by "an old Religious Man" and abdicated his dukedom) addresses the four couples, mirroring Hymen's comments. To the first three pairs, he wishes well: "You to a Love, that your true Faith doth merit/ You to your Land, and Love, and great Allies/ You to a long, and well-deserved Bed." But to Touchstone and Audrey comes a different kind of wish: "And you to Wrangling, for thy loving Voyage is but for two Months victuall'd." The Stratfordian analysis is that this is "one of those good-humored jests to which men of the world on the eve of marriage must laughingly submit."[75]

But to an Oxfordian more seems to have been intended. Why was such a "good-humored jest" made only to Touchstone, and not to any of the other three would-be bridegrooms? Is there significance to the term "two months"? Is it possible that some small window of opportunity, of brief duration, existed within which Oxford might have been able to publish? Five lines later the play ends, followed by Rosalind's epilogue. Although the weddings of the four couples are imminent, no ceremonies actually occur. It would have been sacrilegious to depict a wedding on stage.[76]

To recap, it appears likely that the characters of Audrey and William, and probably Jaques and Touchstone, were added in 1589 to an already extant version of *As You Like It*. If Jaques and Touchstone represent Oxford, if William represents Shakspere of Stratford, and if Audrey represents the dramatic works, the implication is that Oxford and Shakspere were acquainted as early as 1589. Unfortunately, there is little extrinsic evidence to support such a connection. Oxford's exact whereabouts between 1589 and 1592 "remain generally unknown to us."[77]

No letters of his are known to exist between 1585 and August 1590.[78] Curiously, however, he writes to Lord Burghley in May 1591 that "I am weary, of an unsettled life, which is the very pestilence that happens unto Courtiers, that propound unto themselves no end of their time, therein bestowed."[79] This suggests that Oxford may have identified closely with Jaques, who is the one central character not to return to court at the end of *As You Like It*.

As noted above, Ogburn speculates that Oxford may have spent some of this time at Billesley Hall near Stratford-on- Avon. Even less is known of the whereabouts or activities of Shakspere of Stratford; the only verifiable fact of his existence between 1585 and 1596 is that in 1589 he and his father were named in legal proceedings concerning his mother's property in Wilmcote.[80] Whether an opportunity to publish the works actually arose— however tentatively—in 1589 is likewise unknown. The first appearance of the name William Shakespeare as an author is not until 1593, with the publication of the poem *Venus and Adonis*.

Although several Shakespeare plays are published during the 1590s, none carries an author's name until 1598, when *Love's*

Labour's Lost is published, "Newly corrected and augmented by W. Shakespeare." However, Oxfordians have reason to believe that Oxford was known in literary circles as "Willy" in 1590, when Spenser laments in *Tears of the Muses* that "our pleasant Willy" is "dead of late," and "Doth rather choose to sit in idle cell."[81]

This reference supports the speculation that Oxford may have been away from court at this time, and further calls to mind Touchstone's remarks that William is a "fair Name" and that "all your Writers do consent, that ipse is he." Oxford may well have used a similar name as early as 1579, when "Willie" participates in a rhyming contest in Spenser's *The Shepheardes Calendar*. As Shakspere of Stratford was only 15 years old in 1579, it is unlikely that Oxford's choice of name had anything to do with him. There is ample evidence that *As You Like It* was revised, probably more than once.

My conjecture is that one of the author's final touches—probably made after 1598, when the first plays began to appear under the name of William Shakespeare—was the insertion of a line at II,iv.16. As Rosalind, Celia and Touchstone first enter the forest, Touchstone remarks: "Ay, now am I in Arden, the more Fool I." The standard gloss is that Touchstone means that he is now not just a professional fool, but a true fool, or an even greater fool. But, within the context suggested here, the author is also saying, "Now that my works are to be published under the name of the Arden [Stratford] man, the more people will be deceived."

Endnotes

[1] The four titles (*As You Like It, Henry V, Much Ado About Nothing*, and Jonson's *Every Man in His Humour*) are listed on a page bearing the date of August 4, but without a year. Based on the order of other entries in the Register, however, scholars agree that the entry was in 1600. There is no reason to doubt this conclusion.

[2] Kittredge at vii and xvii.

[3] Ogburn at 714.

[4] Dover Wilson grounded his theory on what he detected as blank-verse lines contained in prose passages, certain internal inconsistencies,

and an allusion to Marlowe's death, which occurred on May 30, 1593. Ward at xi. Kittredge dismisses the theory. Kittredge at vii-viii.

[5] Brooke at 155.

[6] Ward at xiv-xv. Prefacing his supposition, Ward states that he is "quite serious."

[7] The popular novel was reprinted in 1592, 1596 and 1598. Ward at ix.

[8] Kittredge (at xi) is certain that Lodge had access to a manuscript copy of the fourteenth century work.

[9] See the Yale Shakespeare edition of *As You Like It* at 119. A more succinct summary is offered by Harold Jenkins: a man dies, leaving three sons, the eldest brother is wicked, the youngest virtuous, and it is he who "wins the princess, herself the victim of a wicked uncle, who has usurped her father's throne." See Halio at 30.

[10] As Stratfordians hardly need to point out, the Forest of Arden is close to Stratfordon-on- Avon, the bard's hometown.

[11] Helen Gardner, "As You Like It," reprinted in Halio at 58.

[12] Thurber & Wetherbee at 106.

[13] Jenkins, reprinted in Halio at 28.

[14] Swinden at 110; Gardner, reprinted in Halio at 56; Ward at viii.

[15] Jenkins, reprinted in Halio at 42. See also Swinden at 115.

[16] Ward at 13.

[17] Halio at 10.

[18] What follows is "an" Oxfordian interpretation, not "the" Oxfordian interpretation. In my view too many questions remain unanswered for Oxfordians to share a common view of the play's date(s) of composition, its relationship to Lodge's novel, or the inspiration or prototypes of all the characters.

[19] Clark at 508-528. Ogburn notes that Stratfordian critic Edward Dowden also dates the play's original composition to 1581, based on the author's style rather than on historical allusions. Ogburn at 714.

[20] Clark further cites Rosalind's encouragement of Orlando before the wrestling match—"Hercules be thy speed" (I,ii.220) — as an allusion to Alençon's given name: Francois Hercules de Valois. Id. At 518.

[21] Simier had loaned Alençon 90,000 crowns; poor Adam loans Orlando 500 crowns (II,iii.38-55). Id. At 523.

[22] In the preface to *Rosalynde*, Lodge offers to the reader, "If you like it, so."

[23] Ogburn at 714.

[24] Kittredge at ix.

[25] Paradise at 36-37.

[26] Smidt at 50.

[27] This is a much more satisfactory explanation than other theories propounded by Stratfordians – that the playwright forgot he had already used the name Jaques when he came to Act II; or that, as he began to develop the character of Jaques, he decided that the character would "work better" if it were not related to Orlando and Oliver, but somehow inadvertently retained the name for the middle brother. See, e.g., Jenkins, reprinted in Halio at 31; Gardner, reprinted in Halio at 58.

[28] Ogburn at 715.

[29] Ogburn at 715. See also Smidt at 196. Oxfordians believe that Oxford coordinated the opposing series of tracts attacking Marprelate. Ogburn at 716.

[30] Smidt at 53. Smidt also detects a break in III,ii., when Celia changes from "thou" to "you" in addressing Rosalind, as Rosalind changes from "you" to "thou" in addressing Celia, and when the two women switch from mentioning ancient gods to mentioning God. Id. At 53-54.

[31] Ward at 26.

[32] Berry at 188.

[33] The thought has occurred to many, though not all, Stratfordians that the characters (especially Jaques) were taken from real life. Halio (at 18) states that the two are created "out of whole cloth." Parrott (at 168) observes that "Shakespeare has taken some pains to individualize [Jaques]. He is the traveler returned from the Continent where, presumably he has, like Greene, practiced 'such a villainy as is abominable to mention' — the Duke calls him 'a libertine as sensual as the brutish sting itself' — and he has come home to sneer at all things English." Lodge's biographer, Paradise (at 90), cites Flora Masson's suggestion that Lodge himself was the source for Jaques, noting that "[h]is melancholy and prevailing mood of discontent, the doleful music of his language, his defense of satire, his medical and nautical figures of speech, and his propensity to travel are all like Lodge." Dowden's view that Shakespeare used Jaques to unload "a weight of melancholy from himself" is shared by Ward (at 27). Jenkins, however, finds it "strange" that "some earlier critics should have thought" that Jaques's "jaundiced view of life . . . might be Shakespeare's." Jenkins, reprinted in Halio at 35.

[34] Jaques's melancholy is hardly a disabling condition. "[I]t is not the fatigue of spirits of the man who has found the world too much for him, but an active principle manifesting itself in tireless and exuberant antics. Far from being a morose person . . . he throws himself into these things with something akin to passion. His misanthropy is a form of self-indulgence." Jenkins, reprinted in Halio at 35. In contemporary psychiatric terms, Jaques seems not depressed, but rather

manicdepressive.

[35] Hughes (at 101) also sees a play on "shakes," the first syllable of the author's last name, "a self-mocking pun."

[36] Ward at 68.

[37] According to the Oxford English Dictionary, the meaning of "touchstone" as a mineral dates from the 1480s, and as a figurative noun dates from the 1530s.

[38] Berry at 187, quoting John Dover Wilson's *Shakespeare's Happy Comedies*.

[39] In *Love's Labour's Lost*, Costard the fool is also "taken with a wench." Kittredge at xiii.

[40] See, e.g., Halio at 18; Barber, reprinted in Halio at 20-21; Mincoff, reprinted in Halio at 101; Mack, reprinted in Halio at 113.

[41] Gardner, reprinted in Halio at 58 and 62. See also Berry at 191.

[42] "The worst side of Touchstone appears in his relation to her, and it was a pity to lower his character. Perhaps Shakespeare felt that Touchstone — who is quite out of place in the forest — needed some pursuit, some amusement to vary a life which bored him; and supplied him with a rustic maid to seduce, and [looking ahead to V,i] a rustic lover to outrival. But the story is quite unnecessary." Brooke at 172.

[43] It is derived from Etheldrida. Interestingly, the word "tawdry" is derived from "St. Audrey's lace," a form of neckwear worn by women in Elizabethan times.

[44] The now-obsolete definition of "feature" as "a form, shape or creation" dates to 1483. Oxford English Dictionary.

[45] Touchstone has been exiled to the forest. Ovid—Shakespeare's chief classical literary source — "was exiled to live among the Getae (Goths), and complained that his works were not understood by these barbarians." Everyman Shakespeare, *As You Like It,* at 134.

[46] "In Book VIII of the *Metamorphoses* Ovid describes a visit by the disguised Jove and Mercury to the cottage of a peasant couple, Philemon and Baucis." Everyman Shakespeare, *As You Like It,* at 136.

[47] In III,v.81-82, Celia quotes two lines from Marlowe's *Hero and Leander*, published in 1598. According to Ward (at xi), this "is the only direct allusion to a contemporary's work in all of Shakespeare." A further reference to *Hero and Leander* may be lurking in IV,i.107-113.

[48] At III,iii.32-33 Audrey plays on the words "fair" and "honest" ("Well, I am not fair, and therefore I pray the Gods make me honest"); earlier in the play, Celia has a similar speech ("for those that [Fortune] makes Fair, she scarce makes Honest, and those that she makes Honest, she makes very ill-favouredly"). I,ii.41-43.

[49] This usage of "foul" dates to the late 1400s. Oxford English

Dictionary.

[50] See, e.g., Smidt at 196 ("his name must have invited ridicule and perhaps topical contempt — unless, of course, a Roman Catholic jibe at the Protestant form of marriage is intended").

[51] Leggatt at 190.

[52] Berry at 191; he earlier notes that "sex is quite unsatisfactory as the sole motive for Touchstone's marriage. The Audreys of the world do not demand a price; the Audrey of this play does not ask it." Id. at 190.

[53] Wilson at 156-157.

[54] Swinden at 115.

[55] Ward at 68.

[56] Jenkins, reprinted in Halio at 40.

[57] Berry at 189.

[58] Jenkins, reprinted in Halio at 40; Gardner, reprinted in Halio at 57 and 62; Halio at 5.

[59] Among the few Stratfordians to have considered the obvious connection is Jonathan Bate, who views the scene as an encounter between the fully mature playwright (personified by Touchstone) and his youthful self (William) as he was before he departed Stratford for London.

[60] Ogburn at 747-749. In addition to William of *As You Like It*, Ogburn notes William Visor, referred to as "an arrant knave," and William Cook, who lost some "sack . . . the other day at Hinkley Fair," both mentioned in *2 Henry IV*. The latter play contains two other references to persons named Will or William, both in III,ii — Shallow's "cousin William is become a good scholar . . . at Oxford"; a few lines later Shallow recalls "Will Squele a Cotswold man." In *2 Henry VI*, II,iii, drunken Peter Thump, the armourer's apprentice, gives his hammer to a fellow apprentice named Will. The other non-historical speaking part is William Page (interesting last name!), the youth who is examined in Latin in *The Merry Wives of Windsor*; as with the William scene of *As You Like It*, it is a curious sidebar to the play itself. Ogburn also notes that there are no non-historical Edwards in the plays.

[61] Ogburn at 655.

[62] Ogburn at 608.

[63] Ogburn at 529.

[64] Ogburn at 712-713. "According to a local rumor, As You Like It was written in Billesley Hall, a rumor most easily accounted for as having originated in fact." Id. at 712. By the 1580s Billesley Hall had been owned by the Trussel family (the family of Oxford's mother) for 400 years. Id.

[65] "To have, is to have" is, of course, a tautology, as elementary a

lesson as can be conceived. Offering an explanation for Touchstone's choice of lesson, Charles Burford points to the Italian translation of the tautology: "Per avere e di avere." The reference to "avere" – a Vere – can hardly be coincidental.

[66] Ogburn at 748; the author notes further that Schoenbaum has treated that hypothesis with "particular scorn."

[67] Ogburn at 748.

[68] Kittredge at 175, citing *The Marriage of Wit and Wisdom*, published in 1579: "In faith I am Ipse, he even the very same? A man of greate estimation in mine owne country."

[69] The Folio word is "Police."

[70] Kittredge at 176.

[71] See, e.g., Kittredge at 180: "To 'go to the world' was a common idiom for to 'get married'. . . . 'The world' seems, in these phrases, to be contrasted with a celibate or monastic life."

[72] Oxford English Dictionary, citing Nashe.

[73] Oxford English Dictionary.

[74] The Folio spelling is "fowl."

[75] Kittredge at 189, quoting Maginn.

[76] Smidt at 57.

[77] Ogburn at 712.

[78] Fowler at 356.

[79] Fowler at 394-395; Ogburn at 721.

[80] Ogburn at 26 & 778.

[81] Ogburn at 719-720.

Bibliography

Andrews, John F. (ed). *As You Like It, The Everyman Shakespeare* (1997, J.M. Dent)Berry, Ralph. *Shakespeare's Comedies — Explorations in Form* (Princeton University Press, 1972).

Bloom, Harold. *William Shakespeare's As You Like It — Modern Critical Interpretations* (New York: Chelsea House, 1988).

Brooke, Stopford A. *On Ten Plays of Shakespeare* (1905, reprinted 1961, Constable and Company).

Burchell, S. C. (ed). *As You Like It, The Yale Shakespeare* (New Haven: Yale Univ. Press, 1954).

Clark, Eva Turner. *Hidden Allusions in Shakespeare's Plays* (Port Washington, NY: Kennikat Press, 1974).

Fowler, William Plumer. *Shakespeare Revealed in Oxford's Letters*

(Portsmouth, NH: Peter Randall Publisher, 1986).

Halio, Jay A. (ed). *Twentieth Century Interpretations of As You Like It* (New York: Prentice-Hall, 1968).

Hughes, Ted. *Shakespeare and the Goddess of Complete Being* (New York: Farrar Straus Giroux, 1992).

Kittredge, George Lyman (ed). *As You Like It It* (Ginn and Company, 1939).

Leggatt, Alexander. *Shakespeare's Comedy of Love* (London: Methuen & Co., 1974).

Ogburn, Charlton. *The Mysterious William Shakespeare — The Myth and the Reality* (McLean, VA: EPM Publications, 1992).

Paradise, N. Burton. *Thomas Lodge — The History of an Elizabethan* (New Haven: Yale University Press, 1931; reprinted 1970, Archon Books).

Parrott, Thomas Marc. *Shakespearean Comedy* (New York: Russell & Russell, 1962).

Smidt, Kristian. *Unconformities in Shakespeare's Later Comedies* (New York: St. Martin's Press, 1993).

Stokes, Francis Griffin. *Who's Who in Shakespeare* (New York: Crescent Books, 1989).

Swinden, Patrick. *An Introduction to Shakespeare's Comedies* (New York: Harper & Row, 1973).

Thurber, Samuel Jr. & Louise Wetherbee. *Shakespeare As You Like It* (Norwood Press, 1992).

Ward, John Powell. *As You Like It, Twayne's New Critical Introductions to Shakespeare* (Twayne Publishers, 1992).

Wilson, John Dover. *Shakespeare's Happy Comedies* (Evanston: Northwestern U. Press, 1962).

.

Chapter 5

The Rival Poet in
Shake-speares Sonnets

Hank Whittemore

This essay is based upon a presentation made at the 2013 Shakespeare Authorship Studies Conference at Concordia University in Portland (OR). The argument set forth here about the rival poet is an expansion of one aspect of the author's complete 900-page study of the Sonnets, The Monument *(2005). See Appendix B for a brief overview of how* The Monument *recasts an understanding of the* Sonnets *through the prism of their historical context being the Essex Rebellion in 1601.*

The phrase "paradigm shift" has become a cliché, but those of us who have been investigating the life of Edward de Vere, seventeenth Earl of Oxford as author of the "Shakespeare" works are involved in bringing about just such an extraordinary change of perspective—one that demands what J. Thomas Looney in 1920 called a "difficult revolution in mental attitude." (Looney, 372)

This transition usually requires strong doubt about the Stratford conception, if not outright rejection of it, but ultimately the more important and compelling stage of the revolution begins with first discovering the correct replacement and then learning as much as possible about his life and his relationship to the poems, plays and sonnets. And the evidence produced by work carried out for nearly a century is that there can be no question that Oxford was the great author. He is such a good fit that we keep finding new information in support, and new insights as a result, leading to much greater (and often astonishing) illumination of the literature and the history. In the process, we have left behind those tired traditional explanations that have been not merely problematic but plainly irrational or oxymoronic.

The Shakespearean works themselves never change; what does profoundly alter, through the Oxfordian lens, is our perception of them; and often the picture is turned inside out or upside down in quite unexpected ways. With Oxford as the model, a light is turned on and we begin exploring avenues that cannot even occur to someone still looking from the old orthodox angle. In effect we have put on new eyeglasses that allow us to "see" differently.

Once that mental revolution occurs, we face the need for many other shifts of perception spinning off from the spine of the Oxford case. This is not about merely changing the author's name on the title pages for another name; in fact the scope and meaning of the change has yet to be fully comprehended. In the process, however, we still have to shake off some of that old baggage, in the form of deeply ingrained assumptions, based on the old model. And even for supposedly open-minded Oxfordians, it's not easy, given that our human nature is to cling to longstanding viewpoints and cherished beliefs as long as possible.

Nowhere is this gravity-pull of tradition stronger than in the matter of the so-called rival poet series of the Sonnets, generally viewed as the sequence from Sonnet 77 or 78 to Sonnet 86. The Stratfordian model forced us to see this series in just one way—namely that other writers, but mainly one particular poet who towers above all the others, is stealing the attentions and affections of the fair youth, generally regarded as Henry Wriothesley, third Earl of Southampton.

When Looney expressed his agreement with the majority of critics that the younger man was Southampton, he pointed to the rival series itself as powerful evidence. First he cited the line in Sonnet 81 about "your name" [i.e., Southampton's name] achieving immortal life [by means of its association with

"Shakespeare"]; and second he cited the "companion" verse, Sonnet 82, in which the author refers to his own "dedicated words" or public dedications of *Venus and Adonis* (1593) and *Lucrece* (1594) to Southampton.

Teams of Rivals

Given then Southampton as the fair youth, Stratfordians have postulated many rivals—Barnes, Chapman, Chaucer, Daniel, Davies, Davison, Drayton, Florio, Golding, Greene, Griffin, Harvey, Jonson, Kyd, Lyly, Markham, Marlowe, Martston, Nashe, Peele, Spenser, the Italian Tasso, Watson. Oxfordians have come up with some overlaps, such as Chapman and Marlowe, while adding the likes of Sir Walter Raleigh and Rober Devereux, the second Earl of Essex. The senior Ogburns in *This Star of England* (1952) thought the rival was both George Chapman and Christopher Marlowe, while their son Charlton Ogburn Jr. in *The Mysterious William Shakespeare* (1984) wisely took no position, instead referring to the rival as "one other poet, whose identity I must leave to the contention of more confident minds." (Ogburn Jr., 328) Meanwhile Peter Moore made a well-researched and detailed case for Essex, summing up this way:

> *Shake-speares Sonnets* describes a rival who was Southampton's friend, a poet, learned, tall, proud, probably a sailor, who had an affable familiar ghost who dealt in intelligence, who received assistance in his writing from friends … who was associated with the word 'virtue' and with cosmetics, who boosted Southampton's fame while being in his debt …. This is quite a detailed portrait, and Essex matches it perfectly. (Moore, 10)

While acknowledging that various lines of the rival poet series may relate to Raleigh or Essex and others, in a more fundamental way I respectfully must disagree with all of the above suggestions. From the viewpoint of Edward de Vere's authorship combined with the context of time and circumstance of Sonnets 27-126 offered by the theory set forth in my edition *The*

Monument (2005), I have come to a radical solution to the rival poet's identity.

Oxford's Double Life

Both the Stratfordian and the Oxfordian views have required the rival poet to be some rather extraordinary individual who wrote poetry and publicly used Southampton's name; but the Oxfordian model opens the door to an entirely new way of looking at the rival poet series itself, resulting in a view of the "better spirit" who "doth use your [Southampton's] name" as none of the individuals mentioned—in fact, as not a *person* at all, but, instead, a *persona*.

In my view the rival poet series represents Oxford's own testimony about the authorship—a grand, poetic, profoundly emotional statement of (1) his dying to the world and (2) his resurrection as a spirit breathing life into the poetical and dramatic luminary known as Shakespeare.

The Stratfordian view gave no reason to look for any kind of authorship statement anywhere, much less in the so-called rival series; but Oxfordians contend precisely that Oxford has split himself into two separate entities—on the one hand, he is Edward de Vere, writing privately in the sonnets; and on the other hand, he is "Shakespeare," the name on the printed page and the mythic figure of a Super Poet shaking the spear of his pen.

At the outset we have pictured Oxford living a double life. We picture the blotting-out or expunging of his true identity and its replacement by a rival identity. We were led to take it for granted that the rival must be some flesh-and-blood individual; but from Looney onward, we have also pictured Oxford as creating his own rival—initially in the form of a pen name or pseudonym, which then takes the form of a character on the world stage, and later as a mask glued to his face, smothering his real identity for all time.

I believe that if not for the Stratfordian baggage that we Oxfordians still carry with us, we would never have postulated a real person as the rival in the first place; we would have known automatically that Oxford is referring to his alter ego. It is not Oxford but "Shakespeare" who signs the dedications to Southampton, which continue to appear in new editions. It is not Oxford but "Shakespeare" who continues to receive the credit. But there's much more to it than that.

The Sacrifice

The clear testimony of the rival poet series is that the author, Oxford, is fading away ... becoming invisible ... and that while dying to the world he is also being resurrected in the persona of "Shakespeare"—making a Christ-like sacrifice to redeem Southampton's sins or crimes, by taking them upon himself, and offering his own identity as ransom, so the younger man may survive and live for as long as men can breathe or eyes can see.

In Sonnets 78 to 86 he is talking about other writers who have dedicated works to Southampton, and praised him, but he means writers in general, whereas he is also and primarily speaking of his own invention or creation, which he inhabits as a spirit. By the end of this series, he considers himself dead to the world while his ghost, his spirit, now lives within the assumed persona of "Shakespeare."

He leads up to the rival series by making clear that his coming death "to all the world" revolves around Southampton – his need to help and protect him and to preserve his memory for posterity, by means of a kind of religious sacrifice. He is not dying in a vacuum, but in relation to Southampton, well before the sequence begins:

> When I perhaps compounded am with clay,
> Do not so much as my poor name rehearse. – 71

> After my death, dear love, forget me quite...
> My name be buried where my body is,
> And live no more to shame nor me nor you. – 72

Each line of Oxford's obliteration is linked to concern for

Southampton. Now begins the rival series with Sonnet 78:

> As every *Alien* pen hath got my use,
> And under thee their posey doth disperse – 78

"Every *Alien* Pen" glances at other poets who have praised Southampton, but it is *E. Ver's* pen name ("Shakespeare") that is alien—not his real identity.

> But now my gracious numbers are decayed,
> And my sick Muse doth give an other place – 79

> *"I yield to Shakespeare. As I decay and disappear, I step aside and let him take my place."*

> O how I faint when I of you do write,
> Knowing a better spirit doth use your name,
> And in the praise thereof spends all his might
> To make me tongue-tied speaking of your fame – 80

This is not hyperbole. Oxford's fainting is an act of losing consciousness or the ability to speak or write. He also faints by feinting, or deceiving—like the feint of a skilled fencer—by assuming an appearance or making a feint to conceal his real identity. He faints by becoming weaker, feebler … less visible. But also in the first line of Sonnet 80 he is crying out to say, directly:

> *"I am the one who is writing to you and using your name. I am fainting in the process, because, while writing in praise of you, I am vanishing into the confines of my pen name. I am undergoing a metamorphosis. I am doing this to myself, feeding my spirit to 'Shakespeare,' so the more I write through him, the more I lose my identity ... and the faster I die to the world. It is through my own spirit that Shakespeare uses your name, and because of his power (ironically the power I give him), I am tongue-tied, silent, and unable to write publicly about you under my own name."*

We have learned in Sonnet 66 that his art has been "tongue-tied by authority"—he is being censored, suppressed; and the force keeping him silent is "authority" or officialdom. The force is the government, as when he writes in *King John* of the monarch's "sovereign greatness and *authority*."

Now in Sonnet 80, extending the same thought, he records that "Shakespeare" is making him tongue-tied, that is, making him "tongue-tied speaking of your [Southampton's] fame." Oxford's own pen name has been turned against him to become *the agent of the authority that is keeping him silent.*

"I, once gone, to all the world must die"

And here the door opens to a larger and more important story than merely Oxford disappearing for no reason. Again back in Sonnet 66, he cites "strength by limping sway disabled"—the government, in the person of the figure now identified as the *limping, swaying* Robert Cecil, a hunchback, is using Oxford's own persona of "Shakespeare" as a weapon against him.

[King James wrote to his ambassadors the Earl of Mar and Edward Bruce on April 8, 1601, two months after the failed Essex rebellion, and referred to the now all-powerful Cecil in England as "Master Secretary, who is king there in effect."] (Akrigg, 175)

Oxford's own better spirit is making him tongue-tied when it comes to "speaking of your fame"—which again refers to the widely read public dedications to Southampton by "Shakespeare," reprinted in every new edition of the narrative poems. "Shakespeare," the "better spirit," is the agent of Oxford's death "to all the world"—as in "I (once gone) to all the world must die" in Sonnet 81—and yet "Shakespeare" is also the means by which, all else having failed, Southampton will attain eternal life.

> My saucy bark, inferior far to his,
> On your broad main doth willfully appear – 80

Steven Booth writes that *willfully* "may have been chosen for its pun on the poet's name: the saucy bark is full of Will." (Booth, 274) I would suggest it's a pun on the poet's *pen* name.

Now in Sonnet 81 come those two famous lines for

Oxfordians which we have already mentioned. These lines sum up the authorship problem and provide the answer to the authorship question.

> Your name from hence immortal life shall have
> Though I (once gone) to all the world must die - 81

If the argument here is correct, then it's no accident that these lines of Sonnet 81 appear in the so-called rival sequence. Southampton's name "from hence" or from this time forward will achieve immortal life, *but not necessarily because of these sonnets.* Henry Wriothesley's name never appears [directly] in the sonnets. From now on, his name will have immortal life because of "Shakespeare's" public dedications to him by name—the only dedications the great author will ever offer to anyone; but by the same token, also because of "Shakespeare," the author's real name or identity will disappear from the world.

And it's in the very next verse, Sonnet 82, where we find Oxford referring to his own 1593-1594 public dedications to Southampton under the "Shakespeare" name, which he used in print for the first time:

> The dedicated words which writers use
> Of their fair subject, blessing every book – 82

> *"The dedications I wrote under the 'Shakespeare' name about the fair youth, Southampton, consecrating E.Ver's (my own) books of 'Venus and Adonis' and 'Lucrece.' "*

This sonnet also contains a remarkable pair of lines from Oxford's private self, playing upon his motto *Nothing Truer than Truth* as if still insisting upon his own identity before it's gone:

> Thou truly fair wert truly sympathized
> In true-plain words by thy true-telling friend – 82

By calling the younger man "fair" in the lines above, he is

64

linking him to the "fair subject" of the dedications mentioned earlier in the same sonnet; and since we know for a fact that Southampton was the subject of those public epistles, we now know equally for certain that he is the subject of the Sonnets.

Oxford is "dumb" or silent and "mute" because he is unable to speak in public:

> Which shall be most my glory, being dumb,
> For I impair not beauty, being mute – 83

He refers in the next sonnet to "both" poets writing to Southampton, that is, both he and his pen name:

> There lives more life in one of your fair eyes
> Than both your poets can in praise devise – 83

Addressing Southampton, he tells about teaching his own pseudonym, "Shakespeare," how to write about Southampton himself:

> Let him but copy what in you is writ,
> Not making worse what nature made so clear,
> And such a counterpart shall fame his wit,
> Making his style admired every where – 84

So here we have Oxford, while using "every" to glance at himself as E.Ver, telling Southampton how to instruct his (Oxford's) alter-ego: *Let him hold the mirror up to your own nature, to copy it, and he will be admired by everyone.*

> My tongue-tied Muse – 85

> *"My Muse and I are silenced."*

> Then others, for the breath of words respect,
> Me for my dumb thoughts, speaking in effect – 85

> *"Respect me for my silent thoughts and for my actions in your behalf."*

The final verse of the series tells the whole story, beginning with its first quatrain:

> Was it the proud full sail of his great verse,
> Bound for the prize of (all too precious) you,
> That did my ripe thoughts in my brain inhearse,
> Making their tomb the womb wherein they grew? - 86

There is only one Super Poet who can force Oxford's thoughts into a tomb in his brain, which is also the tomb of these verses—as in Sonnet 17, "Heaven knows it is but as a tomb which hides your life and shows not half your parts"—and the womb of these verses wherein Southampton can grow—as in Sonnet 115, "To give full life to that which still doth grow."

> Was it his spirit, by spirits taught to write
> Above a mortal pitch, that struck me dead? – 86

No other writer, past or present, has struck Oxford dead—but there it is, in the last sonnet of the sequence, Oxford writing that his identity has been killed.

> No, neither he, nor his compeers by night
> Giving him aid, my verse astonished. – 86

Oxford's own spirit is teaching his public persona to write with the power of Shakespeare.

> He, nor that affable familiar ghost
> Which nightly gulls him with intelligence,
> As victors of my silence cannot boast;
> I was not sick of any fear from thence. - 86

The "affable familiar ghost" is once again Oxford's own spirit, which "nightly" or secretly fills "Shakespeare" the pen name with his substance—or literally with "intelligence" or secret information that Oxford is inserting within the lines of his plays. To "gull" is to cram full, but also to play a trick on, and of course "Shakespeare" the pen name is totally dependent upon Oxford and cannot know what mischief his spirit is up to.

> But when your countenance filled up his line,
> Then lacked I matter, that enfeebled mine. - 86

This final couplet is another direct statement of the authorship problem. As Shakespeare rises in connection with Southampton, so Oxford fades away—as Touchstone in *As You Like It* tells William the country fellow:

> "Drink, being poured out of a cup into a glass, by filling the one doth empty the other."

The so-called rival series is the equivalent of a "movement" of a musical composition, a symphony. It's a separate piece within a larger structure. Its message can be expressed in a line or two, but Oxford wants a *string* of lines. The sequence is a long wail of eloquent mourning.

"Lay on me this cross"

But in fact the actual mourning begins much earlier, with many of the preceding sonnets, which are preoccupied with dying. Death is necessary if there is to be a resurrection. So there is a religious, spiritual aspect, mirroring the sacrifice of Christ.

In fact it goes all the way back to Sonnet 27 where Southampton is "a jewel hung in ghastly night"—the image of a man in prison awaiting execution or, if you will, of a man being "hung" on the cross. In Christian terms a father and his son are separate individuals who, nonetheless, are also inseparable. He writes in Sonnet 27:

> For thee, and for my self, no quiet find

And in Sonnet 42:

> My friend and I are one.

A Poet's Rage

There is a long preparation for the so-called rival series. These words and images are genuinely religious ... spiritual ... devastating. The drumbeat of despair is profound, sorrowful and deeply emotional—what we might expect from a father waiting for his son to be killed by the state and, too, sacrificing his own identity to save him.

Intend a zealous pilgrimage to thee - 27

Clouds do blot the heaven – 28

Look upon myself and curse my fate – 29

Precious friends hid in *death's dateless night* - 30

How many a holy and obsequious tear
Hath dear religious love stolen from mine eye – 31

Thou art the grave where buried love doth live - 31

When that churl death my bones with dust shall cover - 32

Anon permit the basest clouds to ride
With ugly rack on his celestial face - 33

Though thou repent, yet I have still the loss;
The offender's sorrow lends but weak relief
To him that bears the strong offence's cross - 34

So shall those blots that do with me remain
Without thy help, by me be borne alone - 36

Lay on me this cross - 42
To guard the lawful reasons on thy part - 49

'Gainst death and all oblivious enmity
Shall you pace forth – 55

So till the judgment that yourself arise - 55

I (my sovereign) watch the clock for you - 57

Nativity, once in the main of light,
Crawls to maturity, wherewith being crowned,

Crooked eclipses 'gainst his glory fight - 60
To play the watchman ever for thy sake - 61

O fearful meditation! - 65

For restful death I cry - 66

In him those holy antique hours are seen - 68

All tongues, the voice of souls, give thee that due - 69

No longer mourn for me when I am dead - 71

In me thou seest the twilight of such day,
As after Sun-set fadeth in the West - 73

When that fell arrest
Without all bail shall carry me away - 74

Why is my verse so barren of new pride - 76

And here, finally, his verse is like a barren womb, empty of child. Now we have Sonnet 77, a dedicatory verse—with Oxford speaking to Southampton first of "this book" and then, at the end, dedicating it to him as "thy book." This is the real opening of the so-called rival series—ten consecutive sonnets from 77 to 86:

And of this book this learning mayst thou taste…
These offices, so oft as thou wilt look,
Shall profit thee, and much enrich thy book - 77

Yet be most proud of that which I compile,
Whose influence is thine, and born of thee - 78

And in 78, even while "every alien pen hath got my use," he nonetheless tells Southampton to be "most proud" of these sonnets which he is compiling—or arranging—and identifies them as having been influenced or inspired by Southampton and "born" of him, thereby identifying Henry Wriothesley as the "onlie begetter" of the sonnets, "Mr. W.H.," referred to in the dedication.

Meanwhile the nautical imagery has begun a bit earlier, for example:

> When I have seen the hungry ocean gain
> Advantage on the kingdom of the shore ...
> When I have seen such interchange of state
> Or state itself confounded to decay - 64

"'Ocean' or 'sea' as a figure for 'king' is often found in Shakespeare and his fellow-writers," Leslie Hotson observed, citing, for example, "Even to our ocean, to our great King John" in *King John*, 5.4.7 (Hotson, 27) In Sonnet 64 the "hungry Ocean" indicates the royal blood of King James advancing upon England, the "kingdom of the shore," and the coming of the inevitable "interchange of state" or succession upon the death of Queen Elizabeth.

The nautical imagery is based now on Southampton's worth as wide as the Ocean, referring to his royal worth. Metaphorically, Southampton's ocean of royal blood holds up all boats:

> But since your worth (wide as the Ocean is)
> The humble as the proudest sail doth bear - 80

"I may not ever-more acknowledge thee"

I came to this view of the so-called rival by a long and indirect route—hypothesizing that the fair youth sonnets are in fact chronologically arranged from Sonnet 1 to Sonnet 126; and that they lead up to, and away from, Sonnet 107, when Southampton is released from the Tower in April 1603 after being "supposed as forfeit to a confined doom."

That so-called "dating" sonnet (referring to its obvious allusions to topical events in the spring of 1603) involves not only the liberation of Southampton, but also the death of Elizabeth, the succession of James and the fall of the Tudor dynasty. If the other sonnets have no relationship to that enormously serious, political subject matter, then Sonnet 107 would be one huge anomaly within the series.

A simple question therefore became obvious. Given that Shakespeare is a masterful storyteller, and given that the high point of this story is Southampton getting *out of* the Tower, it stands to reason that he must have marked the time when Southampton went *into* the Tower. Otherwise there is no story at all, no suspense, and his liberation comes out of the blue, apropos of nothing.

Moving downward along the consecutively numbered verses from the high point of Sonnet 107, and following the allusions to legal matters and imprisonment as well as the dark language of suffering, I landed back at Sonnet 27 as marking that time on the night of February 8, 1601 when Southampton had entered the Tower expecting execution—when the author envisions him as *"a Jewel hung in ghastly night."* Then, moving forward or upward toward Sonnet 107 again, I tracked sonnets reflecting those crucial days after the failed Essex rebellion until the moment of Southampton's reprieve from execution in March 1601. And in that context it became clear that Oxford had made a deal with Robert Cecil to save the younger earl, a secret agreement that required complete severance of the relationship between himself and Southampton, which he recorded for posterity:

I may not ever-more acknowledge thee – 36

Oxford is sacrificing his identity to gain Southampton's life; he is dying to the world and undergoing a resurrection as "Shakespeare." And once the rival series comes to its conclusion with Sonnet 86, the very first word of Sonnet 87, appropriately, is "farewell":

Farwell, thou art too dear for my possessing ...
My bonds in thee are all determinate - 87

"Our connection to each other is hereby severed. The deal is done."

Adopting the pen name in 1593 had been Edward de Vere's way of lending public support to Southampton from behind the scenes; now in 1601, to save Southampton's life and gain his eventual freedom, he has agreed to make the pen name permanent. From now on, even after his death, the rest is silence.

The enormity of Oxford's sacrifice—completely severing his relationship with Southampton, losing his identity as the great writer—the dashing of his hopes involving succession to Elizabeth and the future of England – his death to the world and resurrection as "Shakespeare" to save Southampton and redeem his sins and ensure his life in the eyes of posterity—the enormity of this sacrifice demands a use of words that, in most any other scenario, would seem to be sheer hyperbole, nothing more than "a poet's rage and stretched meter of an antique song":

> *"My gracious numbers are decayed ... my sick muse ... O how I faint .... Being wracked, I am a worthless boat ... the earth can yield me but a common grave ... most my glory, being dumb ... being mute ... my tongue-tied muse ... my dumb thoughts."*

This is, in fact, a poet's rage—but when viewed within the correct context, as part of the correctly perceived picture, the rage is no longer fatuous or "over the top"; instead it becomes honest and real, written in reaction to major events affecting England's contemporary history, in a supreme effort to leave behind a *witnessing* to otherwise secret happenings; and so, too, the words expressing these urgent matters become not merely appropriate but, as well, used with accuracy and precision. Clearly the rival poet series deserves a "difficult revolution in mental attitude."

Works Cited

Akrigg, G.P.V., *Letters of King James VI & I* (U. of Cal. Press) 1984

Booth, Stephen, *Shakespeare's Sonnets* (Yale U. Press) 1977

Hotson, Leslie, *Mr. W.H.* (Knopf) 1965

Looney, J. Thomas, *"Shakespeare" Identified* (Cecil Palmer) 1920

Moore, Peter R., *The Lame Storyteller, Poor and Despised* (Verlag Uwe Laugwitz) 2009

Ogburn, Dorothy/Charlton, *This Star of England* (Coward) 1952

Ogburn Jr., Charlton, *The Mysterious William Shakespeare* (EMP) 1984

Whittemore, Hank. *The Monument* (Meadow Geese Press) 2005

Chapter 6

Southampton's Tower Poem

Hank Whittemore

This essay is based upon a presentation made at the 2013
Shakespeare Authorship Studies Conference
at Concordia University in Portland (OR).

Henry Wriothesley, third Earl of Southampton wrote a 74-line poem from his prison room in the Tower of London to Queen Elizabeth in February or March of 1601, begging for royal mercy. I would like to present strong evidence that during this same period in the Tower he received some of the private Shakespearean sonnets from Edward de Vere, seventeenth Earl of Oxford that helped to guide him in the composition of his poem to the Queen.

The Tower

He had been imprisoned on the night of February 8, 1601, after the so-called rebellion of that day had failed; he and Robert Devereux, second Earl of Essex stood trial eleven days later; both were found guilty of high treason and sentenced to be executed. Essex was beheaded six days later, on the morning of February twenty-fifth; and then Southampton began to languish in his prison room waiting to be executed. The earl wrote his poem to Elizabeth during the next three or four weeks, until no later than the twentieth of March, the approximate time when he was unexpectedly spared the death penalty. His sentence was quietly commuted to perpetual imprisonment—not only quietly, but secretly, because no official record of the reprieve has ever been found.

His poem written in the Tower was discovered by Lara Crowley, assistant professor of English at Texas Tech University, and printed in the winter 2011 issue of *English Literary Renaissance*. Professor Crowley found the poem in the British Library, in a collection of miscellaneous folios prepared in the 1620s or 1630s. It was preserved as a scribal copy entitled *"The Earl of Southampton prisoner, and condemned, to Queen Elizabeth."* The 74 lines consist of 37 rhymed couplets in iambic pentameter—as in the lines of the Shakespeare sonnets (five feet or 10 beats per line) and more specifically as in the rhymed couplets of Sonnet 126, the envoy or postscript to the fair youth series written to and about Southampton. The newly recovered scribal copy represents the only poem Southampton is known to have written. [The poem is reprinted in full at the end of this essay.]

Professor Crowley calls it a "verse letter" to the Queen— although a literary work, it is nonetheless *nonfictional* and *functional*—intended as a means of communication and persuasion. Crowley also refers to it as a "heartfelt plea" by Henry Wriothesley for his life and focuses on several key issues.

One is the *authenticity* of the poem. In this regard she cites certain details within the poem that would be known only to Southampton himself and just a few others—the prison doctor, the Lieutenant of the Tower and Secretary Robert Cecil. Also favoring authenticity is that Southampton wrote several letters to the Privy Council, as well as one to Cecil, and many of the key words in the poem are also employed in these letters.

A second issue is the question whether Southampton wrote the poem all by himself or with someone's help. Is it even possible, Crowley wonders, that some more "practiced" poet wrote it for him? Could such help have come from Mr. Shakespeare?

Highly improbable, given the restricted access to Southampton, but she puts forth the question and lets it float out there.

A third matter to which she gives attention is the *literary quality* of the poem. Crowley notes the work is "unpolished," adding however that we might predict such lack of polish from a man expecting to face the executioner's axe at any moment. However imperfect it may be, she writes, *"the poem proves lyrical, powerful and persuasive."*

Robert Cecil

Most important to Crowley is that the poem triggers a historical question that has never been satisfactorily answered: *Why was Southampton spared?* There must have been a concrete *reason*; but there is nothing in the record, from the government or from anywhere else, with an explanation of what happened. The professor dismisses any idea that Cecil was moved to save Southampton out of sympathy. At this point he had the power—apparently even over Elizabeth—to make, or not make, this decision; and if he *did* make sure that a convicted traitor was spared, he would have demanded something that he dearly wanted in return.

Of course, what he dearly wanted now was to bring James of Scotland to the throne. At stake was Cecil's own position behind the throne, not to mention his life; and now he faced a long, uncertain time of waiting for the Queen to die, during which time he had to conduct a secret and even treasonous correspondence with James that her Majesty might discover at any moment. It would take more than two years—a period of almost unbearable tension for Robert Cecil; and the question, given these high stakes, is what he might have demanded and gotten in return for sparing Southampton's life.

The Southampton Tower Poem was of interest to me right away, because I realized it could have some bearing upon the theory of the Shakespeare sonnets as expressed in my book *The Monument*. A central aspect of the theory is that on the night of the failed rebellion, Edward de Vere began to write a string of sonnets—a sequence that he ultimately arranged in correspondence with each day (or night, if you will) until Southampton was either executed or given a reprieve. Oxford knew that Southampton's fate would be determined sooner rather than later; in fact it took approximately forty days and forty nights until the reprieve; and in my view, no matter what the precise number of days, Oxford *deliberately lined up exactly forty sonnets* from number 27 to number 66.

I believe he arranged this sequence to equal forty sonnets in order to have it correspond with the *forty days and forty* nights that Jesus spent fasting in the wilderness, as in the Gospel of Matthew:

> "And when he had fasted *forty days and forty nights* ... And when the tempter came to him ... he answered and said, 'It is written, Man shall not live by bread alone, but by *every word* that proceedeth from the mouth of God'" —Matthew, 4.4

And ten sonnets later in Sonnet 76, at the very center of Oxford's "century" of one hundred sonnets numbered 27 to 126, he writes in blatant correspondence with that Gospel verse:

> "That *every word* doth almost tell my name, showing their birth, and where they did *proceed*" —Sonnet 76 [1]

Now if those forty sonnets correspond with the forty days from the eighth of February 1601 to the nineteenth of March 1601, *we then have Southampton in the Tower during the very same time, waiting to learn his fate*—and we know that in those days and nights he wrote his letters to the Council and to Cecil and additionally his poem to Elizabeth, pleading for mercy. So if the theory of forty sonnets (27 to 66) during that time is correct, *we should be able to predict that we'll find some relationship* between Oxford's sonnets to Southampton and Southampton's poem to the Queen.

First, a few markers:

"When to the Sessions of sweet silent thought
I summon up remembrance of things past" – Sonnet 30

Given the premise that the sonnet is written just when Oxford
is *summoned to the sessions or treason trial*, it would seem to be
extraordinary corroboration.

Thy adverse party is thy Advocate—Sonnet 35

["Your (legal) opponent is also your (legal) defender."—Katherine
Duncan-Jones, editor, the *Arden* edition]

"Thy adverse party is thy Advocate" would describe Oxford's
role on the tribunal at the trial, having to be Southampton's
adverse party by voting to find him guilty and sentence him to
death, but also promising to work behind the scenes as his
advocate or legal defender.

To my knowledge, this is the only explanation of that line
that *links it to a specific historical and biographical event* – that is,
the trial, and Oxford's role on the tribunal—and also in terms of
its accuracy and precision as a recognized legal reference.
Moreover the line serves to suggest that *Oxford had some way of
helping Southampton*—helping him write those letters to the
Council, not only with words but with guidance about what to say
to the queen – and that he may have urged Southampton to plead
with Elizabeth through poetry in the first place. It would be logical
to infer that in playing his role as "advocate" or defense counsel,
Oxford either helped him write the poem, or at least suggested its
themes if not its words.

Essex wrote a much longer poem to Elizabeth from the
Tower, during the few days between the trial and his execution. In
that case, however, it was absolutely necessary for Cecil to destroy
Essex by sending him to his death; therefore I would think it fairly
certain that he made sure Elizabeth *never did see* the Essex poem.
In Oxford's case, however, *the proposition here is that he made a
deal with Cecil*, which included lending his support (and work
behind the scenes) for the succession of King James of Scotland to

the English throne … not to mention severing his relationship to "Shakespeare" and any connection to Southampton. In return Cecil would make it possible for Oxford to help Southampton gain a reprieve. And given the likelihood that Oxford advised Southampton to write a poem to her Majesty, the question is *how he might have helped him*—which brings us to another marker, this one in Sonnet 45, when Oxford refers to:

> Those swift messengers returned from thee,
> Who even but now come back again assured
> Of thy fair health, recounting it to me. —Sonnet 45

There are two topics here—one, he appears to be referring to *messengers on horseback* riding back and forth between Oxford's home in Hackney and the Tower—and this may well indicate that he's been able to get copies of sonnets delivered to Southampton. This suggestion, in my view, is quite in the realm of the possible and even the probable—first because of Oxford's high rank and seeming ability to get away with so much, apparently because the Queen protected him; second because John Peyton, Lieutenant of the Tower, had been appointed by Cecil back in 1598, and owed his allegiance to him; and third because if Oxford made a deal with Cecil, it was in the Secretary's best interest to *enable* such communication between Oxford and Southampton, so that Oxford could play his part by helping him. And this would include the proposition here that, as part of such communication, *copies of the sonnets got into Southampton's possession in the Tower.*

The other aspect of these two lines of Sonnet 45 is the clear reference to Southampton's health. It is on the record that he had fevers and swellings in his legs and other parts of his body; but he was being treated and apparently his health was steadily improving. In his poem to the Queen, Southampton refers specifically to his leg problem.

> I've left my going since my legs' strength decayed …

In addition there is a strong overall correspondence between Oxford's Shakespearean sonnets and Southampton's Tower poem, as predicted. At least 47 key words in the Sonnets also appear in Southampton's poem, of which the following twenty-four words might be emphasized:

> *Blood, Buried, Cancel, Condemned, Crimes, Dead, Die, Faults, Grave, Grief, Ill, Liberty, Loss, Mercy, Offenses, Pardon, Power, Princes, Prison, Sorrow, Stain, Tears, Tombs...*

At least four distinct themes are shared by the Sonnets and the Southampton poem:

1. **The Crime** – *Fault – Offence – Ill Deed*
2. **The Grief** – *Loss – Sorrow – Tears*
3. **The Prison** – *Death – Tomb – Buried*
4. **The Plea** – *Mercy – Pardon – Liberty*

Following are some examples of these themes as expressed by both Oxford and Southampton:

(1) The Crime

Traditional scholars tend to view specific words in the Sonnets such as "fault" and "offence" as metaphors for some sexual transgression or betrayal. In Southampton's poem, however, they are *not metaphorical but literal*. The view here is that *the same words used in the Sonnets are also literal*; and here are some examples of their usage in both the Sonnets and in the Southampton poem:

> "The *offender's* sorrow lends but weak relief
>   To him that bears the strong *offence's* cross."
> (Sonnet 34)

> "I beg liberty to cancel old *offences*...
>   Better go ten such voyages than once *offend*
>   The majesty of a Prince, where all things end"
> (Southampton)

-"All men make *faults,* and even I in this"
(Sonnet 35)

"Where *faults* weigh down the scale"
(Southampton)

"To you it doth belong
 Yourself to pardon of self-doing *crime*"
(Sonnet 58)

"Let grace so...
 Swim above all my *crimes*"
(Southampton)

(2) The Grief

Another aspect of traditional commentary is the tendency to overlook the true emotional depth of the "grief" and "loss" and "sorrow" in the Sonnets; but when viewed within the context of Southampton's imprisonment, such depth of suffering becomes apparent:

"But day doth daily draw my *sorrows* longer,
 And night doth nightly make *grief's* length seem stronger"
(Sonnet 28)

"*Sorrow,* such ruins, as where a flood hath been
 On all my parts afflicted, hath been seen:
 My face which *grief* plowed..."
(Southampton)

"Though thou repent, yet I have still the *loss*"
(Sonnet 34)

"And I with eating do no more engross
 Than one that plays small game after great *loss*"
(Southampton)

"To *dry the rain* on *my storm-beaten face*"
(Sonnet 34)

"And *in the wrinkles of my cheeks, tears* lie
Like furrows *filled with rain*, and no more *dry*"
(Southampton)

(3) The Prisoner

Oxford in the Sonnets pictures Southampton and his friends in the Tower prison. They are not yet executed, but exist unseen in the darkness of their expected death; and he weeps while picturing Southampton himself as a living grave:

"Then can I drown an eye (un-used to flow)
For precious friends *hid in death's dateless night*
(Sonnet 30)

How many a holy and obsequious tear
Hath dear *religious* love stolen from mine eye…
Thou art the grave where buried love doth live
(Sonnet 31)

Southampton in turn pictures the prison itself as a grave or tomb, in which he is buried alive, and legally a dead mean -- that is, found guilty of treason and condemned to death:

"While I yet breathe, and sense and motion have
(For this a *prison* differs from a *grave*),
Prisons are living men's tombs, who there go
As one may, sith say *the dead* walk so.
There *I am buried quick*: hence one may draw
I am *religious* because *dead in law*."
(Southampton)

(4) The Plea

Given the unique power of a king or queen to grant a royal pardon to those convicted of serious crimes including high treason, Oxford writes as if Southampton himself is a royal prince or a king who is somehow able to help himself:

81

"The *imprisoned absence of your liberty*...
To you it doth belong
Yourself to *pardon* of self-doing *crime*"
(Sonnet 58)

And Southampton writes to Elizabeth within the same royal context:

"Not to live more at ease (Dear Prince) of thee
But with new merits, *I beg liberty*...
If faults were not, how could great Princes then
Approach so near God in *pardoning* men?"
(Southampton)

We have a record of Oxford's concept of the monarch being able to substitute mercy for justice—in his letter to Cecil on May 7, 1603, soon after Elizabeth's funeral, when Southampton had already been liberated by such mercy from James, whom Oxford appears to be thanking indirectly through the Secretary:

"Nothing adorns a king more than justice, nor in anything doth a King more resemble God than in justice, which is the head of all virtue..."

Southampton expresses the same idea by writing that "mercy" is an "antidote to justice"—mercy as a remedy to ensure the *right kind* of justice:

Wisdom and valor common men have known,
But only *mercy* is the Prince's own.
Mercy's an antidote to justice...
(Southampton)

He associates the Queen with the miracle worker who cured *Naaman's* condition, and mentions the River Jordan, thereby linking Elizabeth with Christ, the ultimate exemplar of mercy.

Had I the leprosy of *Naaman,*

Your mercy hath the same effects as Jordan.
(Southampton)

The vast majority of these key words fall not only within the first forty verses numbered Sonnet 27 to Sonnet 66, but, moreover, virtually all the key words from the Shakespeare sonnets used by Southampton come from *the first twenty of these*. And most of those words are actually located within the first ten sonnets[2] — within the sequence of Sonnet 27 to Sonnet 36—and the key words from these ten sonnets are also used by Southampton in his poem to the Queen:

Sonnets 27 to 36:

Sonnet 28 – *Sorrows, Grief*

Sonnet 30 –*Death, Grieve, Moan, Losses, Sorrows*

Sonnet 31 – *Dead, Buried, Tear, Religious, The Dead, Grave, Buried*

Sonnet 32 – *Death, Died*

Sonnet 33 – *Stain, Staineth*

Sonnet 34 – *Rain, Grief, Loss, Offender, Sorrow, Offence, Tears, Ill*

Sonnet 35 – *Grieved, Stain, Faults, Fault, Plea*

Sonnet 36 – *Blots* [stains]

The proposition suggested here is that upon the night of the failed rebellion, Edward de Vere began to write and compile sonnets that would ultimately correspond with the days and nights of waiting to see if Southampton would live or die by execution. The further proposition is that Oxford, while trying to work a deal with Cecil to save Southampton's life, was able to send messages—including messages within some of these sonnets—to Southampton in the Tower.

Now, with the existence of a poem that Southampton himself wrote to the Queen, the added proposition is that he drew upon Oxford's sonnets for words, concepts and themes as well as inspiration. And given the preponderance of such words and themes within the first forty sonnets 27 to 66, covering those forty days, the further proposition is that Southampton drew mainly from these particular sonnets, which, as a practical matter, would have been delivered to him in the Tower before any of the others.

I suggest that the foregoing evidence amounts to very near certainty, if not absolute proof, that the real-life context of these particular Shakespearean sonnets is in fact the plight of Southampton in prison after the failed Essex Rebellion and his desperate need for a reprieve from the Queen; and that—in this context of time and circumstance—Elizabeth becomes the so-called Dark Lady of Sonnets 127 to 152, wherein we find:

"Straight in her heart did *mercy* come" – Sonnet 145

Endnotes

[1] The center of the "century" occurs at Sonnets 76-77, dividing the hundred verses into two halves as 27-76 and 77-126.

[2] In my book *The Monument* the "century" of sonnets from 27 to 126 is divided into ten "chapters" of ten sonnets apiece, starting with Sonnets 27-36.

Below is a modern-English version of the Southampton Tower Poem (February-March 1601), with the couplets separated.

Emphasized are key words that also appear (in one form or another) within the Shakespearean "century" of Sonnets numbered 27 to 126.

The Earl of Southampton Prisoner, and Condemned, to Queen Elizabeth:

Not to live more at ease (Dear Prince) of thee
But with new merits, I beg *liberty*

To *cancel* old *offences*; let grace so
(As oil all liquor else will overflow)

Swim above all my *crimes*. In lawn, a *stain*
Well taken forth may be made serve again.

Perseverance in *ill* is all the ill. The horses may,
That stumbled in the morn, go well all day.

If *faults* were not, how could great Princes then
Approach so near God, in *pardoning* men?

Wisdom and valor, common men have known,
But only mercy is the Prince's own.

Mercy's an antidote to justice, and will,
Like a true *blood*-stone, keep their bleeding still.

Where *faults* weigh down the scale, one grain of this
Will make it wise, until the beam it kiss.

Had I the leprosy of Naaman,
Your mercy hath the same effects as Jordan.

As surgeons cut and take from the sound part
That which is *rotten*, and beyond all art

Of healing, see (which time hath since revealed),
Limbs have been cut which might else have been healed.

A Poet's Rage

While I yet breath and sense and motion have
(For this a *prison* differs from a *grave*),

Prisons are living men's *tombs*, who there go
As one may, sith say the *dead* walk so.

There I am *buried* quick: hence one may draw
I am *religious* because *dead* in *law*.

One of the old Anchorites, by me may be expressed:
A vial hath more room laid in a *chest*:

Prisoners condemned, like fish within shells lie
Cleaving to walls, which when they're opened, *die*:

So they, when taken forth, unless a *pardon*
(As a worm takes a bullet from a gun)

Take them from thence, and so deceive the sprights
Of people, *curious* after rueful sights.

Sorrow, such *ruins*, as where a flood hath been
On all my parts afflicted, hath been seen:

My face which *grief* plowed, and mine eyes when they
Stand full like two nine-holes, where at boys play

And so their fires went out like Iron hot
And put into the forge, and then is not

And in the *wrinkles* of my *cheeks, tears* lie
Like *furrows* filled with *rain,* and no more *dry*:

Mine arms like hammers to an anvil go
Upon my breast: now *lamed* with beating so

Stand as clock-hammers, which strike once an hour
Without such intermission they want power.

I've left my going since my legs' *strength decayed*
Like one, whose stock being spent give over trade.

And I with eating do no more engross
Than one that plays small game after great loss

Is like to get his own: or then a pit
With shovels emptied, and hath spoons to fill it.

And so sleep visits me, when *night*'s half spent
As one, that means nothing but complement.

Horror and fear, like cold in ice, dwell here;
And hope (like lightning) gone ere it appear:

With less than half these miseries, a man
Might have twice shot the Straits of Magellan;

Better go ten such voyages than once *offend*
The Majesty of a Prince, where all things end

And begin: why whose sacred prerogative
He as he list, we as we ought live.

All mankind lives to serve a few: the throne
(To which all bow) is sewed to by each one.

Life, which I now beg, wer't to proceed
From else whoso'er, I'd first choose to bleed

But now, the cause, why life I do implore
Is that I think you worthy to give more.

The light of your countenance, and that same
Morning of the Court favor, where at all aim,

Vouchsafe unto me, and be moved by my *groans*,
For my *tears* have already worn these stones.

3rd Earl of Southampton in the Tower

Chapter 7

Unveiling the *Sonnets*

William Boyle

The following paper was first published in 2009 in Discovering
Shakespeare. *It is based on preparations for a panel discussion on*
Shake-speares Sonnets *at the 2006 Shakespeare Authorship Studies
Conference at Concordia University in Portland, Oregon. I appeared
there with author Hank Whittemore to present and defend Whittemore's
"Monument Theory" on the meaning and purpose of the Sonnets. As a
friend and colleague of Whittemore for 20 years, and as an editor of
his work in the* Shakespeare Oxford Newsletter *and* Shakespeare Matters,
*this was not the first time we had worked together or participated in
joint presentations on the Monument Theory (the theory is explained
in Appendix B). My purpose here is to provide—based upon this
theory—a perspective on how a bona fide historical context
influences the interpretation of certain words in several of the
sonnets, thereby transforming interpretation of the sonnets
themselves from mere speculation or guessing into sound theorizing.*

In an article in *Modern Language Notes* in 1917, Henry David
Gray neatly captured the dilemma of all commentators who
dare take on the infamous sonnet enigma; his words ring
as true today as they did 89 years ago:

> [One might do well to introduce himself thus] . . . "I am a
> Southamptonite, dating the Sonnets with Sarrazin from 1592 to
> 1596, accepting with Dowden the quarto order of the first 125 as
> chronological, with Massey identifying the Dark Lady as Elizabeth
> Vernon, and with Wyndham proclaiming the Rival Poet to be

Drayton." Or, "I am a Pembrokist, dating the Sonnets with Mackail from 1598 to 1603, with Tyler identifying the Dark Lady as Mary Fitton, and holding with Minto that the Rival Poet is Chapman." Or, "I agree with Sir Sidney Lee that the Sonnets are literary exercises which do not record the poet's own experiences; I believe with Alden that it is impertinent to try to identify the Dark Lady; I think with Fleay that W.H. is not the youth to whom the First Series is addressed at all but Thorpe's "only procurer" of them; I am confident, with Walsh, that the order is wholly haphazard and must be completely readjusted to make the Sonnets intelligible; I haven't the faintest idea who the Rival Poet could have been, for I hold with Rolfe, that many of the First Series may have been addressed to a woman." Or finally: "I am a free lance among the Sonnets' critics with a special set of conjectures all my own; though I do agree with Butler that W.H. is William Hughes, with Acheson that the Dark Lady is Mistress Davenant, and with Montgomery that the Rival Poet is Spenser; I realize, with Beeching, that Sonnet 107 must refer to the death of Elizabeth, though the majority, as McClumpha shows, are contemporary with *Romeo and Juliet* and *Love's Labour's Lost*." Having thus, or by some similar formula, presented his credentials, the new champion may enter the lists and proceed to break his spear against the Veiled Knight who guards the Mystery of the Sonnets. (17-18)

Little has changed since Gray's time, even with the subsequent identification, by J.T. Looney, of Edward de Vere, the 17th Earl of Oxford, as Shakespeare, for Oxfordians have battled each other just as furiously over these same points as have any groupings of Stratfordians or anti-Stratfordians. But identifying who's who in the Sonnets is just half the task of the Sonnet Mystery; the other half is resolving the question of "Just what is the story?" Indeed, one might ask (and many have): "Is there any story at all?" Theories that suggest a story range from speculations on love trysts to love triangles to peculiar forms of adultery, to suggestions that the Sonnets are all about man-on-man love, most often referred to as homosexual love. The only point on which most can agree is that the poet exhibits deep passion and deep anguish over something.

More recently, writing on Sonnet 29 in the *Durham University Journal*, David Thatcher covers some of this "what is the story" ground in what he describes—quoting Harold Bloom—as engagements in "strong misreading" that only complicate and add to already "weak and repetitious ones [i.e., other interpretive scenarios] still at large" (59-60). Thatcher offers (echoing Sonnet 66, while still talking about readings and misreadings), that he, too, is "tired, especially with biographical interpretations." Yet Thatcher, peeling away successive layers of Sonnet 29 to prompt questions like "What is this?" and "Why is that?" seems to contradict the basis for his exasperation, for, in posing such questions to us, he surely must recognize that, in the end, such questions, of course, can only be answered by knowing who is writing to whom and about what. For example, Thatcher notes that

> [a] crucial ambivalence the poem[Sonnet 29] never resolves is whether the disgrace is real or illusory, deserved or undeserved, making it difficult for the reader to know if sympathy towards the speaker (the conventional reaction) is really an appropriate and justified response. Theoretically, only an historical human narratee, if there had been one, might have been in a position to know what precisely the narrator was referring to in this opening line. . . . But such knowledge is irrecoverable. (61)

There we have the sonnet dilemma in a nutshell: "Such knowledge is irrecoverable." But what if such knowledge were not irrecoverable? What if there were a correct answer to the entire Sonnet Mystery, and all that one needed to achieve it were the proper set of interpretive tools?

Sonnet commentary background

These essays by Gray and Thatcher are just two of the thousands of writings to have been published over the past two centuries on Shakespeare's Sonnets. In a recent book of critical essays on the Sonnets,[1] James Schiffer introduces the collection with an excellent sixty- eight page essay that surveys the history of sonnet commentary, making several interesting points along the way.

Perhaps most helpful in Schiffer's survey is its presentation of a history that has ebbed and flowed more than once over the "biographical vs. fictive" schools of interpretation, and, as part of the larger sonnet debate, advances the notion that appreciating the Sonnets' themes does not require knowing the particular events in the author's life that may have inspired any particular verse. This notion is summed up in a 1907 quote from commentator Walter Raleigh:

> It would help us but little to know the names of the beautiful youth and the dark woman; no public records could reflect even faintly those vicissitudes of experience, exultations and abysses of feeling which have their sole and sufficient record in the Sonnets. . . . Poetry is not biography; and the value of the Sonnets to the modern reader is independent of all knowledge of their occasion. That they were made from the material of experience is certain: Shakespeare was no puny imitative rhymster. But the processes of art have changed the tear to a pearl, which remains to decorate new sorrows. The Sonnets speak to all who have known the chances and changes of human life. Their occasion is a thing of the past; their time is eternal. (qtd. in Schiffer 32)

Schiffer then comments that "such attention to theme divorced from . . . biography, while not exactly new, would become a dominant note as sonnets criticism moved into the twentieth century" (33). But it is this "divorce" of theme from biography that really is at the heart of the Sonnets' mystery, and demonstrates—even if unknowingly—the overriding importance of the authorship debate in any commentary on *Shake-speares Sonnets*. Without having "real" known biographical facts with which to buttress any biographical interpretation, all interpretations become thematic musings, with any biographical implications being nothing more than attempts to recover the "irrecoverable knowledge," the absence of which Thatcher laments but which Raleigh says is irrelevant anyway.

So the traditional critical approach to the Sonnets that has evolved from this situation is that all that needs to be done is to identify a Fair Youth and a Dark Lady, and then proceed to hypothesize unknown events into a story of some sort—or else, as

Raleigh wrote, ignore the story of the Poet, the Youth and the Dark Lady altogether and just enjoy the eternal pearl of the poems' lyrical beauty. For Stratfordians, of course, this approach can never he tempered with the idea that it is Shakespeare himself (the Poet) who needs to be "correctly" identified before any progress can he made, but this is where the authorship debate and anti-Stratfordian Sonnet commentary become factors in our hopes of achieving as full an understanding of the Sonnets as possible.

Yet for all Sonnet commentators (Stratfordian and anti-Stratfordian) the equally important task of identifying an actual history involving the parties (Poet, Fair Youth, Dark Lady) about which the Poet was writing has presented a seemingly insurmountable obstacle. And it has been attempts to overcome this obstacle that have resulted in an abundance of commentary that "hypothesizes" what this actual history "must" have been based only on what any given Sonnet "seems" to be about to the interpreter of those Sonnets.

All this highly subjective, impressionistic criticism has led to the current state of the traditional sonnet debate. For example, Joseph Pequigney's *Such is My Love* (1985), with its homoerotic reading of the Sonnets, has won many converts. Yet Pequigney's reading coexists with those of Booth (1977), Kerrigan (1986), Vendler (1997) and Duncan-Jones (1998), all of which steer clear of going down the autobiographical road in interpreting the Sonnets.

One of the gems in Schiffer's essay is the story of an early round of sonnet commentary in which Edmund Malone responded to George Steevens' moral revulsion over Shakespeare's declaration to his addressee in Sonnet 20 that he is "the master-mistress of my passion." In his 1783 edition of Shakespeare, Steevens had written that "[i]t is impossible to read this fulsome panegyrick, addressed to a male object, without an equal mixture of disgust and indignation." Malone responded in 1790 that "[s]ome part of this indignation might perhaps have been abated if it had been considered that such addresses to men, however indelicate, were customary in our author's time, and neither imported criminality, nor were esteemed indecorous . . . ." He added that "Master-mistress" does not mean "man-mistress," but [rather] "Sovereign mistress" (the same two words are used together in Sonnet 126, line 5). Little did he know (as we shall see) the import of what he was saying, because while he was certainly not promoting the youth as really "sovereign" in any sense, he nonetheless introduced into the equation a thesis that has resonated for the past 150 years among many anti-Stratfordian commentators (notably Oxfordians, but before them, Baconians). In rejecting possibly homosexual allusions, Malone found royal allusions (qtd in Schiffer 21-23).

That initial showdown over interpreting a single line in one sonnet set the stage for the next 200 years, with the central point of contention always being whether to accept the words as literally true and autobiographical (and hence, as some commentators maintain, "diminish" Shakespeare since the perceived man-to-man love could, to them, only be homosexual) or adopt more benign interpretations that are not autobiographical and thereby "protect" Shakespeare from any suggestion that he was gay or bisexual (Schiffer 27-31). This "true/diminishing" vs. "benign/protecting" dichotomy has also bedeviled anti-Stratfordian commentary, for the suggestion that the Poet was being "real" when he calls the Youth "my sovereign" in Sonnet 57 (one of many royal allusions throughout the sonnets[2]) has been every bit as contentious for some anti-Stratfordians as the homosexual thesis has been for Stratfordians.

The notion of the royal allusions being real was introduced into the Oxfordian movement in the 1930s by B. M. Ward and Percy Allen.[3] Their theory was that the Poet/Fair Youth relationship was not one of an older lover and a younger lover but rather one of father and son—and that the son was a prince, seen by the father as the rightful heir to Elizabeth (the Dark Lady).

This theory—generally referred to among contemporary Oxfordians as the "Prince Tudor" theory (Whittemore xxxv-xxxvi)—has divided the Oxfordian movement ever since it was first proposed, not least because there seems to be no independent historical evidence for it, but also because it seems, to many, so outrageously "over the top," or "hopelessly romantic," or — worst of all—conspiratorial.

This theory of the Sonnets was aptly summed up by Charlton Ogburn, Jr.:

> We are left with a compelling question raised by the Sonnets. It is a question that is inescapable and one that traditional scholarship is resolved upon escaping at all costs .... How is it that the Poet of the Sonnets can—as he unmistakably does—address the fair youth as an adoring and deeply concerned father would address his son and as a subject would his liege-lord? (75)

The "royal" theory has been the source of much contention among Oxfordians over the past seventy years. The exact details of who may have slept with whom to create such a scenario we will leave to another day,[4] but the import of demonstrating the "royal" theory, if it can be demonstrated, is crucial to the resolution of the Shakespeare Mystery, as this is the one issue that divides Oxfordian scholars more than any other contested issue within the Oxfordian community.

A proposed solution

Writing in support of Hank Whittemore's "Monument Theory" of the Sonnets' meaning and purpose in the Summer 2004 *Shakespeare Matters* (in an article titled "With the Sonnets Now Solved..."), I chose a headline that boldly declared the Sonnets Mystery solved. In response, Lynne Kositsky and Roger Stritmatter submitted an article, "Critique of the Monument Theory," for publication in the Fall 2004 issue of *Shakespeare Matters*. In the years since the publication of that article, the debate has raged, with opponents of the Monument Theory (with its royalist "Prince Tudor" implications) contending that one cannot claim the Sonnets are "solved," or that there is no answer to the sonnet enigma.

Therefore, let me justify the above headline by restating it: I think the sonnets can be solved if one has the right elements in place, and I submit that, in Whittemore's work, they have been solved. By "solved" let me be clear about what I mean, for it goes hack to Thatcher's contention that "only an historical human narratee . . . knows what was being referred to . . . but that knowledge is irrecoverable." I believe that knowledge is indeed "recoverable," and that several particular words within the sonnets, when read in the light of their actual historical context—as opposed to the subjective guesses of de-historicized impressionistic readers—reveal the true story. The key to recovering this true story lies in correctly identifying the narrator (Poet), the narratee (Fair Youth), the Dark Lady, and the historical circumstances. All these elements must he identified before anyone can dare declare, "Sonnets solved."

Unlike all previous sonnet theories, the Monument Theory accomplishes this. It hypothesizes "Poet" identity (Edward de Vere, 17th Earl of Oxford), "Fair Youth" identity (Henry Wriothesley, 3rd Earl of Southampton), "Dark Lady" identity (Queen Elizabeth I) and documented historical circumstances that are applicable to the entire sonnet sequence while bringing to the foreground key words that appear in the sonnets but have never been understood in contextual terms, i.e., a bona fide historical context. Briefly, I believe that the key to the solution lies in both the primary historical context identified by Whittemore—the Essex Rebellion of 1601—and in the relationship of the Poet to the Fair Youth as one of father to royal son. Further, it is important to note that both father and son were involved in the Rebellion and that both suffered its consequences.

In my 2004 article supporting the Monument Theory, I focused on three sonnets (35, 87, 120), and I wish to revisit them in this essay in more detail to make the point that the answer to the mystery of the sonnets has been embedded in the sonnets the whole time, hiding in plain sight, waiting to be found. When one places the royal allusions (Hotson Ch. 2-3, Whittemore 773-777) and the abundance of legal language (Whittemore xlvii) in the sonnets side-by-side with the royal succession agenda and the subsequent treason trials of the Essex Rebellion, the meaning of the Sonnets comes into focus.

Essex Rebellion background

Before delving into these three sonnets, let's first look at some of the history surrounding the Essex Rebellion, since it is posited as being central to the Monument Theory. As I wrote in 2004, one important question that seldom has been asked (let alone answered) about the Essex Rebellion is why the life of its co-leader, the 3rd Earl of Southampton, was spared (he was tried with Essex, convicted of treason and sentenced to die). A second question is why the author, Shakespeare, was not rounded up, tried and punished—or even interrogated—when his play *Richard II*, depicting the deposition of a monarch, was used to set the stage for the Rebellion. A third question focuses on just what the conspirators' goals were that day (i.e., were they, in fact, advancing James's claim as Elizabeth's successor?). And a final question asks what Essex had been up to in the years leading up to the rebellion, a period during which he was often perceived as a contemporary Bolingbroke to Elizabeth's Richard II. Much of this history has been written about in Essex biographies and other histories of the period, but always from a conventional viewpoint in which neither Shakespeare nor Southampton is seen as having any stake in the succession debate.

A recent article by Chris Fitter in *Early Modern Literary Studies* sheds some light on this last question (about Essex), and, of special significance, Fritter attempts to comprehend what Shakespeare was up to as he wrote and rewrote *Richard II* over a period of five years leading up to the Rebellion (Fitter never considers that Shakespeare could have been revising work written before 1596).

After the Rebellion's failure, it was recorded at the rebels' trial that Prosecutor Edward Coke said Essex had designs on becoming King Robert the First (Camden par. 18) and that Robert Cecil had stated that Essex wished to set himself up as King (Harrison 151). In fact, some of Cecil's words seem remarkable, considering that Essex had no blood claim to the throne whatsoever (Bolingbroke, at least, was Richard II's cousin, the son of one of his uncles):

> And had I not seen your [Essex's] ambitious affections inclined to usurpation, I could have gone on my knees to her Majesty to have done you good .... You, my good lords, counselors of state, have had many conferences, and I do confess I have said the King of Scots is a competitor, and the King of Spain is a competitor, and you [i.e. Essex] I have said are a competitor: you would depose the Queen, you would be king of England, and call a Parliament. (qtd in Keeton 55-56)

Here is Cecil mentioning Essex right in the company of the two most powerful claimants angling to succeed Elizabeth. How could this perception of Essex as a "would be king of England" have developed in the years leading up to 1601 without Essex ever having faced any serious rebuke? Neither the Privy Council hearing in the Fall of 1599 nor the quasi-official "commission" hearing in June 1600—both of which did begin to take action in response to these perceptions, precipitated by the dedication to Essex in Dr. John Hayward's 1599 *History of Henry the Fourth*— seem sufficiently serious forums for consideration of the risks allied to a potential usurper. And consider further that Essex's almost year-long house arrest during this period was just that— house arrest, not the Tower (which is where Hayward was sent and remained until Elizabeth died). Moreover, it was just six months after his release from house arrest that the Rebellion took place. It is even recorded that Robert Cecil had seen *Richard II* in 1597 and that, upon learning of this fact, Essex was "wonderful merry" at Cecil's reaction to the play (we have no direct evidence of what Cecil's reaction was, just that Essex commented upon it). Chris Fitter's take on this (Fitter pars. 31-32, 36- 37)—the main point of his essay, in fact—is that Shakespeare actually is sabotaging the overreaching earl more than seriously promoting his Bolingbroke-like ambitions, so perhaps Cecil is enjoying a laugh at Essex's expense. If so, he must have overlooked the depose-and-kill-the-monarch ending of the play, or perhaps—in the realpolitik world of Elizabethan statecraft—he had a different ending in mind.

Fitter's article makes clear what dangerous times these were with the politics of succession so unsettled, and how risky it was for anyone to speak out. Yet speak out is exactly what some (including Shakespeare) did. Robert Parson's *Conference About the Next Succession to the Crowne of England* (1594/1595) contained a dedication to Essex that Fitter describes as "treasonably suggesting him to be Elizabeth's next heir" (Fitter par. 7). As noted above, the dedication to Essex in Hayward's 1599 *History of Henry the Fourth* had landed the author in the Tower for his daring. Yet, even as Fitter makes the case for Shakespeare's active involvement in such dangerous politics with his *Richard II*, he never asks how Shakespeare could have—or why he would have—dared to do so. At one point, Fitter cites a letter from Rowland Whyte to Robert Sidney in which Whyte says, "To wryte of these Things are [sic] dangerous in so perillous a Tyme." And in the next sentence Fitter writes, "And this is precisely what Shakespeare now did" (Fitter pars. 39-40).

One final note on Fitter's intriguing examination of the period: he never mentions the Earl of Southampton. Considering that he is explicating Shakespeare's political agenda on the succession, the Queen, and the Earl of Essex, and given the sudden appearance of Shakespeare on the literary scene in 1593-1594 (coincident with the rise of Essex) with two long poems dedicated to Southampton, Fitter's omission seems strange. It does seem to reflect the larger problem that Oxfordians have frequently noted over the years—namely, that if one has the wrong Shakespeare, then any history involving him cannot be fully, or correctly, understood. Southampton was definitely involved with Essex throughout this period, and was, in fact, a co-leader and co-conspirator in the Rebellion. If, as Fitter speculates, Shakespeare was actually sabotaging Essex during this critical period when Essex was openly seen as a Bolingbroke-like challenger in the succession sweepstakes, how can Fitter not wonder how Southampton (publicly linked to Shakespeare through the popular *Venus and Adonis* and *Lucrece* poems) factors into all of this?

The unanswered question here—if Fitter is right in his speculation about Shakespeare and Essex—is, then, what was Shakespeare up to? Just what are his concerns in *Richard II* about the succession crisis of the 1590s? His play does seem to suggest approval of the notion of Bolingbroke usurping a monarch such as Richard, but if Shakespeare didn't approve of Essex as an Elizabethan Bolingbroke, did he have another Bolingbroke in mind? After all, the future of the Elizabethan state was at stake in these years; would there be a peaceful succession or civil war if the Tudor Dynasty were to disappear without an heir having been named before the Queen's death?

Why was Southampton spared?

To return to the Southampton side of the equation in the Essex Rebellion, we must ask how, in the *quid pro quo* world of Elizabethan justice, Southampton's life was spared without any record of something having been done, either by him or by someone acting for him. For all the other conspirators there is a record of their swift executions following their trials (Essex, Blount, Meyrick, Danvers and Cuffe), or of staggering fines being assessed and—for the most part—paid (e.g., by Rutland, Bedford, Neville, and many others), or, in the interesting case of Sir John Davis, of full cooperation with the state that secured the death penalty for himself and the four others tried with him (Blount, Meyrick, Danvers, and Cuffe), yet as these other four went to their deaths within weeks of their trial, he (Davis) was spared and eventually granted a pardon by the Queen in 1602 (Devereux 198); was this a *quid pro quo* for his cooperation? And was it the only one exacted following the Rebellion? After all, what was it that saved the co-leader of the Rebellion itself: Henry Wriothesley, 3rd Earl of Southampton?

Charlotte Stopes, in her biography of Southampton, mentions this *quid pro quo* system:

> As soon as the Privy Council felt safe by the apprehension of the chief offender, they turned their attention towards possible mercy, in

order to ingratiate themselves with the people. This rarely meant politic mercy, as in the case of Mountjoy, who was needed where he was; or even compassionate mercy, as in the case of the Earl of Southampton. It in general expressed itself as *mercantile mercy*, measured in proportion, not to the degree of the offender's guilt, but of his capacity to pay. (233; emphasis added)

Although Stopes notes the "mercantile" nature of the system, in the absence of any record of a *quid pro quo* for Southampton, she concludes that it was "compassion" alone that spared him. In the face of the enormity of Southampton's crime, however, is such a sentimental conclusion credible?

A closer examination of the extant records involving Southampton tells a different story than that offered by Stopes. The primary records are Southampton's letters to the Privy Council in February and March of 1601. While these letters (in which "her Majiestie" and "mercy" are mentioned often) are reproduced in their entirety by Stopes (225-231), they are curiously absent in both Rowse's and Akrigg's biographies (perhaps—however difficult it is to imagine—because neither saw Southampton's reprieve as a story worth reviewing in detail). The story that these letters tell is of a man who seems to have a defense counsel (his "advocate" [Sonnet 35]) hovering over his shoulder, telling him exactly what to say and how to say it. The letters, even as they beg for mercy for his "fawte" [fault], reflect a perfect understanding of the legal difference between "treason" and the lesser charge of "misprision of treason" as it was used at this time. When Southampton writes that he had no idea what Essex was up to, and no idea that events were headed toward treason, he sets himself up to be plea-bargained from treason and death to "misprision of treason" and life in prison ("supposed as forfeit to a confined doom" [Sonnet 107]). That precise legal mechanism had been perfected throughout the 120-year Tudor dynasty, whereby treason charges could be, at the discretion of the Crown, reduced to "misprision of treason" (Bellamy 30; Rastell 153).[5]

Finally, while the phrase "misprision of treason" cannot be directly linked to a reduction in sentence to account for the failure of the State to execute Southampton with the other conspirators sentenced to die, it has been used to refer to the fate of one of his fellow conspirators: Sir Henry Neville. In a 1978 article by Clayton Roberts and Owen Duncan about the English Parliament circa 1614, Neville is mentioned, and a reference is made by the authors to his having been accused of "misprision of treason" in the Essex Rebellion and thereby imprisoned. The article does not cite any contemporary source for using this phrase, but it does state that although he knew of the plot, he did not inform Cecil, and that Neville, "for this was accused of misprision of treason and sent to the Tower" (494).[6] Southampton, in his pleading letters to the Privy Council, not only acknowledged not informing anyone, but even claimed that he really didn't know where the events for which he had been convicted were headed—almost as if he were asking how he could have informed anyone. And Neville, though he was released on the same day as Southampton (10 April 1603), had his lands restored and also was pardoned (James and Rubinstein 147), still had to pay a substantial portion of his original £10,000 fine (estimated at £3,000 [James and Rubinstein 146]). Further, as Neville's biographers note, Neville was tainted by the Rebellion for the rest of his life and barred from high office. Neville's punitive treatment highlights how Southampton—the co-leader of the rebellion—stood alone among all the conspirators as apparently having been required to perform nothing and pay nothing for his special treatment. In fact, not only was Southampton not punished; he was fully restored, pardoned, and even honored upon his release; he even was made a Knight of the Garter.

So, was Southampton as disconnected from intimate association with Essex and the conspirators of the Rebellion as his pleading letters to the Privy Council would indicate? I think not. The historical record seems to belie his words, beginning with his unarguably close association with Essex in the years leading up to the Rebellion. Both of them, after all—and more than once—had been arraigned before and were in frequent trouble with the Queen over their disobedient behavior. There is also an intriguing account from John Nichols about an event in the spring of 1603, shortly after Southampton's release and pardon (Akrigg 136-137; Massey 77-78) that is illuminating. Nichols reports that Southampton told James' wife, Queen Anne, that the Rebellion could have—perhaps would have—succeeded if only they could have followed through with their plans. The Nichols report relates how Queen Anne remarked "in amazement" that "so many great men did so little for themselves," a remark to which (in Akrigg's words), "Southampton had a ready reply: they [the Essex Rebellion conspirators] had no choice but to yield, since their sovereign had sided with their enemies" (136).

Lord Grey, an Essex/Southampton opponent in the years leading up to the Rebellion (one of "their enemies"), is then reported to interrupt, saying (in Akrigg's words) that "he and his friends could have done much more than the Essexians" (137). Argument ensued, and Grey and Southampton were sent briefly to the Tower. But consider what this moment in 1603 reveals: Southampton is still fighting the same fight and justifying what occurred in 1601—and this from someone who had claimed in his letters to the Privy Council that he didn't even know what was going on! The tone of the exchange (as reported) seems to cast in doubt that the placement of James of Scotland on the throne of England was the goal of the Rebellion; otherwise, what are they arguing over? Why would Queen Anne say that so many great men did so little for themselves if they were doing it for James? Southampton's words, uttered just months after his release, are not the same words one finds in his obsequious letters written two and one-half years earlier.

Also of interest in this matter of the Essex-Southampton relationship is an attempt by Captain Thomas Lee, just days after the Rebellion, to find a way to get both Essex and Southampton out of the Tower and into the presence of the Queen to explain themselves (Lacey 298; Myers 48). Lee, a notorious assassin involved with Essex in Ireland, was caught, and within two days tried, convicted and executed for treason. James P. Myers, writing about Lee in a 1991 article, reports that at his trial[7] he said his only intention was "with the aid of a half dozen resolute men [to] step unto the queen, and kneel before her, and never rise till she had signed a warrant . . . and never stir till the earls of Essex and Southampton were brought to the queen's presence" (qtd. in Myers 48). Myers comments that Lee's true intentions may never he known and that he was reported to have died "still [denying] the treason for which he was executed" (48). Myers further notes that Lee's trial also does not make apparent that Lee "until the Essex Rebellion, had enjoyed repute as the Crown's creature, a successful mercenary and assassin . .. Evidence in the state papers suggests that someone [other than his brother Sir Henry], possibly the Cecils or the queen or even all three, had for almost twenty years protected him . . . " (48). Myers then notes:

> Given, moreover, the residual popularity of Essex and the lingering potential for further disturbances, Lee's treason could conveniently be made to pressure the vacillating monarch into authorizing Essex's death. The ploy succeeded: Cecil, writing of Essex's execution to the lord deputy of Ireland on 26 February, pointedly observed that the earl's death 'was the more hastened by the bloody practice of 'Thom' Lee'. (49)

Myers' speculation leaves open the possibility that the entire Lee episode was a Cecil ploy from the beginning. If so, it would reinforce and reaffirm how cutthroat and double-dealing were the politics of this era, especially the politics surrounding the Rebellion. Lee's claim that he wished only to bring both Essex and Southampton before the Queen is noteworthy, but who it was who put him up to risking and losing his life in this cause to present Essex and Southampton before Elizabeth is unknown.

In both of these instances, we can see that Essex and Southampton were, indeed, co-leaders of the Rebellion. Southampton's protestations to the Privy Council were transparently false, but they were necessary if he were to hope to secure a reprieve from his death sentence. However—and astonishingly—there is no written record in Southampton's case of exactly how or why his sentence alone was commuted when all of the other conspirators were punished in severe degree. The upshot of all this history is that Rebellion co-leader Southampton was clearly unique in how his case was handled. History has yet to explain why he received such special and unaccounted-for leniency. If Southampton did not have to pay for his acts with his life, did someone else pay Cecil's, i.e., the State's, price for the young earl's life? With some of this background in place, let's take a look at how Sonnets 35, 87 and 120 may be concerned with those events and their consequences.

"That which thou has't done"

Sonnet 35 begins, "No more be grieved at that which thou has't done." The word "that" clearly refers to "something done" which, in turn, is the key to the "story." But how can we ever know what "that" is which has been done? Isn't it "irrecoverable knowledge"? Consider, however, that "that" is referenced again in the same sonnet—both as a "trespass" and as a "sensual fault":

> All men make faults, and even I in this
> Authorizing thy trespass with compare (ll. 5-6)

> For to thy sensual fault I bring in sense
> (Thy adverse party is thy advocate) (9-10)

Consider further that "trespass" is repeated once later in the sequence (Sonnet 120) in which we observe that "trespass" and "crime" are used interchangeably:

> To weigh how once I suffered in your crime (8)

> But that your trespass now becomes a fee,
> Mine ransom yours, and yours must ransom me (13-14)

So, using just these two sonnets, one could propose a straightforward formula:

> that = fault = trespass (Sonnet 35) = crime = trespass (Sonnet 120)

By this, we can see that "that which thou has't done" refers not to just a minor offense of some sort, but to a crime (and "crime" also appears in Sonnet 58 [12] as the Youth's "self-doing crime"). Is there a Fair Youth candidate who is known to have committed a crime? Yes: Henry Wriothesley, 3rd Earl of Southampton, was convicted of treason in the Essex Rebellion and sentenced to death.[8] And considering that the range of Sonnets between 35 and 120 covers almost the entire 100 middle-sonnet sequence (27-126), it seems reasonable to consider that the only thing being discussed between the Poet and the Youth throughout this entire sequence is just this one thing: "that which thou hast done," i.e., the crime which you have committed.[9]

The other key word/concept that can be gleaned from these sonnets (35, 120 and also Sonnet 34) is "ransom" as some form of expiation of the Fair Youth's crime. Our chief consideration here is to recall that—with Southampton posited as the Fair Youth—we have a Fair Youth who had been convicted of a crime and sentenced to die but was later reprieved. In a world where "ransom and fines" were almost always paid to obtain commutations by convicts who could afford them, there is no record of any ransom or fine being paid by the youthful Southampton for his commutation. But might a ransom have been paid for him by another? Is it possible that the Sonnets may provide the missing explanation for Southampton's freedom and what price was paid— and by whom—to obtain it? We will return to this point later.

Trespass and treason

Kositsky and Stritmatter point out in their article critiquing the Monument Theory that the word "treason" does not appear in Sonnet 35 (11) nor even in the middle century of sonnets (27-126), the sequence postulated by Whittemore to he a chronological diary and record of Shakespeare, Southampton and the Essex Rebellion. Therefore, they contend, there is no reason to gloss the words "trespass" or "fault" as references to Southampton's treason. It should be noted here that Whittemore, however, provides in his book several examples from Shakespeare's plays where Shakespeare treated these words interchangeably (Whittemore 478-479).[10]

However, there is another Shakespearean work which uses "trespass" and "fault," plus the words "treason" and "crime," interchangeably: *The Rape of Lucrece*. In fact, those four words are used throughout that poem in reference only to the one event being discussed: Tarquin's acts of bursting into Lucrece's bedroom and raping her (the actual word count is: Treason=6, Trespass=6, fault=12, crime=5 [Furness]). Significantly, although those words are used to discuss a single event, their usage actually is differentiated within the poem: "treason" is associated exclusively with Tarquin (in his own words or those of the poet/narrator), while "fault" and "trespass" are used principally—though not exclusively—to describe Lucrece (in her own words or those of the poet/narrator). The usage of "crime" is split evenly between Tarquin and Lucrece, with two instances of Lucrece speaking of "his" crime—i.e., Tarquin's crime—and two instances of her speaking of "my" crime, plus one instance of the poet/narrator saying "Though men can cover crimes with bold stern looks / Poor women's faces are their own faults' books" (1252-53).

This word usage results in a "Rashomon" effect of how two people see the same event. For Tarquin, it clearly was treason to do what he did—as he acknowledges before and after the fact—fully considering (like Hamlet) the consequences of what he wants to do but then (unlike Hamlet) acting anyway ("a disputation / 'Tween frozen conscience and hot-burning will," 246-47). But Lucrece feels complicit and talks of "my trespass," "my fault," and "my crime" in (she thinks) "leading Tarquin on" or "allowing" the rape. The extended diversion within the poem where she views the painting of the Fall of Troy reinforces this point, allowing her to curse Helen for her "trespass" (line 1476) in arousing a passion in Paris that caused him to kidnap her.

These distinctions in *Lucrece* demonstrate that the same words in the Sonnets may show how the several parties actually saw and reacted to the events of "that which thou has't done" and what the nuanced use of these words may suggest about these reactions. Tarquin, having spent the first third of the poem talking "sense" to himself about what he was thinking of doing, then goes and does it (his rational "sense" gives way to his emotional "sensual" act). This, I submit, is his "sensual fault," his "treason" (perhaps anticipating Sonnet 35, "to thy sensual fault I bring sense").[11] I should emphasize, too, that I do not mean here "sensuous," which some erroneously equate with "sensual" ("sensuous" means loving, while "sensual" means willful[12]). This poem recounts, after all, not a love story but a rape. Then, as now, rape is not about sex; it is about the tyrannical use of power. Tarquin's soliloquies about it underscore that fact: he wants to possess what someone else has, even at the risk of "dispossessing" himself.[13] In fact, the consequences of Tarquin's treason are political disaster for two families: his own, and Lucrece's (when she commits suicide in defense of her chastity).

Sonnet 87 and "misprision"

With this hypothesis in place, i.e., the "that" over which the youth must "no more be grieved" is his "trespass / sensual fault / crime" in the Essex Rebellion (referred to by Shakespeare as "thy trespass" and "your trespass" in sonnets 35 and 120), other sonnets in the central century-sonnet sequence (27-126) can be read in a proper light. One of the most important of these sonnets is 87, about which Kositsky and Stritmatter write, "In many ways, the crux of Whittemore's argument can be found in a single word in Sonnet 87 [misprision]" (12). While acknowledging that Southampton's death sentence might have been commuted to "misprision of treason," they note that "of treason" is not in the poem,[14] and they claim that 87 is a sonnet about simple "emotional leave-taking." Further, they note that the sonnet is full of financial metaphors (dear, possessing, estimate, charter, bonds, granting, worth, riches, gift, patent) and therefore conclude:

> If we want to understand "misprision" in its actual, as opposed to hypothetical, context, we should read the word in relation to this financial schema. Stephen Booth notes that one definition of "misprision" is "undervaluation," which accords perfectly with the language of the sonnet without recourse to the meaning Boyle and Whittemore depend on to make their thesis . . . The context of the

sonnet does not support [glossing "misprision" as "misprision of treason"]. Instead, the preferred meaning is clearly "undervaluation." To accept the meaning supplied by Boyle and Whittemore requires us to ignore the obvious context (with its extensive monetary metaphors) of the sonnet itself in favor of a hypothetical context, which the sonnet, without the misconstruction of the word "misprision," entirely fails to support. (12; emphasis added)

This critique illustrates much that has been misdirected in Sonnet scholarship for almost two centuries. Although Kositsky and Stritmatter argue for a supposedly "obvious" context that trumps a "hypothetical" context, they at the same time also postulate that such an obvious context must be understood only within this sonnet's internal context, not the larger, external context provided by the other sonnets in the sequence (e.g., by "trespass" equaling "treason" in sonnets 35 and 120) let alone any genuine historical context within which the Poet lived, wrote, and—most especially—interacted with the Fair Youth.

Apart from Shakespeare's own parallel usage of these words (trespass and treason),[15] it should be noted here that there is, in fact, an independent contemporaneous linkage of the words "misprision" and "trespass" that should settle any questions about whether the word "trespass" could be used to describe a high crime (rather than a misdemeanor or some other petty offense). In a 1567 legal lexicon there appears a revealing entry for "Misprision of felonie or trespasse" (Rastell 152). The entry states

> ... that in every treason or felonie is included *misprision*, and where any hath committed treason or felonie the [Queen] may cause the same to be indited and [arraigned] but of *misprision only* if she will. (Rastell 153; emphasis added).[16]

The usage of "misprision," coupled with "trespass," in this entry, is evidence, therefore, that "trespass" was synonymous with "felonie," and, accordingly, it is not unreasonable to see how Shakespeare could also equate it with "treason," especially in light of his usage of those words in *Lucrece*, as if they described degrees of guilt/culpability over the same offense—similar to determining whether a killing was manslaughter or murder.

Although such usage of "trespass" may have been slipping into obscurity by 1567, the timing would be a perfect fit for those, like Oxfordians, who believe that Shakespeare was seventeen years old in 1567 and being trained in the law at that time at Gray's Inn. It also is especially interesting to note, in this context, that the Queen could commute any indictment of treason or felony to misprision at her will—an important point for the argument that converting Southampton's conviction for treason to "misprision" is exactly what Southampton was seeking in his letters to the Queen.

Turning to some of the more recent mainstream Sonnet commentaries, we find that Helen Vendler has nothing to say about the word "misprision," while Booth (as previously noted) glosses it as "undervaluation" (291) and Duncan-Jones declares it "a false estimate" (284).[17] It is true that there is nothing within Sonnet 87 alone that would compel a reader to think "misprision of treason" solely by the appearance of the word "misprision." But this is where the element of historical context must he considered, together with the context provided by considering all of *Shake-speares Sonnets* to be in authorial sequence and telling a single story. As noted earlier, the key words "trespass" and "fault," linked with the word "crime," lead us outside the Sonnets and into an event in history: the Essex Rebellion. For anyone who postulates Southampton as the Fair Youth, this event must, in my view, come first and foremost in any consideration of the "that" which the Fair Youth has done. Let me also suggest that if the words "misprision of treason" had ever been associated with Southampton in the historical record, or by any of his biographers, Sonnet commentary would long ago have picked up on it, and there would be no question about it.

The Southampton mystery

Finally, to get to the heart of Sonnet 87, even after identifying Southampton as the Fair Youth of the Sonnets (as many commentators have), we need to ask ourselves, "Who is Southampton? What is his relationship to Shakespeare? Why is he allied with Essex, and what is their relationship?" Establishing these contexts mean, therefore, not only recognizing that Southampton was a co-leader of the Essex Rebellion but affirms the need to inquire into the many unanswered questions about the Rebellion and its leaders and explore what Shakespeare's perspectives on these persons and events were.

As we noted earlier, Essex's name had been bandied throughout the 1590s as one who might play a possible late-sixteenth-century Bolingbroke to Elizabeth's Richard II; indeed, he was accused at his trial of seeking to become King Robert I. Shakespeare's *Richard II* had been performed, on Essex's and Southampton's orders, the night before the attempted coup, seemingly both to justify a monarch's downfall and to rally support for the coming coup. Yet the author, Shakespeare, was never mentioned during the post-rebellion trials, nor was he ever party to those involved in the play and its production who were questioned, tried and punished for participating, however indirectly, in the Rebellion. And Southampton, notably, once sentenced to die, was inexplicably spared—a point where the Shakespeare problem, i.e., the Shakespeare authorship problem, seems to intersect with this little-noticed Southampton mystery. Historians cannot say for certain why Southampton was spared in 1601 anymore than they can say for certain why Shakespeare was never held to account for his role in the Essex Rebellion.

These curiosities lead us back to the "Prince Tudor" theory, i.e., the thesis that Southampton himself may have harbored his own royal aspirations as the unacknowledged son of the Queen and the poet, Oxford/Shakespeare. In addition to the previously-noted curiosities in the Sonnets' references to the Fair Youth, we are told by Shakespeare that the youth has a "charter of his worth" (87:3), and other sonnets also provide a backdrop to this boy's "charter of worth," such as the Poet's astonishing address to him as "my sovereign" in Sonnet 57. Indeed, as also noted earlier, "royal language" is used throughout the sonnet sequence to describe the Youth. Add to this an historical context (the Essex Rebellion) concerned with royal succession and, I believe, we have before us—achieved within a defined historical context—the revelation of what Sonnet 87 is all about.

Kings and a king

Sonnet 87 is not the only instance in the sonnets of a "king" being mentioned in a discussion of value and worth. In Sonnet 29, Shakespeare declares, "For thy sweet love remembered such wealth brings / That then I scorn to change my state with kings" (13-14). So, Shakespeare tells us, there are things in this world more valuable than kingship.

As we noted earlier in looking at the Essex Rebellion, Southampton was convicted of treason and sentenced to death, but was then reprieved from his death sentence. At the trial of Essex and Southampton, Essex was accused of seeking to set himself up as King, yet no record exists of Southampton's motives in the Rebellion—other than his letters to the Privy Council, wherein he pleads for mercy and proclaims that he only was involved out of his "love for Essex" (Stopes 225-231).[18]

With these key elements in place, we can now look at the final lines of Sonnet 87—"Thus have I had thee as a dream doth flatter, / In sleep a king, but waking no such matter" (13-14)—and ask why these particular verses appear here. Turning to Helen Vendler's comments, we find:

> The deposed-by-daylight king of the last line generates the several puns of the closing: mist-a-king [line 10], m-a-king [line 12], wa-king [line 14], the "nutshells" hiding the nut, a king, which is phonetically speaking, close to "aching." (381)

In fact, Vendler notes, ten of the sonnet's fourteen lines end in verbs with "-ing." It's as if the whole sonnet could be entitled, "To a King—not." Vendler also remarks on the legal terms used in the sonnet, emphasizing that these terms represent exchanges between Poet and Youth, which she calls "the giving-and-recalling, or swerving [line 8], of what was, or seemed to be, a gift" [lines 7, 11]. She calls it a "gift of love," and notes that it is a "keyword" in

112

the sonnets, with "gift," "gives," "gav'st," and "gift" again appearing in each quatrain, but then becoming suddenly absent from the couplet (making it, in her overall scheme of sonnet analysis, a "defective key word").

Yet neither Vendler (in noting this "gift of love") nor Kositsky/Stritmatter (in noting what they call the sonnet's "financial schema") consider that a "king" itself is a thing of value (being the Youth's own "worth"), and if what is occurring in Sonnet 87 is an "exchange" involving "gifts" or "giving," then we must remember that Shakespeare has already noted, back in Sonnet 29, that "love" (and I would add "life") is more valuable than kingship. The "gift of love" could, in fact, be worth a king's ransom.

Let's make a deal

Continuing with Sonnet 87, it is reasonable at this point, I believe, to infer that the word "misprision" ("So thy great gift, upon misprision growing," line 11) alludes to a "deal"—a legal maneuver—that saved Southampton's life, not to a "false estimate" or an "undervaluation" as more traditional glosses would have it. Furthermore, let us consider that this deal may be the financial transaction alluded to in the sonnet. Southampton, after all, had "risked" his life in the Rebellion—"his own worth then not knowing"—and, in fact, had *lost his life* by receiving a death sentence. The Poet, in turn, has given him back his life ("...thy great gift, *upon misprision growing*" in line 11 being not a further reference to something going from Youth to Poet, but rather from Poet to Youth; emphasis added).[19] However, the consequence of the deal is that, from now on, the youth is a king in (the Poet's and his) dreams only. Kingship has been surrendered in exchange for life, echoing Sonnet 29. Sonnet 87 records a deal concluded ("My bonds in thee are all determinate") and the end of a dynasty ("In sleep a king ... "). And lest we doubt that the most important word in this sonnet is "king," we can thank Helen Vendler for her insight on the phonetic clues that lead us repeatedly to that word (382-383).

113

But much as I like what Vendler says about this sonnet, she also has this to say:

> The *universal appeal* of this much-anthologized sonnet springs from its very *lack of particular detail*: there are no sexually precise pronouns, no references to a new sexual or affectional or poetic rival, and (because of the modern persistence of its legal vocabulary) no *estranging historical allusions*. (383; emphasis added)

No "estranging historical allusions?" This comment from one of the leading authorities on the sonnets perfectly illustrates all that is at stake in the authorship debate, and, moreover, it illustrates that to correctly interpret a sonnet (its "universal appeal" notwithstanding), one must have the correct historical context—the "particular detail"—about which the Poet is writing. *Standing alone, the sonnet cannot fully explain itself.* What Vendler says is similar to what the critic Walter Raleigh had written in 1907 when he declared that "the value of the Sonnets to the modern reader is independent of all knowledge of their occasion . . . for [once] the processes of art have changed the tear to a pearl [echoing Sonnet 34, line 13] their occasion is a thing of the past; their theme is eternal" (qtd. in Schiffer 32). Thus Vendler is being true to her mission to gloss the sonnets independent of any consideration for their having been composed within the context of an external story (the "occasion")[20] by which the authorial intent of the composition might be derived.

Similarly, the Kositsky/Stritmatter assertion that Sonnet 87 has its "own context," and that therefore it is "obvious" what is being talked about by looking at this lone sonnet divorced from its context and its place within the series, is, in effect, to claim to know the occasion that inspired the writing without actually knowing the history. This, however, is just another manifestation of "old paradigm" thinking, i.e., "This is a self-evident love sonnet—and only a love sonnet, period"—and, as such, everything about it is obvious (since everyone knows all about love) and the occasion that inspired it, if we care to know anything about it, can be deduced from the "sonnet pearl" without having any knowledge about the cause of the particular "tears" that become that "pearl."

But how can there be a Sonnet Mystery if everything is obvious? Absent a genuine historical context, everything in such an interpretive universe can only be—indeed, *must* be—confined to conjecture and empty speculation. In contrast, the Monument Theory introduces a documented historical context, i.e., the Essex Rebellion—with its genuine "tears" over a known "occasion" that never has been part of any previous sonnet commentary.[21] Raleigh and Vendler may eschew contemplation or investigation of the "occasion" behind the Sonnets, but anyone engaged in the authorship debate cannot.

Finally, let us consider the word "deal" that I've been using. As already noted earlier in this essay, there is no official record about any "deal" to save Southampton. And yet Southampton was spared. Even with the skilled legal advice he must have gotten in order to compose his Privy Council letters, was more done to rescue him from the headsman? If so, what?—and by whom? Were ransom and fines paid by anyone for Southampton, as happened for the other surviving conspirators? Again, there is no official record of it, but unless the State was determined simply to release the convicted leader of a rebellion against the Crown without the imposition of any penalty or ransom, we have no alternative but to conclude that a ransom of some kind was paid, by someone.

Sonnet 120

We now come to the idea that the sonnets can furnish historical information not found in official records. Such a notion is, of course, premised on the Monument Theory's recognition that the middle 100 sonnets (27-126) are a diary of events surrounding the Essex Rebellion. I believe that the depth of analysis contained in *The Monument* makes such a case, with Whittemore's extensive research on the meanings and uses of words in each Sonnet— meanings and uses confirmed not by a reader's subjective or impressionistic appraisal but by comparing the uses of those words used elsewhere by Shakespeare himself. Accordingly, Whittemore makes an overwhelmingly persuasive case that these verses are about actual historical, political events in the participants' lives that disclose, definitively, the identities of those participants—including the Poet, Shakespeare.

In the Sonnets, the word "ransom" appears twice: in Sonnets 120 and 34 (and Sonnet 87 talks of something of value being exchanged). Sonnet 120 also uses the words "crime" and "trespass" interchangeably. More significant, however, is how Sonnet 120 links the occasion of "trespass" and "ransom" in its couplet: "But that your trespass now becomes a fee; / Mine ransoms yours, and yours must ransom me" (13-14). Here, historical context informs a reading and yields far more intelligible results than commentators, left to historical guessing or purely impressionistic musings, have so far proposed. Of the three most recent commentators on the Sonnets that I have been citing, only Booth analyzes the couplet in detail. He notes that "trespass" must refer to the "crime" mentioned in line 8, and declares that "becomes" likely means "turns into" or "takes on the nature of," although he adds that it also could mean "is suitable to" or "is becoming to." He concludes with a purely literary construct on the whole problem however, noting that Shakespeare has skillfully made two separate but intertwined statements: "I feel your pain because my own pain was once as great," and "I do not feel your pain because my own pain was once as great." In other words, the "fee" that the trespass has required is offset by the poet's own trespass, i.e., you offended me, and then I offended you, so we're even (Booth 290- 291). This is similar to the glosses of Duncan-Jones ("the speaker's trespass cancels out that of his friend." ([350]) and Vendler ("[my trespass] 'buys back' yours" [510]). None of them, however, considers that "Mine" in line 14, refers, in fact, to the "fee" to be paid—not to the "trespass"—and that "and yours . . ." in line 14 therefore must he saying "and your fee is to ransom me." But within a context of "trespass, treason, crime = conviction for crime," a fee is exactly what is needed to "ransom" the trespasser and get the convicted off the hook! The Essex Rebellion's context for the composition of this poem makes perfect sense of such a reading, but, even more importantly, it tells us something we didn't know: that Southampton didn't receive "compassionate mercy" (as Stopes had speculated); rather, we learn that a ransom was paid—and paid by the Poet, Oxford/Shakespeare. Shakespeare, indeed, is telling us in straightforward language that he has paid the fee to ransom Southampton's trespass, and now "your—Southampton's—fee must ransom me." A ransom has been paid—and it truly was a king's ransom.

Ransom "me," not "mine"

So, why did the Poet write, "ransom me"? Is Shakespeare telling us something by using "me" rather than "mine"? He could easily have written the couplet as, "But that your trespass becomes a fine / Mine ransoms yours, and yours must ransom mine." But if written that way, he would be saying that he, too, had committed a trespass. Clearly, he did not see it that way. He wrote in Sonnet 35 that "all men make faults, and even I in this, authorizing thy trespass with compare . . ." (emphasis mine). In other words, "I may have committed a fault, but not quite the trespass you committed, and certainly not the treason for which you were convicted" (an offense which, I suspect, Oxford/Shakespeare felt was not actually treason). This parsing of words echoes *The Rape of Lucrece*, where Tarquin's rape is called treason, but Lucrece feels complicit and speaks of her "fault" and her "trespass" in describing the same event.

The ransom payment that Oxford-Shakespeare made was not one of money, but himself. Not only was Southampton's claim to the throne surrendered in the deal to save Southampton ("In sleep a king, but waking no such matter" [Sonnet 87]), but also Oxford's claim to the authorship of his anonymous and pseudonymous works ("I, once gone, to all the world must die" [Sonnet 81]). Like Lucrece, seeing himself as complicit in the Essex Rebellion ("authorizing thy trespass with compare" [Sonnet 35]), he commits a form of suicide—literary suicide: he agrees to be consigned, forever, to oblivion. It was done under great duress, with Southampton being held hostage in the Tower and the only acceptable ransom being, in effect, a "hostage swap." But he did it, and that is why he doesn't ask for a ransom for "my trespass [mine]," but rather just for himself ("me"). He knew that a political dynasty—the Tudors—would expire with him. And if Southampton were indeed an unacknowledged Tudor heir, then Elizabeth herself had also played Lucrece, placing her reputation for chastity—her political persona as the Queen married only to her country—above all else, ending her life as a phoenix that *would not* arise from its ashes, "leaving no posterity ... " (from *The Phoenix and the Turtle*, lines 59-61).[22]

Conclusion

To conclude, I would assert that we, with confidence, now can say, in the words of Henry David Gray—with whose words I opened this essay—that the "Veiled Knight who guards the Mystery of the Sonnets" (18) is, of course, the author himself. Yet even Oxfordians, who identify Shakespeare as Oxford (and most of whom affirm that the Fair Youth is Southampton), still have come up short and been at sixes-and-sevens in attempts to solve the mystery because of their inability unanimously to affirm the need to recognize the historical context of these verses as the means by which their right meaning can be discovered. Fortunately, Hank Whittemore's Monument Theory now has provided the context that completes the unveiling, exposing, in unprecedented detail, the connection between the verses and their historical context, thus resolving the mystery and "solving" the sonnets.

In concentrating on only three sonnets (35, 87, and 120), I hope I have made the point that—absent context—individual words and individual sonnets can be (and have been—and are!) interpreted to mean almost anything. Without a comprehensive context, meaning, indeed, is always going to be utterly subjective and remain solely in the eye of the beholder. With context, however, multiple musings and imaginings can he discarded and replaced with the provision of the author's purpose and the context for the work's correct interpretation, for only with a clearly defined external historical context can anyone hope to "unveil" the author's intent in writing these sonnets.

Of greater significance is that the Monument Theory provides, for the first time, a unified theory of how the Shakespeare authorship problem came into existence, and in so doing provides answers to two outstanding unanswered questions from the history of the Essex Rebellion: why Southampton was spared execution, and why Shakespeare was spared punishment for his supporting role in those events. The simple answer to both these questions—an answer that only Oxfordians can provide—is that the true Shakespeare (Edward de Vere, 17th Earl of Oxford) was punished—virtually erased from history—and it was his punishment, his sacrifice, that saved Southampton. "Shakespeare" died so that Southampton could live.

Such a simple and elegant solution to the authorship problem is just what Supreme Court Justice John Paul Stevens called for over twenty years ago in Washington, DC, at the 1987 Moot Court Trial on the Shakespeare Authorship Question. In his closing statement, Justice Stevens declared that while he suspected a conspiracy involving the Queen and Burghley could be behind this incredible story, Oxfordians had yet to articulate an all-encompassing account:

> I would submit that, if their [Oxfordians'] thesis is sound, . . . one has to assume that the conspiracy—[and] *I would not hesitate to call it a conspiracy*, because there is nothing necessarily invidious about the desire to keep the true authorship secret . . . . [T]he strongest theory of the case requires an assumption, *for some reason we don't understand*, that the Queen and her Prime Minister decided, 'We want this man to be writing under a pseudonym.' . . . Of course *this thesis may be so improbable that it is not worth even thinking about*; but I would think that the Oxfordians really have not yet put together a concise, coherent theory that they are prepared to defend in all respects. (qtd in Boyle, "The 1987 Moot Court Trial" 7-8; emphasis added)

The Monument Theory of the Sonnets provides this "concise,

coherent" theory, but because of the still controversial nature of the "Prince Tudor" aspect of the theory—not to mention a general aversion by some to the suggestion that the Shakespeare problem is the result of a (gasp!) conspiracy—the question remains: is it a theory that can be defended? That Justice Stevens himself, even as he postulated a possible conspiracy and called for a "concise, coherent theory," could also suggest that such a theory might be "improbable" confirms just how vexing the Shakespeare authorship debate really is and likely will continue to be.

Meanwhile, with a theory in hand that would seem to solve the Sonnet mystery, and also solve the "how and why of the authorship problem,"[23] I would now submit that it is now up to others to refute—if they can—rather than reactionarily reject what Whittemore has accomplished. I do not think, however, that that is any more likely to happen than we are to see a refutation of Copernicus's heliocentric model of the solar system or a refutation of Watson and Crick's double helix solution to the mysteries of how genes work: the sun is at the center of our solar system and things revolve around it; two complementary strands of chemicals drive the reproduction of life, and that is how genes work. But discovery is discovery, and facts discovered will remain facts to the end of time ("For truth is truth though never so old, and time cannot make that false which was once true," as Edward de Vere once wrote [qtd. in Fowler, *Letters* 771]).

It is time to build on what Whittemore has discovered and defined in his "monumental" study and complete our work in gaining the world's acceptance of Edward de Vere as Shakespeare with attendant appreciation for the reasons this writer wrote what he did and allowed his name to be buried these many centuries, in expectation of a time when "eyes to be" could behold his work and "tongues to be" could salute his noble purpose.

Endnotes

[1] *Shakespeare's Sonnets: Critical Essays*. Ed, James Schiffer. New York: Garland, 1999. Schiffer notes that Herbert S. Donow's 1981 bibliography on the Sonnets lists 1,898 items, and in a footnote (n.2, p. 57) also mentions that a 1972 book by Ball State University Professor

Tetsumaro Hayashi, entitled *Shakespeare's Sonnets: A Record of 20th-Century Criticism*, lists even more-2,503 entries. Such a number of books and articles written on Shake-speares Sonnets testify to readers' and scholars' intense and persistent attraction to these enigmatic verses.

[2] Leslie Hotson, for example, offers a detailed catalog of these royal allusions in Chapters 2 and 3 of *Mr. W. H.* Of course, being a Statfordian, Hotson had to invent a Fair Youth connection (he proposes William Hatcliffe as W.H.) and a royal context (Hotson imagines Hatcliffe as a "Prince of Purpoole" during Christmas celebrations at Gray's Inn) to which, he suggests, the royal allusions refer. His work is mentioned—dismissively—by Schiffer as demonstrative of "the flaw in evidential logic that Schoenbaum describes is a frequent problem in biographical criticism" (42). Whittemore, however, notes that no less venerable a critic as G. Wilson Knight made extended observations on the royal imagery of the Sonnets, calling the Sonnets the" heart of Shakespeare's royal poetry" (Whittemore 806).

[3] These thoughts were first published in a 1937 pamphlet by Percy Allen and B. M. Ward: *An Enquiry into the Relations between Lord Oxford as "Shakespeare," Queen Elizabeth, and the Fair Youth of Shakespeare's Sonnets* (cited in a 24-page supplement to the April 1939 issue of *The Shakespeare Fellowship News-letter* in which Allen and Ward debated Canon G. H. Rendall and Mr. T. M. Aitken about their theory). Whittemore gives an updated overview on the Tudor Heir theory on pages xxxv-xxxvi of *The Monument.* Baconians also had considered the royal factor in their analysis of the Sonnets and contemplated how that factor figured into the authorship debate, often by concluding that when Shakespeare speaks of something as "royal," he means it literally.

[4] Another variation of this theory is that Oxford himself is a son of Elizabeth who, born in 1548, was her first child at a time when rumors circulated of her possible impregnation by the Lord Admiral, Thomas Seymour; in response, the 30-year old William Cecil (later Lord Burghley) came to her aid during this crisis and remained at her side for the next 50 years, sheltering and educating Oxford—eventually even marrying Oxford to his daughter. If Oxford, however, were both the son of Elizabeth and the father of Southampton by her, that would constitute incest—a sexual practice far more common in the Elizabethan world than often supposed, but hateful to the ears of Victorian-minded moralists who are scandalized that Shakespeare could have been a practitioner of such a sexual abomination. Many studies, however, have been written on the extensive theme of incest in Shakespeare. If incest is the deep, dark secret at the core of the Shakespeare problem, that would explain, of course, much about the imposition of secrecy on the authorship then and account for the perpetuity of the secrecy and reluctance to pursue its implication that continues today; for more on this, refer to Professor Daniel Wright's address to the Shakespeare Oxford Society in October

2008, "All My Children: Royal Bastards and Royal Policy."

[5] Throughout the Tudor dynasty, especially after Henry VIII's break with Rome, treason charges against political opponents became the standard means of applying political control, and the lesser charge of "misprision of treason" became a useful bargaining chip for the Crown, utilized on a case-by case basis. See Bellamy's *The Tudor Law of Treason* for a history of how this practice evolved.

[6] Southampton then embarked upon a storied political career that culminated in his becoming a political opponent of James in the early 1620s, allied with—surprisingly?—the 18th Earl of Oxford, Henry de Vere. And at this same moment in history the First Folio (1623) was published.

[7] Myers cites from *Cobbett's Complete Collection of State Trials* (London, 1809-28) as his source on Lee's trial.

[8] This is where, in my view, Joseph Pequigney and his version of the homosexual theory of the sonnets (and, for that matter, all the gay sexual theorists of the Sonnets) wander astray, for although Pequigney also looks at the connections among these same key words, he departs in many conjectural directions after doing so. For example, on page 104 of *Such is My Love*, while discussing Sonnet 35, he observes that "trespass" (35.6), some "ill-deed" (34.14) and a "sensual fault" (35.9) constitute the cause of the quarrel [between the Poet and the Youth]:' He then notes, however, that E.A.M. Coleman, in *The Dramatic Use of Bawdy in Shakespeare*, has remarked that "fault" frequently occurs in early modern English with a "sexual flavour" and so concludes that the modifier "sensual" confirms that the "fault" is somehow sexual.

Here, therefore, is someone who looks at this same linkage of words ("trespass" and "fault") as clear referents to something that is going on between the Poet and the Youth, but who provides only subjective speculation with no historical context outside the Sonnet to inform his interpretation. As we shall see, Southampton himself referred, in writing, to his participation in the Rebellion as his "fawte, i.e., fault," and Whittemore, in his glosses on Sonnet 35, supplies several examples of "sensual" being used within this period in distinctly non-sexual contexts—including one derived from William Cecil, Lord Burghley, who wrote in 1584 that favor no sensual & willful recusants" (qtd in *The Monument* 250).

[9] None of the major recent books on the sonnets—Booth (1977); Kerrigan (1986); Vendler (1997); Duncan-Jones (1998)—has anything to say about Shakespeare's meaning in using the word "crime." It is not even mentioned in their extensive glosses of words in the Sonnets. This absence of any discussion about "crime"—and its centrality in interpreting the meaning of the Sonnets—shows how the absence of a real historical context clouds the judgment of anyone tackling the Sonnet

mystery. It also is of interest to note that both Booth and Duncan-Jones, in discussing Sonnet 120, observe that comparisons can be made back to Sonnet 34. Duncan-Jones specifically suggests that the use of the word "salve" in both sonnets may be related. But neither Booth nor Duncan-Jones ventures any farther than this, and they do not consider the possible interconnections between such vital words as "ransom" in Sonnet 34, "trespass" in Sonnet 35, and the use of both words ("ransom" and "trespass") in Sonnet 120. So the notion that the Poet is talking about the same event, using the same language in Sonnets 34-35 and 120, is absent from their commentary, let alone any consideration that both instances of "trespass" may be referring to a real crime."

[10] Kositsky and Stritmatter wrote in response to articles by William Boyle and Hank Whittemore in *Shakespeare Matters* (Summer 2004)— not to Whittemore's *The Monument*, which had not yet been published— and so were unaware of Whittemore's explanation for this. Yet, astonishingly, they dismissively write in their article: "Doubtless reply will be made that we have not waited to evaluate the entirety of the evidence contained in Mr. Whittemore's book. This is true but also irrelevant. No larger case which depends on the kind of examples cited in these two articles can be regarded as a sound one" (13).

[11] It is interesting to note how this aspect of Tarquin can be seen more in Essex than Southampton. Chris Fitter, commenting on how he sees Essex reflected in *Richard II*, writes, "Shakespeare's motivation for freezing the career of the hot and headlong young nobleman in a lucid frost of maximal suspicion must remain, of course, conjectural" (Fitter par. 45), and in describing Essex as "hot and headlong," he also could be describing Tarquin in *Lucrece*. This view of Essex and its possible parallel with Tarquin touches on my growing suspicion that the "graver labor" of *Lucrece* may also (like *Richard II*) have been part of a broader 1590s succession politics agenda, perhaps intended as a cautionary tale that may well have been anticipating what came to pass in 1601 and warning Southampton to beware of his relationship with Essex.

[12] In *Webster's New World Dictionary*, "sensuous" is defined as follows: "1. Of, derived from, or perceived by the senses, 2. Enjoying sensation." "Sensual" is defined as: "1. Of the body and the senses as distinguished from the intellect [emphasis added]. 2. Connected or occupied with sexual pleasure." It is this first definition of "sensual" that is closest, I believe, to Shakespeare's intent in depicting Tarquin's thinking as he anticipates taking (raping) Lucrece. This is why so much of the poem begins with his "soliloquy," preoccupied with the consequences of what he is about to do, but with his intellect unable to control his senses.

[13] A 2001 article ("Tarquin Dispossessed") in *Shakespeare Quarterly* by Catherine Belsey contains many interesting observations on the political ramifications of Tarquin's act, Lucrece's response and the

subsequent political fallout. I have drawn much from her observations, especially regarding the notion of what it means to be "dispossessed." She does not, however, discuss the semantic—and possibly legal—subtleties of "treason" vs. "trespass."

[14] There are several good reasons why of treason" would not be used. First, it would make the actual historical context too obvious. Second, it may not scan right for the poet in composing this sonnet. Third, if Shakespeare's use of the words "treason" and "trespass" do represent a difference in his mind—and perhaps also in law—over degrees of culpability (as in *Lucrece*), then that is one more reason not to use the word "treason" in the middle hundred sonnets, particularly if he genuinely believes that Southampton did not actually commit a treasonable offense (his judicial conviction notwithstanding). It also is interesting to note that the only appearance of the word "treason" in the Sonnets is in Sonnet 151, where it appears along with the only three instances of the word" conscience." Its usage here (" ... I do betray / My nobler part to my gross body's treason"—lines 5-6) may correspond to what we have been considering about Tarquin in *Lucrece*, i.e., that his "treason" is his surrender to his "sensual" urges because of his "frozen conscience." There is not space in this essay to explore the larger meaning of this sole appearance of the word "treason," coupled with "conscience," nor why the Poet uses it to describe himself vis a vis the Dark Lady (Elizabeth) rather than the Youth (Southampton) who was convicted of that crime.

[15] Whittemore provides several examples from the Shakespeare plays in *The Monument* (see, for example, p. 248).

[16] The well-known legal concept of misprision is repeated over the centuries in such authorities as Edward Coke's *Institutes of the Laws of England* and William Blackstone's *Commentaries on the Laws of England*.

[17] The exact quote from Duncan-Jones (in her gloss of line 11) is: " 'upon misprision growing' means coming into existence as the result of a false estimate" (284).

[18] Southampton's letters, as Whittemore notes in *The Monument* (301-302), are virtually Shakespearean in their pleas for mercy from the Queen, but they are also savvy in laying the groundwork for a commutation of his conviction for treason to one of conviction for "misprision of treason" and its accompanying life sentence rather than death sentence (301-302).

[19] Sir Walter Raleigh, in a letter to the Privy Council begging for his life after his conviction for treason in November 1603, wrote, "For a greater gift none can give, or receive, than life ..." (qtd in Hume 199). Raleigh's death sentence was, indeed, later commuted to misprision of treason, which, incredibly, is what Attorney General Edward Coke said is

all that he was accusing him of in the first place. Raleigh's treason conviction was, however, reinstated (as it could be, since he was never pardoned), and he was executed in 1618 (Hume 281).

[20] It is interesting to note that Professor Helen Vendler had been sent an early draft of Whittemore's work in spring 1999, and she wrote a letter to Shakespeare Oxford Society Trustee Elliott Stone in reply, declaring, "I am no historian, and have by now learned the limits of my own interests, which are rhetorical and not historical."

[21] For the record, we should note that Stritmatter believes that Southampton likely was a putative Tudor heir, as demonstrated most recently in his 2004 article on *Venus and Adonis* in the Tennessee Law Review (216). Lynne Kositsky, his co-author in critique of the Monument Theory, does not, however, accept the "Tudor Heir" theory. And as readers may have discerned by now, it is being postulated in this essay that the Monument Theory of the Sonnets (with the Essex Rebellion at its center) is a clinching argument both for Oxford being Shakespeare and for Southampton being the Fair Youth and a candidate for the succession.

[22] The Essex Rebellion context of *The Phoenix and Turtle* has been explicated in Anthea Hume's "Love's Martyr, The Phoenix and Turtle, and the Aftermath of the Essex Rebellion." While the author is primarily concerned with Robert Chester's *Love's Martyr* as a political allegory about the failed Essex Rebellion and the succession issue (with the Phoenix representing the Queen, and the Turtle the "loyal and loving subjects of the Queen"[157]), she also discusses Shakespeare's role in the 1601 collection and his unique take on the succession issue (Shakespeare's Phoenix alone *does not arise from its ashes*, but is instead described as "leaving no posterity ... t'was married chastity,"11. 59-60). Oxfordians William Plumer Fowler, Dorothy Ogburn and Professor Daniel Wright also have discoursed on this poem, making sense of its enigmas by positing that it is about Oxford (Turtle), Elizabeth (Phoenix) and Southampton (Rarity) and the end of a dynasty (Tudor) because the Phoenix *will not acknowledge her posterity*. Hume posits that the Turtle is the people of England, which explains how the chaste Virgin Queen could leave "no posteritie." Oxfordians Fowler, Ogburn and Wright, however, argue that "married chastity" and "no posterity" represent something more tangible, i.e., a real but unacknowledged heir. Still, all four (Hume, Fowler, Ogburn and Wright) agree that the outcome was the same—the Tudor dynasty "unofficially" ended with the Essex Rebellion.

[23] By the "how and why of the authorship problem" I mean the situation that occurred after the author's death. It is a "given" for all anti-Stratfordians that the true author wrote anonymously during his lifetime. The greater mystery, heretofore, is why the attribution to the Stratford man took place, and why it has, until now, endured for four centuries. The Monument Theory of the sonnets, plus the Tudor Heir theory

regarding the crisis of the succession, provide compelling "reasons of state" for this situation, i.e., the attribution of the works of "Shakespeare" to the Stratford man, Shaksper, in order to de-politicize the works and leave them sanitized of any supposed relationship to politics and people at the Court.

Works Cited

Akrigg, G.P.V. *Shakespeare and the Earl of Southampton*. Cambridge: Harvard, 1968.

Allen, Percy and B.M Ward. *An Enquiry into the Relations between Lord Oxford as "Shakespeare," Queen Elizabeth and the Fair Youth of Shake-speare's Sonnets*. London, 1937.

Bellamy, John. *The Tudor Law of Treason*. London: Routledge, 1979.

Belsey, Catherine "Tarquin Dispossessed; Expropriation and Consent in The Rape of Lucrece."*Shakespeare Quarterly* 52.3 (2001): 315-335.

Blackstone, William. *Commentaries on the Laws of England*. Oxford: Clarendon, 1765.

Booth, Stephen. *Shakespeare's Sonnets*. New Haven: Yale, 1977.

Boyle, William. "With the Sonnets Now Solved" *Shakespeare Matters* 3.4 (2004): 1, 11-15.

-. "The 1987 Moot Court Trial." *Shakespeare Oxford Newsletter* 33.3 (1997): 1, 6-8.

Camden, William. *Anno Domini* 1601.
<http://www.philological.bham.ac.uk/camden/1601e.html>

Cobbett, William and T.B. Howell, eds. *Cobbett's Complete Collection of State Trials*. 34 vols. London, 1809-28.

Coke, Edward. Institutes of the Laws of England. London, 1628.

Colman, E.A.M. *The Dramatic Use of Bawdy in Shakespeare*. London: Longman, 1974.

Devereux, Walter Bourchier. Lives and Letters of the Earls of Essex in the Reigns of Elizabeth, James I and Charles I. 2 vols. London: Murray, 1853.
<http://books.google.com/books?dq=devereux+lives+and+letters&pr intsec=frontcover&source=web&sig=RVjfVx3vOcAmtLORbHDqE fxT_U&id=loc3EN7A75wC&ots=p7tgINA2sx&o utput=htm>.

Donrow, Herbert S. *The Sonnets in England and America: A Bibliography of Criticism*. Westport: Greenwood, 1982

Duncan, Owen. "The Political Career of Sir Henry Neville." Diss., Ohio State University, 1974.

Duncan-Jones, Katherine. *Shakespeare's Sonnets* London: Nelson, 1997.

Fitter, Chris. "Historicising Shakespeare's *Richard II*: Current Events, Dating and the Sabotage of Essex" *Early Modern Literary Studies* 11.2 (2005). <http://purl.ocic.org/emls/11-2/fittric2.htm>.

Fowler, William Plumer. *Shakespeare Revealed in Oxford's Letters*. Portsmouth: Peter Randall, 1986.

-.*Shakespeare's "Phoenix and Turtle"* : An Interpretation by William Plumer Fowler, with a Supplementary Exegesis by Dorothy Ogburn. Portsmouth: Peter *Randall*, 1986.

Furness, Mrs. Howard Horace. *A Concordance to Shakespeare Poems*. 1874. New York: AMS, 1972.

Gray, Henry David. "Shakespeare's Last Sonnets." *Modern Language Notes* 32.1 (1917): 17-21.

Harrison, G.B. *The Elizabethan Journals*. London: Routledge, 1938.

Hayashi, Tetsumaro. *Shakespeare's Sonnets: A Record of 20th Century Criticism*. Metuchen, NJ: Scarecrow, 1972.

Hotson, Leslie. *Mr. W. H.* London: Rupert Hart-Davis, 1962.

Hume, Anthea."Love's Martyr, The Phoenix and Turtle, and the Aftermath of the Essex Rebellion," *Review of English Studies* 40.157 (1989): 48-71.

Hume, Martin. *Sir Walter Raleigh*. New York: Knopf, 1926.

James, Brenda, and William D. Rubinstein. *The Truth Will Out*. Harlow: Longman, 2005.

Keeton, George W. *Trial for Treason*. London: MacDonald, 1959.

Kerrigan, John. *Shakespeare's Sonnets*. London: Penguin, 1986.

Kositsky, Lynne, and Roger Stritmatter. "Critique of the Monument Theory." *Shakespeare Matters* 4.1 (Fall 2004): 1, 10-14.

Lacey, Robert. Robert, Earl of Essex. London: History Book Club, 1970.

Massey, Gerald. *Shakespeare's Sonnets Never Before Interpreted*. London: Longmans, 1866.

Myers, James P. " 'Murdering Heart Murdering Hand': Captain Thomas Lee of Ireland, Elizabethan Assassin." *Sixteenth Century Journal* 22.1 (1991): 47-60.

Nichols, John. *The Progresses, Processions and Magnificent Festivities, of King James the First, His Royal Consort, Family and Court*. 4 vols. London, 1828.

Ogburn, Charlton Jr. *The Man Who Was Shakespeare*. McLean, VA.: EPM, 1995.

Parsons, Robert. *Conference about the Next Succession to the Crowne of England*. Amsterdam, 1594; London, 1595.

Pequigney, Joseph. *Such is My Love*. Chicago: University of Chicago, 1985.

Rastell, John. *The Exposicions of the Termes of the Lawes of England.* London: Richard Tottell, 1567.

Roberts, Clayton, and Owen Duncan. "The Parliamentary Undertaking of 1614." *English Historical Review.* 93.368 (1978): 481-498.

Rowse, A. L. *Shakespeare's Southampton.* New York: Harper & Row, 1965.

Schiffer, James."Reading New Life into Shakespeare's Sonnets: A Survey of Criticism." *Shakespeare's Sonnets: Critical Essays.* Ed. James Schiffer. New York: Garland, 1999.3-71.

Shakespeare, William. *Rape of Lucrece.* From *The Riverside Shakespeare.* New York: Houghton Mifflin, 1974.

Shakespeare, William. *Shake-speares Sonnets.* 1609. London: Thomas Thorpe, 1977.

Stopes, Charlotte C. *The Life of Henry, Third Earl of Southampton.* 1922. New York: AMS, 1969.

Stritmatter, Roger. "A Law Case in Verse: *Venus and Adonis* and the Authorship Question." *Tennessee Law Review* 72.1 (2004): 171-219.

Thatcher, David, "What a Lark: The Undoing of Sonnet 29." *Durham University Journal* 55.1 (1994): 59-66.

Vendler, Helen. *The Art of Shakespeare's Sonnets.* Cambridge: Harvard, 1997.

-. Letter to Elliott Stone. 8 June 1999.

Whittemore, Hank. *The Monument.* Marshfield, MA: Meadow Geese Press, 2005.

Wright, Daniel L."All My Children: Royal Bastards and Royal Policy:' The Shakespeare Oxford Society / Shakespeare Fellowship Annual Conference. White Plains, NY. 9 October 2008.

—"Phoenix Rising: Recovering Authorial Intent in Interpreting Shakespeare's 'Phoenix and Turtle'" The 13th Annual Shakespeare Authorship Studies Conference. Concordia University. Portland, OR. 18 April 2009.

Chapter 8

The Phoenix and Turtle

William Plumer Fowler

*This essay was first published in 1986 as a pamphlet under the
title* Shake-speare's "Phoenix and Turtle." *The original 1986 pamphlet
also included Dorothy Ogburn's views on the poem, as originally
published in* This Star of England *(1952). Fowler's essay is
reprinted here with the permission of the Fowler family.*

PHOENIX AND TURTLE

Let the bird of loudest lay
On the sole *Arabian* tree,
Herald sad and trumpet be:
To whose sound chaste wings obey.

But thou shrieking harbinger,
Foul precurrer of the fiend,
Augur of the fevers end,
To this troupe come thou not near.

From this Session interdict
Every fowl of tyrant wing,
Save the Eagle, feath'red King,
Keep the obsequy so strict.

Let the Priest in Surplice white,
That defunctive Music can,
Be the death-divining Swan,
Lest the *Requiem* lack his right.

And thou treble dated Crow,
That thy sable gender mak'st,
With the breath thou giv'st and tak'st,
Mongst our mourners shalt thou go.

Here the Anthem cloth commence,
Love and Constancy is dead,
Phoenix and the *Turtle* fled,
In a mutual flame from hence.

So they loved as love in twain,
Had the essence but in one,
Two distincts, Division none,
Number there in love was slain.

Hearts remote, yet not asunder;
Distance and no space was seen,
Twixt this *Turtle* and his Queen;
But in them it were a wonder.

So between them Love did shine,
That the *Turtle* saw his right,
Flaming in the *Phoenix* sight;
Either was the others mine.

Property was thus appalled,
That the self was not the same;
Single Natures double name,
Neither two nor one was called.

Reason in itself confounded,
Saw Division grow together,
To themselves yet either neither,
Simple were so well compounded.

That it cried, how true a twain,
Seemeth this concordant one,
Love hath Reason, Reason none,
If what parts, can so remain.

Whereupon it made this *Threne*,
To the *Phoenix* and the *Dove*,
Co-supremes and stars of Love,
As *Chorus* to their Tragic Scene.

Threnos

Beauty, Truth, and Rarity,
Grace in all simplicity,
Here enclosed, in cinders lie.

Death is now the *Phoenix* nest,
And the *Turtles* loyal breast,
To eternity doth rest.

Leaving no posterity,
'Twas not their infirmity,
It was married Chastity.

Truth may seem, but cannot be,
Beauty brag, but tis not she,
Truth and Beauty buried be.

To this urn let those repair,
That are either true or fair,
For these dead Birds, sigh a prayer.

William Shake-speare

(Editor's note: original typeface and punctuation preserved)

This allegorical and majestic dirge has long presented a difficult and insoluble enigma to Shakespearean commentators, who have wrongly attributed its authorship to the simple theater-worker, William Shaksper of Stratford. They have failed, however, to take into consideration the significance of the hyphenated name, William Shake-speare, subscribed in italics to the first printing of this poem in Robert Chester's *Love's Martyr: or Rosalins Complaint*, a book appearing shortly after the Essex Rebellion of February 8, 1601, and containing also poems by others including Marston, Chapman, and Ben Jonson. It remained for Percy Allen, Esq., in the 1930's to recognize the hyphenated name as the pseudonym for Edward de Vere, the 17th Earl of Oxford[1], and to appreciate the sonorous music of what Mr. Allen terms "the loveliest of all Shakespeare's poems." It has been only since 1920, with the publication of J. Thomas Looney's *Shakespeare Identified in Edward de Vere, the Seventeenth Earl of Oxford*, that thoughtful people have begun to realize that Oxford was, with little doubt, the true author of the Shakespearean works. And it is only through the Oxford theory that *The Phoenix and the Turtle* becomes meaningful.

"The first point that strikes one, in reading this exalted dirge," writes Mr. Allen (in his pamphlet, "Who Were the Dark Lady and Fair Youth?"[2]) "is the solemn majesty of the verse, combined with the serene, sunset glory of vision discoverable in no other Shakespearean work, saving only *Antony and Cleopatra*, written about the same time, by the same pen, and about the same pair."

Percy Allen stresses the significance of the poet's statements, referring to the Turtle, that the Phoenix is "his Queen"; and that, in the radiance of their mutual love, we can see "his right"—his dynastic right—"flaming in the Phoenix sight." The Phoenix and Turtle, according to Mr. Allen, "is a final renunciation of all worldly hopes and aspirations." It is Oxford's memorial to Queen Elizabeth, as *Antony and Cleopatra* is his tribute.

But this poem, with its all-pervasive sadness, is still more. It is Oxford's reaction to the Essex Rebellion—the final and greatest tragedy of his life—when the "Fair Youth," Henry Wriothesley, the 3rd Earl of Southampton, who (if we accept a well-documented hypothesis[3]) was apparently Oxford's and Queen Elizabeth's carefully concealed son, whom Oxford had hoped to get legitimized and named as the Queen's successor, joined with Essex in a nearly successful attempt to dethrone Elizabeth, with the result that Oxford, as England's premier earl, was forced to sit on the panel of Lords that sentenced both Essex and Southampton (who was second in command) to death for treason. Southampton's sentence was, however, commuted by Queen Elizabeth to life imprisonment in the Tower, while Essex's head rolled off on the block two weeks later. The timing of the first publication of "The Phoenix and Turtle" on the heels of the Essex Rebellion thus becomes fundamental to its understanding.

The poem is divided into three parts: a five-stanza prologue, an eight-stanza anthem, and a five-stanza threnody or choral requiem.

The prologue introduces the setting of an allegorical funeral service that is the reverse of the classical Phoenix myth, wherein the 500-year old Phoenix is consumed by flames, with her successor—a newly hatched Phoenix—rising from the ashes of her cremation. Here, not only the Phoenix, but also her mate and offspring, perish in the same fire. The service takes place at the Phoenix' nest or throne, "the sole Arabian tree" referred to in *The Tempest* (111,3,22) where Sebastian states his belief that:

> " . . . in Arabia
> There is one tree, the phoenix' throne, one phoenix
> At this hour reigning there."

In this poem, the "sole Arabian tree" stands for England's dynastic family tree of the Plantagenets, with Queen Elizabeth reigning there.

She is also called "the Phoenix" in Vennard's *The Miracle of Nature*, and is referred to as "that rare Arabian Phoenix" in Anthony Munday's *Zelauto*. Oxford is writing the funeral service in advance for both Queen Elizabeth as the Phoenix and himself as the Turtle dove.[4]

Let us now consider the opening stanza:

> "Let the bird of loudest lay,
> On the sole Arabian tree,
> Herald sad and trumpet be:
> To whose sound chaste wings obey."

Here the "bird of loudest lay" who serves as "herald sad and trumpet" appears to be the same bird as the fourth stanza's "death-divining Swan" or trumpeter swan, who, in his dual capacity as "the Priest in Surplice white," conducts the service. Both references are allegorical for Oxford himself, saddened by his son's treason.

In the next stanza—

"But thou shrieking harbinger,
Foul precurrer of the fiend,
Augur of the fever's end,
To this troupe come thou not near."—

the "shrieking harbinger" is the screech owl heralding the "fiend" of death on the route to the underworld. He is told to keep away from the service. There is little question but that this "shrieking harbinger . . . Augur of the fever's end" (or, of E. Ver's end) stands for the hard-screeching Ben Jonson, who had written a poem about a screech owl and had already started to caricature Oxford (as Shake-speare) in *Everyman Out of His Humour* and other plays, and was threatening to supplant Oxford (i.e., Shake-speare) as the chief dramatic composer of the dawning 17th Century.

"From this Session interdict
Every fowl of tyrant wing,
Save the Eagle, feath'red King,
Keep the obsequy so strict."

Those invited to the strict obsequies are limited to birds of "chaste wings," or Oxford's closest associates connected with the writing of Shakespeare's works. The inclusion of "the Eagle, feath'red King," or king of the birds, applies to William Stanley, the 6th Earl of Derby, Oxford's son-in-law, whose crest was Jove's eagle carrying off Ganymede, and who is believed to have collaborated in the composition of *Love's Labour's Lost*, *Measure for Measure*, *A Midsummer Night's Dream*, *Cymbeline*, *The Tempest*, and possibly other plays of Shakespeare.

134

"Let the Priest in Surplice white
That defunctive Music can,
Be the death-divining Swan,
Lest the Requiem lack his right."

Only the "death-divining Swan" could foresee that Elizabeth and Oxford would both die shortly thereafter, she in 1603, and he in 1604. And only England's leading poet and dramatist—the "Swan of Avon"[5]—would have the "right" and capability to compose and conduct the funeral service for this distinguished pair. This Swan is the same swan referred to in *The Merchant of Venice* (111,2,44) by Portia, in her remark about Bassanio, prior to his making a choice of caskets:

"Then, if he lose, he makes a swanlike end,
Fading in music . . ."—

the "defunctive Music" of this poem.

"And thou treble-dated Crow,
That thy sable gender mak'st,
With the breath thou giv'st and tak'st,
Mongst our mourners shalt thou go."

At the very last, the "treble-dated Crow," Southampton himself, is invited to attend. The word "crow"[6] in Elizabethan times was a reference to either an actor or nobleman, Southampton having been an amateur actor as well as an Earl. His three dates are: (a) first, October 6, 1573, the reputed date of his birth, but really that of the birth of the Second Countess of Southampton's (his purported mother's) first son[7] who either died or disappeared; (b) second, about June 30, 1574, the conjectured date of Southampton's actual birth to Queen Elizabeth, prior to his being substituted as "a little changeling boy"[8] for the son born of the Countess of Southampton on October 6, 1573; and (c) third, February 8, 1601, the date of the Essex Rebellion, when Southampton, by turning against his biological mother, Queen

Elizabeth, made his own "sable gender" or black birth. Sable or
black is the recognized heraldic symbol for bastardy. What has
emerged from the nest in the "sole Arabian tree" is not a newborn
Phoenix, as in the myth, but a "crow" blackened by the flames of
his own rebellion, which have destroyed forever his dynastic right
to be legitimized by his mother, "the Phoenix" or Queen, and
named as her successor to the throne. The appropriateness of the
reference to Southampton as a "Crow" making his own sable
gender becomes apparent as we proceed into the Anthem and find
him declared dynastically dead, with the Phoenix and Turtle—his
carefully concealed parents—utterly crushed and fleeing in the
mutual flame of the Rebellion that forever blackened him.
Commentators in the past have been far afield in trying to explain
the "treble-dated Crow" in relation to the bird itself rather than by
its profound allegorical significance.

> "Here the Anthem doth commence,
> Love and Constancy is dead,
> Phoenix and the Turtle fled,
> In a mutual flame from hence."

The Anthem is introduced with a flat statement. The line,
"Love and Constancy is dead," refers not only to the death of these
qualities in Southampton but also, in view of the singular verb, to
Southampton himself, who is now figuratively dead because under
sentence of death commuted to life imprisonment, and here
dynastically disavowed. The Phoenix and Turtle have "fled" in the
"mutual flame" of his Rebellion. Similar references to
Southampton's love and constancy occur in two sonnets: first, in
Sonnet 117 (14) where the poet, addressing him, writes of "The
constancy and virtue of your love"; and again in Sonnet 152 (10)
in which the poet tells him, "For I have sworn deep oaths of thy deep
kindness, / Oaths of *thy love, thy truth, thy constancy*."

> "So they loved as love in twain,
> Had the essence but in one,
> Two distincts, Division none,

136

Number there in love was slain."

This stanza reflects the resumption of Oxford's and Elizabeth's earlier consuming love, begun when he was a youth 17 years her junior, and of which the single "essence" was Southampton. Their closeness is now rekindled as a result of their mutual tragedy. The line, "Number there in love was slain," again refers to their dynastic disavowal[9] of Southampton, their carefully concealed son, whether or not the word "there" is to be taken as an anagram for "three."

> "Hearts remote, yet not asunder;
> Distance and no space was seen,
> 'Twixt this *Turtle* and his Queen;
> But in them it were a wonder."

This stanza specifically names the Queen as the Turtle's beloved. Despite the physical distance between them, their mutual unity endures, and "in them it were a wonder."

> "So between them Love did shine
> That the *Turtle* saw his right,
> Flaming in the Phoenix sight;
> Either was the others mine."

Here the poet re-emphasizes the strength of this unity, which was so great that Oxford was able to see his dynastic "right" (to have Southampton legitimized and named as the Queen's successor) going up in flames in sight of the Phoenix, or the Queen, herself. The "mine" may be read either as a possessive pronoun or as a noun, in the latter case with the "mine" of one providing the ore to enrich the other's life. The poet was a master of multiple meaning.

> "Property was thus appalled,
> That the self was not the same;
> Single Natures double name,
> Neither two nor one was called."

"Property" here is to be construed in its archaic sense of "propriety," or, as in logic, as something ancillary to the essence. "That the self was not the same" reverses Queen Elizabeth's motto, "*Semper eadem,*" or "Always the same"; while "Single Natures double name" is an allusion to Oxford's double name as Shakespeare, a name having no relationship to either the true poet or the Queen.

> "Reason in itself confounded,
> Saw Division grow together,
> To themselves yet either neither,
> Simple were so well compounded."

Here, contrary to all reason, after years of division, Oxford and Elizabeth are reunited by their mutual tragedy, but without losing their individualities. The term "simple" is used in its archaic sense of a single pure ingredient in a medicinal compound. Through Oxford's love for his Queen and country, the minds of these two distinct individuals are compounded into a single entity.

> "That it cried, how true a twain,
> Seemeth this concordant one;
> Love hath Reason, Reason none,
> If what parts, can so remain."

In this, the Anthem's penultimate stanza, the compounded or united mind of this pair cries in amazement at how true a couple they seem in their concordance. Despite the abstruseness of this passage, the poet seems to be indicating that the reason for their Love's resurgence in this great tragedy is that the strength of their youthful love had not entirely died, and was able to revive despite their long parting, which has now ended.

> "Whereupon it made this *Threne*,
> To the *Phoenix* and the *Dove*,
> Co-supremes and stars of Love,
> As *Chorus* to their Tragic Scene."

The Anthem ends by specifically introducing the "threne" or threnody as a chorus to the "Tragic Scene" of the "Co-supremes"—the Phoenix and the Dove—Elizabeth as England's Queen and supreme ruler and Oxford as its supreme poet and dramatist. They are also "stars of Love." The mention of their "Tragic Scene" stresses the magnitude of their personal tragedy in having to witness and act upon their natural son's treason. Note also in this stanza the introduction of the term "Dove" denoting the Turtle-dove, and forming here an anagram of the initials of Edward de Vere Oxford.

The heart of the matter follows in the "threne" or threnody:

Threnos.

"Beauty, Truth, and Rarity,
Grace in all simplicity,
Here enclosed, in cinders lie."

Here in the threnody—even as the prologue's "treble-dated Crow" (Southampton) became "Love and Constancy" in the Anthem—the three defunctive allegorical birds are represented also in the abstract, with "Beauty" (a variant of Betty) standing for Elizabeth, "Truth" (in its Anglicization of Vere) for Oxford, and "Rarity" (a variation of the "Rose-ly" pronunciation of Wriothesley, Southampton's family name) for the Fair Youth. All three now lie enclosed in cinders.

"Death is now the Phoenix nest,
And the Turtles loyall[10] breast,
To eternity doth rest."

As a result of the Rebellion and consequent disavowal, the "Phoenix nest" bears no successor and becomes a place of death rather than one of birth; and Oxford (the Turtle) maintains his feudal loyalty to his Queen (the Phoenix) until death.

"Leaving no posterity,
'Twas not their infirmity,
It was married Chastity."

"Leaving no posterity" reverses both the myth and the poet's statement to Southampton in Sonnet VI (12): "Leaving thee living in posterity." Southampton is dynastically disavowed and figuratively dead, bereft of his potential immortality. "Twas not their infirmity" shows that the Queen, contrary to official reports, as well as Oxford, was capable of having had a child; while "It was married Chastity" reflects Queen Elizabeth's insistence on being known as the "Virgin Queen," a political necessity in uniting her people against Spain.

"Truth may seem, but cannot be,
Beauty brag, but tis not she,
Truth and Beauty buried be."

These are the requiem's saddest lines. We find Oxford, despite his worship of truth, being forced to live a lie, with the truth behind the name "William Shakespeare" and Oxford's relationship to Southampton suppressed. While in "Beauty brag, but tis not she," we have Elizabeth still maintaining her epithet of "Virgin Queen," even though it isn't valid. In "Truth and Beauty buried be," we have the fulfillment of the doom prophesied to Southampton in the concluding couplet of Sonnet XIV in reference to the same pair:

"But from thine eyes my knowledge I derive,
And *constant stars*, in them I read such art
As *truth and beauty* shall together thrive,
If from thyself to store thou wouldst convert.
Or else of thee this I prognosticate:
Thy end is truth's and beauty's doom and date."

We come now to the final stanza:

"To this urn let those repair,
That are either true or fair,
For these dead Birds, sigh a prayer."

The poignancy of these verses of lamentation is brought out when the curtain falls, and those "That are either true or fair " are called upon to "sigh a prayer" at the urn containing the ashes of "these dead Birds"—the Phoenix as Queen Elizabeth and the Turtle-dove as Edward de Vere, Oxford. Invited are not only members of de Vere's family, in their Latin version of "true" and their variant pronunciation of "fair" as Vere , but also members of the "fair" youth's family, and of Beauty's or Elizabeth's, in their description as "fair." The invitation also includes in its breadth all the world's "true" or "fair" individuals, that is, all those who support the "true" in the face of the false, and who are "fair" to Edward de Vere, the 17th Earl of Oxford—the true Shakespeare.

This sad but powerful dirge corroborates the Oxford theory of the authorship of Shakespeare, by which alone it becomes understandable despite its abstruseness. It also supports the hypothesis of Southampton's royal parentage, whether or not one is willing to accept it. Above all, it clarifies the Sonnets' emphasis on "Truth and Beauty" through its alternate references to Oxford, the "Turtle," as "Truth," and to "his Queen," the "Phoenix," as "Beauty" (like Betty) for Elizabeth. We are left with a sense of tragedy more grievous even than Hamlet's, Othello's, or Lear's.

Endnotes

[1] Oxford's crest as Lord Bulbec, before becoming an earl, was a lion shaking a broken spear in token of victory. [since this essay was first published in 1986 more recent research has shown that this particular crest (of the lion shaking the broken spear) probably was first used after Oxford's lifetime].

[2] Dorothy and Charlton Ogburn, *This Star of England*, page 1171.

[3] Dorothy and Charlton Ogburn, *This Star of England*, Chapter 61.

[4] It was then not unusual to speak of the turtledove simply as "the turtle," as in the Biblical Song of Solomon (Ch.2, verse 12): "The voice of the turtle is heard in our land."

[5] Oxford owned an estate on the River Avon.

[6] Cf. Robert Greene's "upstart crow," in *A Groatsworth of Wit*, 1592.

[7] Charlotte C. Stopes, in her research for the life of Southampton, was unable to discover an explanation for prevalent local tradition that Southampton (the 3rd Earl) was the second, not the first, son of the 2nd Earl.

[8] See *A Midsummer Night's Dream*, (II, 1,23; 1,210; IV, 1, 59).

[9] When this poem was written, Oxford had no idea that he would, two years later, reaffirm his love for Southampton upon his being released from his "confined doom" in the Tower by King James on his succeeding Elizabeth on her death on March 24, 1603; whereupon Oxford wrote in Sonnet 107 :

> "Not mine own fears, nor the prophetic soul
> Of the wide world dreaming on things to come,
> Can yet the lease of my true love control,
> *Supposed as forfeit to a confined doom*."

[10] Feudal loyalty to his queen was one of Oxford's outstanding characteristics. He was so careful to protect Elizabeth that it has .taken three centuries for their relationship to be realized.

Chapter 9

Bitter Fruit: Troilus and Cressida in the Court of Elizabeth

Charles Boyle

This seminar paper was presented at the 1993 Shakespeare Association of America annual conference. It was first published in The Elizabethan Review *(Autumn 1994, Vol. 2, no. 2, 11-18).*

In his introduction to the Folger edition of *Troilus and Cressida* Louis B. Wright wrote, "Some scholars have been tempted to see a precise parallel between the situation in the Grecian camp and conditions in England during the period of the Earl of Essex's quarrel with the Queen and his subsequent rebellion. Such an interpretation, however, raises many problems... [the author] would not have been so unwise as to put his neck in a noose by writing a thinly disguised political allegory certain to bring down upon his head the wrath of the authorities."

Later, however, he makes this observation: "One reason for [the story of Troy's] popularity was the belief that Englishmen were 'true Trojans,' that London had been founded by Brutus, the great-grandson of Aeneas, and that the English nation had sprung from this noble Trojan."[1] R.A. Foakes amplifies this with the observation that the Elizabthan writers Heywood, Spenser, and Drayton also affirmed the London-Troy connection. "These poets were all celebrating the famous origins of Britain, and the ancestry of Queen Elizabeth ... The Queen even quartered the arms of a mythical Trojan in one version of her official coat of arms."[2]

Certainly the author of *T&C* makes little attempt to conceal the contemporary background of his bitter satire, most strikingly in its closing lines when Pandarus recalls "some galled goose of Winchester," a blatantly insulting reference to the Bishop of Winchester, under whose wing brothels so flourished that a prostitute was commonly called a "Winchester goose." The author means for us to understand that, in this play, Troy is London.

In fact, allegory was the accepted literary device for those who wished to comment on the political scene. This was Spenser's method. Indeed, in an age of near total press control ("Art made tongue-tied by authority," as Sonnet 66 complains) what other method would be left? Not that the authorities didn't understand.

Take the case of Elizabeth I and *Richard II*. When reminded that members of the Essex faction had arranged a performance of this play (in which a vain and effeminate Monarch is deposed by the virile rebel Henry Bolingbroke) as prelude to the ill-fated rebellion of her favorite (who had often been compared to Bolingbroke), she is said to have snapped, "I am Richard II. Know ye not that?"

Then there was the mysterious uproar that surrounded a 1597 play called *The Isle* of *Dogs*. England is an isle, of course, and "dogs" was Elizabethan slang for playwrights, but this play was filled with such terrible yet never explained "seditious and slanderous matter" that the authorities wiped all trace of its text from the public record.

In light of this it would be fair to take at his word the declaration Shakespeare put in the mouth of his truth-loving Prince Hamlet when he warns the Queen's chief councilor, Polonius, "The players ... are the abstract and brief chronicles of the time." (II.ii) Later, he informs the deceiving daughter of this scheming politician, "The players cannot keep counsel; they'll tell all." (III.ii)

This from a character, nominally the prince of a Danish Court long past, who will banter elsewhere about London theater gossip of the years immediately following the Essex Rebellion, including specific reference to the Globe Theater and the "late innovation" (i.e., rebellion). (II.ii)

That Shakespeare was playing the same game as many of his fellow writers is self-evident. But the audacity of his political satire has rarely been explored.

It was as far back as 1869 that the scholar George Russell French first identified the character of Polonius as a lampoon of William Cecil, Lord Burghley, Queen Elizabeth's principal minister. French even went on to note that Burghley's son, Robert, and daughter, Anne, might be taken for Laertes and Ophelia.[3] Sir Edmund K. Chambers later concurred.[4] Since then, the evidence for this identification has continued to accumulate to the point where it is conclusive.

Following the declaration of Hamlet, I am inclined to study Shakespeare's plays as abstracts and brief chronicles of his time. I find they make a tapestry that provides an illuminating real world background to his art, an art in which the drama of court life is vibrantly reflected. In pursuing this I will cite a number of scholars who have detected patterns of imagery and incident interconnecting the plays and poems of Shakespeare. My assumption will always be that the author was inspired by reality.

The general consensus has been that the plays *Twelfth Night, As You Like It, Hamlet, T&C*, and the enigmatic poem *The Phoenix and the Turtle* were all composed in the years prior to and following the Essex Rebellion, that is, between 1599 and 1602. These are the works we will look at.

In *The Question of Hamlet,* Harry Levin rightly observed, "*Troilus and Cressida* has close affinities with *Hamlet* in composition and in temper."[5] In his Introduction to the Signet edition of *T&C*, the late Daniel Seltzer continues this line of thought: "It may be helpful to observe .... that many of the problems that challenge Hamlet's mind are paralleled by those that confuse the Trojan princes and the Greek generals. In both [plays] the authority of law is opposed by individual desire or private principle ... the definition of honor, 'to be great,' is strenuously argued by those who have most at stake."[6]

D.A. Traversi, in *An Approach to Shakespeare*, develops this theme. "The devotion to honor ... is devotion to an abstraction that has no sufficient in reason ... but to abandon honor for its lack of rational foundation is to expose oneself to the danger of lethargy, to a rooted disinclination to act at all." He then notes, "The relation of this to *Hamlet*, and in particular to such a soliloquy as, 'How all occasions do inform against me' ☐ (IV.iv) is worth careful consideration."[7]

My immediate concern here is to consider the close relationship between the characters Troilus and Hamlet, as well as the respective courts in which they operate. Both young men are princes of the realm, romantic idealists with a keen sense of honor and a great hunger for truth (Truth is a word never far from Troilus' lips). Both experience deep love for women of doubtful constancy. For Hamlet, both Ophelia and the Queen are not to be trusted. Troilus will eventually discover there is little difference between his Cressida and the adulterous Helen of Troy who, like Gertrude, is a central figure in her court.

Some might object that Troilus lacks the stature of Hamlet. He has been described by Jusserand in *A Literary History of the English People* as "a whining babbler."[8] But L.A. Richards demonstrates in an essay published in *Speculative Instruments* that that characterization is mistaken.[9]

Ulysses, a man in touch with the "mystery" (i.e., the secrets) of the Trojan state as well as his own, describes Troilus to his king as "a true knight ... firm of word ... his heart and hand both open and both free ... manly as Hector, but more dangerous." (IV.v.96-104)

It is in his handling of Cressida's betrayal that Troilus reveals his true depth of character. Richards argues that Shakespeare, either "through the Language or the Tradition," was familiar with Plato's *Republic* and used it extensively in this play. He then quotes from it: "...a good man who is ruled by reason will take such blows of fate as the loss of a son or anything very dear to him less hardly than other people.... Reason says that nothing in man's existence is to be taken so seriously, and our grief keeps us back from the very thing we need as quickly as possible in such times, [which is] to take thought on the event...." (ibid.).

Richards goes on to show how Troilus, when he witnesses Cressida's betrayal (V.ii), goes through the changes advised. He is not torn apart by this profound wounding of his heart. Instead, as Coleridge wrote, "having a depth of calmer element in a will stronger than desire, more entire than choice ... the same moral energy is represented as snatching him aloof from all neighborhood with her dishonor."

Troilus is no "whining babbler," he is Hamlet's ideal, the man "that is not passion's slave." (*Hamlet* III.ii)

Add to this that the speech Hamlet requests of the Player King laments the fall of Troy. Or recall Troilus' uncanny echoing of Hamlet's response to a nosy Polonius on what he reads— "Words, words, words..." (*Hamlet*, II.ii.192)—with his own response to an equally nosy Pandarus—"words, words, mere words; no matter..." (*T&C*, V.iii.108).

But for the alert reader these two scenes, considered together, can yield much interesting matter. In Hamlet's scene he is treating Polonius as a man who would pander his own daughter to a prince. He calls him "a fishmonger," and soon follows this with the extraordinary line, "For if the sun [Sun God, King] breed maggots in a dead dog, being a god [King] kissing carrion --- Have you such a daughter?" (II.ii.181-2) Such evaluations of character do not deter the ever ambitious Polonius. Only a little later, in an aside, he tells us he will "contrive the means of meeting between him and my daughter." (II.ii.211)

Lest we dismiss this as coincidence, we are given in these same scenes additional echoes, linking both the princes and their busybody advisors. The book Hamlet reads, written by a "satirical rogue," reports "old men have grey beards; that their faces are wrinkled, their eyes purging thick amber and plumtree gum; and that they have a plentiful lack of wit, together with most weak hams." (196-200) Compare this with the complaining self-pity of Pandarus: "A whoreson rascally tisick so troubles me ... that I shall leave you one o' th's days. And I have a rheum in mine eyes too, and such an ache in my bones that, unless a man were cursed, I cannot tell what to think on't." (101-106)

Did the author find in these two a common inspiration? Unless it was he who suffered from a "lack of wit," I think so. There are other subtle touches linking Pandarus to Polonius and his prototype, Burghley.

As the power behind the throne of Elizabeth, William Cecil and Robert, the son he groomed to succeed him, were figures of extraordinary cunning and ambition. The bond the father forged with Elizabeth began when she was a defenseless girl accused of carrying the child of the treasonous Thomas Seymour and Cecil the shrewdest of the court lawyers sent to interrogate her. It lasted with unbroken intimacy till the day Cecil died. On the Continent, diplomats jokingly referred to England under him as "Cecilium."[10] After Robert Cecil had crushed Essex, James of Scotland advised his ambassadors in London that the little man was "king there *in effect*."[11]

In *T&C* there is a comic encounter (III.i) between a servant and Pandarus where much is made of confusion concerning Lords, rank and God's anointed. After mixing up the Lords of Troy with the Lord above, the servant tries to pin down Pandarus and the condition of his "honor." "You are in the state of grace," he would know. The misunderstanding in the old man's response is telling.

"Grace? Not so friend. Honor and lordship are my titles." Pandarus has not heard what others would have, that is, a reference to the spiritual state necessary for salvation. Instinctively, he has modestly demurred from a title—Grace—for those of royal blood. That he assumes the meaning tells the joke, another pointed jab at the Cecil family's ascendancy over the English aristocracy, represented by Essex.

A number of scholars, including Dover Wilson, have suggested Essex as the model for Hamlet.[12] G. Wilson Knight, however, speaks for a whole tradition when, in *Shakespeare and Religion*, he finds "...the satire in *Troilus and Cressida* far too insulting for a poet whose tragic period was partly brought about by a sense of loss at Essex's fall. And if Hamlet was so clear an

Essex portrait, Polonius a study of Burghley, surely Gertrude or Claudius must have seemed to correspond to Queen Elizabeth, and would not this have been suicidal?"[13]

So runs the conventional wisdom and so has it stymied all reasonable inquiry into Shakespeare's relationship to the world he lived in and his favorite setting, the court. But what does the author tell us that could shed some light on this problem?

Daniel Seltzer makes some telling links between the steps Troilus takes on the path to self-knowledge, and those Shakespeare delineates in one of his most personal poems:

> The subject matter of this poem clarifies the nature of Shakespeare's thematic concerns in [*T&C*]... *The Phoenix and the Turtle* describes the remarkable union of the mythical Phoenix and the Turtledove, in which love was so complete that even Reason stands amazed at the sight. In this mating, we are told, "number ... in love was stain," for two separate lovers became one, and "Property" itself—the defining essence of the individual thing—was "appalled." These two lovers, in themselves all "Beauty, truth and rarity," do not survive their own union, but are consumed "In a mutual flame," even as each finds absolute perfection in the other. In this play no miraculous marriage of "Truth and Beauty" deserves the repose of death. What Troilus sees, though the truth, runs counter to his ideal, and to this ideal, he is as constant as any genuinely tragic hero [such as Hamlet]. His vocabulary, as he tries to convince both himself and Ulysses that what he has seen cannot actually have taken place, is very similar to that of *The Phoenix and the Turtle.* "If there be rule in unity itself," he cries, "This was not she" (V.ii.138-39)— recalling the paradox in the poem that number (i.e., that "one" cannot be "two") "was slain," that the lovers merged into one entity, yet preserved their distinct essences. Building upon the conceit that there must be two Cressidas ["This is, and is not, Cressid."], he elaborates the most painful truth in the play: that what has seemed glorious and admirable, is not so. (op. cit., xxxiv-v)

No one would suggest Shakespeare wrote *The Phoenix* about birds. Obviously, they stand for real people. Troilus compares himself to that emblem of eternally faithful love, the turtledove (III.ii.179). Hallett Smith, writing in *The Riverside Shakespeare,* comments, "Some critics have thought that the phoenix and the turtle darkly hint at Queen Elizabeth (who was often represented symbolically by the phoenix) and the Earl of Essex."[14]

The great Lord Burghley ridiculed as Polonius and Pandarus? The Virgin Queen of sacred memory scorned as a faithless strumpet? For some scholars these are dark waters indeed. Again, G. Wilson Knight would speak for them. "The whole argument about the Shakespeare-Essex relation is shadowy and without evidence." (ibid)

Yet most of what touches the actual life of Shakespeare is shadowy and without evidence. But if the court of Queen Elizabeth and the Queen herself was his true subject, then this lack of evidence is not surprising, particularly if what Shakespeare has to say is true. Early in the play, Cressida and Pandarus have a curious exchange. He says, "You are such a woman a man knows not at what ward you lie." (Ward is a position of defense in swordplay.) She replies, "Upon my back, to defend my belly; upon my wit, to defend my wiles; upon my secrecy, to defend mine honesty; my mask, to defend my beauty; and you, to defend all these." (I.ii)

Honesty, of course, means chastity. She seems to imply that her reputation for that depends on secrecy and the backing of this key advisor. Is this the Virgin Queen and Burghley in private conversation? I think so.

We have grown used to the idea that Richard III's reputation was blackened by Tudor propaganda and subsequent English historians who followed that line. It has been said that Shakespeare was one of this ilk—though his *Richard III* may, in reality, be a portrait of the crook-backed Robert Cecil. However that may be, it is only very recently that we have come to see how artificially whitened Elizabeth's own reputation has been. The figure drawn by Carolly Erickson in her 1983 book, *The First Elizabeth,* is far closer to a Gertrude or Cressida than the sanitized tradition has ever allowed.

As Seltzer notes, Shakespeare does indeed elaborate the most painful truths in this plays: "what has seemed glorious and admirable, is not so."

One may well wonder how Shakespeare knew—and how he

escaped getting his head put in a noose for daring to "tell all."

Two plays placed in the years immediately preceding the ones under discussion are *As You Like It* and *Twelfth Night.* In both appear fools, Touchstone and Feste, as "all-licensed" as the nameless Fool in *King Lear* And in both plays Shakespeare has other characters admire in glowing terms the professional fool's ability to speak truth to power and "cleanse the foul body of the infected world if they will patiently receive my medicine." *(AYLI,* II.vii.61-62*)*, In this regard, it is significant to recall that Olivia reminds her offended servant that Feste is her "allowed fool" (*TN,* I.v) just as Achilles must remind Patroclus, his favorite, that the scurrilous Thersites "is a privileged man." (II.iii) At Elsinore the only fool referred to is the beloved "poor Yorick" whose skull the Prince holds in such proximity to his own. Perhaps there is no Fool in *Hamlet* because Hamlet is the Fool.

A disgruntled Polonius does complain to the Queen, "Tell him his pranks have been too broad to bear with / And that your Grace hath screened and stood between / Much heat and him." (*Hamlet* III.iv)

I believe Shakespeare drew from life. Like other great writers he wrote what he knew. Since his subject was court life, he tells us plainly he enjoyed the protection of some great patron.

Polonius and Pandarus are Burghley, Gertrude and Cressida the Queen. Hamlet and Troilus may have been inspired in part by Essex but they are clearly mixed with elements of the author himself, the most amazing court jester who lived. Who he truly was remains an open question.

Endnotes

[1] Louis B. Wright, *Troilus and Cressida* (1966).

[2] K A. Foakes, "Troilus and Cressida Reconsidered," *University of Toronto Quarterly* 32 (1963).

[3] George Russell French quoted in Tom Bethell's "The Case for Oxford," *The Atlantic Monthly* 268:4 (October 1991).

[4] Ibid.

[5] Harry Levin, *The Question of Hamlet* (1959).

[6] Daniel Seltzer (ed), *Troilus and Cressida* (Signet Classics, 1963).

[7] D.A. Traversi, *An Approach to Shakespeare,* 2nd ed., revised (1956).

[8] Jusserand, *A Literary History of the English People,* iii, 253.

[9] I.A. Richards, *Speculative Instruments* (1955).

[10] Charlton Ogburn, *The Mysterious William Shakespeare (1984).*

[11] Charlotte Stopes, *The Life of Henry Wriosley, the 3rd Earl of Southampton* (Cambridge, *1922).*

[12] Dover Wilson, *What Happens in Hamlet* (Cambridge, 1935).

[13] G. Wilson Knight, *Shakespeare and Religion* (1967).

[14] Hallett Smith, *The Phoenix and the Turtle,* introduction (Riverside, 1974).

Chapter 10

"I am I, howe'er I was begot":
King John's Bastard Prince

Prof. Daniel Wright, Ph.D.

*This paper was presented at the 2013 Shakespeare Authorship Studies
Conference at Concordia University, Portland, Oregon.*

"There's the not-so that reveals the so…"
- Philip Roth, *Exit Ghost*

No one is more aware than an Oxfordian of what a liar Shakespeare is. When he reports history to us, he tells us nothing so much as what it was *not*. And while many Stratfordians protest that Shakespeare's inaccurate historical reportage is nothing more than a testament to Shakespeare's fundamental lack of learning—a consequence of his inability, having never studied history, to sort out truth from fiction in his many chronicle plays—Oxfordians, of course, know better.[1] Shakespeare, in recounting events that never were and the lives of men and women who never lived, actually demonstrates great care, not carelessness, in his craft.

Far from being reckless in composing his dramatic narratives, Shakespeare, through the history plays, demonstrates his dedication to one of the cardinal principles of Renaissance historiography for, as argued by no lesser authority than the great Renaissance poet, Sir Philip Sidney, a Poet, in his historical writing, asserts and comments upon that which *should* have been (by reshaping what *had been*) into forms that reveal how persons and events of the past *ought* to be interpreted—not in the dim light of the past but in the bright and modern light of the playwright's audience's *present*. Shakespeare—as a Poet, a Maker, a Shaper—is clearly at one with this doctrine. Indeed, he may be its most well-known practitioner, and in Shakespeare's history plays we can readily observe his process of creative selection in choosing his chronicle sources and determining what new things to do with them (when, of course, he elects to use those sources rather than overthrow them in favor of wholly supplanting established historical accounts with characters, deeds and narratives of his personal invention). As Sidney, in his monumental *Defense of Poesie*, describes the poet's work on historical matters:

> The Poet…citeth not authorities of other Histories, but eve[n] for his entry calleth the sweete Muses to inspire unto him a good invention. In troth, not laboring to tell you what is, or is not, but what should [be], or should not…. (50)

Indeed, suggests Sidney, the Historian *qua* Historian, as opposed to the Poet—given the Historian's task—is a writer of limited and mundane purpose and therefore merits, at best, restrained praise. This must be so, argues Sidney, because the Historian, who dispassionately records that which *was*, is dedicated to mere reportage—a low task, a baser labor than the Poet's—for in Sidney's appraisal, the Historian, in the proper exercise of his office, must be satisfied with recording the follies of the world rather than worthily engaging himself, like the Poet, in the noble cause of edifying his reader. This neglect of a virtuous resolve in the Historian, according to Sidney, is corrected by the Poet who, if his subject is History, properly reshapes that History to a right purpose in order that his readers might be instructed and edified—not by being shown what *was* but by showing what *ought to be* or what *should have been.* As Sidney himself puts it,

> [T]he Historian…is so tied, not to what should be, but to what is, to the particular truth of things, and not to the general reason

154

> of things, that his example draweth no necessarie consequence, and therefore a lesse fruitfull doctrine. Now doth the peerless Poet perform both, for whatsoever the Philosopher saith should be done, he gives a perfect picture of it...[for] he coupleth the general notion with the particular example. (22)

The doctrine, not insignificantly, is shared by Shakespeare's contemporary and Spanish counterpart, Miguel de Cervantes. In *Don Quijote*, for example, we discover Sidney's distinction between the Poet and the Historian in the words Cervantes gives to Samson Carrasco, the Salamancan graduate:

> [I]t's one thing to write as a poet, and very different to write as a historian. The poet can show us things not as they actually happened, but as they should have happened, but the historian has to record them not as they ought to have been, but as they actually were . . . . (376)

It is with this Renaissance sensibility[2] that we have to read Shakespeare's history plays—not as "exercises in analytical neutrality" (Canino 13), disinterested reportage or objective accounts of the past, of which they, even to the lightly-tutored eye, are nothing of the sort – but as chronicles shaped by art that re-imagines the past in the light of the present. As such, they are not transparent windows but reflective mirrors—windows less into England's past than mirrors of Shakespeare's Elizabethan present—and even more specifically, as Professor Lily B. Campbell has put it in her famous study of Shakespeare's histories, mirrors of Elizabethan policy.[3]

Comprehended as such, the discerning critic acknowledges that Shakespeare was anything but a writer of commonplace entertainments or an indifferent recorder of history. He was, instead, an informed commentator on the contemporary *political* scene, an expositor of *political* conviction and an advocate for *policy* that, often enough, contravened or challenged Government—which is to say "Cecilian"—philosophy and practice. How else can we explain Shakespeare's daring self-assignation as political tutor and non-adulatory critic by writing, in large part, as Professor Campbell has put it, "not about the admirable rulers of England and their times, but…about those rulers who had sowed the wind and reaped the whirlwind" (11)?

Why, too, if Shakespeare were only an ambitious, socially-aspirant former butcher or tradesman-turned-playwright who wished to make money, "fly under the political radar" and ruffle none of officialdom's feathers, would he be about the business of putting before the public eye sceptred lunatics and royal ineffectuals of England's past—addled monarchs like Lear, Cymbeline and Henry VI; fiends, degenerates, tyrants and usurpers like Richard III and Macbeth; an enthusiastic adulterer and lecherous wanton like Edward IV; and a narcissistic, vainglorious romantic like Richard II?

Why, if Shakespeare purposed to ingratiate himself with the Crown and the Court would he give over so much of his historical writing to foregrounding an ambitious and devious but tormented and haunted conspirator like the insecure and dissembling Henry Bolingbroke, who, brazenly boasting of his theft of the Crown, gloats, "[T]hen I stole all courtesy from heaven,/And dress'd myself in such humility/That I did pluck allegiance from men's hearts" [*1H4* III.ii.50-52] and who, in a similarly arrogant celebration of his ignoble triumph, offers his son corrosive counsel that is centuries ahead of Karl Rove's cynical political playbook: "[B]usy giddy minds/ With foreign quarrels, that action, hence borne out / May waste the memory of…former days" (*2H4* III.v.213-15)? [4]

Shakespeare's Political Voice

Given all this, and despite the irrepressible stream of conventional apologists for Shakespeare's allegedly fuzzy grasp of history (Shakespeare, left school, after all, declares no less a Stratfordian authority than J. Halliwell-Phillipps, "destitute of all polished accomplishments" [qtd in Sams 18]), it is relatively easy for us to see why a growing number of leading scholars have begun to recognize the Shakespeare plays' lofty and sophisticated political voice. They have sought to anchor their interpretations of

Shakespeare's works within decidedly political contexts, often pointing to Shakespeare's unyielding attentiveness to, and his exploration of, the politics of succession, right rule and the qualities of a candidate's fitness for the authority conferred by the Crown. They concede that Shakespeare's politics reveal uncomfortable patterns of thematic preoccupation and development that gnaw obsessively at the periphery—and sometimes at the center—of almost all of the Shakespeare plays.

Discerning critics, accordingly, will not subscribe to the preposterous assumption that Shakespeare wrote solely for ignorant spectators, as one who, himself, possessed no insider knowledge of higher politics or rarefied understandings of political controversy and court intrigue. Max Meredith Reese, in *The Cease of Majesty*, cautions, for example, that "it is surely a grave misunderstanding of [Shakespeare's] purpose to suppose that the great cycle of English historical drama was written just as a poetic exercise" (111), and the late Allan Bloom and Professor (now Emeritus) Harry Jaffa, in their observations of Shakespeare's histories, go even farther in emphasizing that Shakespeare was an "eminently political author" (4), who wrote with political purpose and, as a learnéd expositor and interpreter of history, "had a pedagogic intention" (10).

The late great theatre critic, Jan Kott, acknowledged, too, that most of Shakespeare's histories were anything but celebratory; Shakespeare's darker histories, he observed, uniformly follow a particular thematic arc in that "[e]ach of the . . . great historical tragedies begins with a struggle for the throne, or for its consolidation. Each ends with the monarch's death and a new coronation" (4). In confirmation of that observation, therefore, we do well to look closely at one of those histories—*King John*—a lesser-known Shakespearean play and one based on an even more youthful (though officially anonymous) work that likely, in large part, was Shakespeare's as well: *The Troublesome Raigne of King John.*[5]

King John and history

Given the unappealing character of John and his reign, what, one might well ask, would have been Shakespeare's purpose in dramatizing this "history" of one of England's more self-centered and ignoble kings? To one looking at this play with little more than superficial awareness of the era, Shakespeare's *King John* might even seem to be about some subject other, and probably more, than what it purports to be, for to a reader or spectator with any understanding of the Angevin dynasty, Shakespeare's "history" of *King John* is obviously less a faithful record of John's reign and more a descant on the character of besotted, degraded monarchy itself—with a particularly stern and not-too-muted indictment of English sovereignty that has whored itself to disrepute and betrayed its duty to posterity by failing to provide England not only with selfless rule but with an heir both worthy and capable—a sovereign's most sacred responsibility and the one inviolable duty to the nation that he or she must perform.

Shakespeare's *King John*, unlike its predecessor drama, presents to its audience an otiose English monarch of dubious title and little foresight who, as Ralph Turner records, ruled with impunity, "maintained power through cruelty and fear" (198) and does not so much glorify England by a heroic defiance of Rome (as is the case in *Troublesome Raigne*) as shame himself and England by selfishly failing to look to the good of England's future.

To Kristian Smidt, the principal issue of the play is evident: "The opening speeches of *King John*," he points out, "go straight to the central issue of the drama: King John's possession of the crown of England and the threats to his hold of it by claimants who urge a better title" (72). The tragic diminishment of royal dignity grows in prominence disproportionate to the King's frenzied attempt to secure and confirm his claim as we behold the pathetic spectacle of an arguably illegitimate king scrambling, first and foremost, to protect what his own mother acknowledges to be his "strong possession much more than [his] right" (I.i.39).

The degradation of the King's dignity and his lack of interest in the vitality of the Kingdom's life beyond the maintenance of his own tyranny is illustrated by an accelerated downward movement in Shakespeare's play as John is given over to immoral connivance and base compromise. He finally is compelled, by his weakness, to squander the larger part of his reign in staving off civil insurrection and foreign invasion – all the while willfully overlooking the solution to the problem of his contested legitimacy that would solve his and his nation's troubles (principally the threat of foreign invasion) by settling the succession on a royal offspring of perfect virtue, military distinction and regal blood who, *alone amongst all the characters in the play*, has England's true interests at heart. As G. R. Hibbard summarizes it, "*King John* is about the . . . conflict between an unlawful king, in possession of a throne he has seized, and a lawful claimant to that throne, who has no power of his own to make his claim good . . ." (133).

Shakespeare's preoccupation with this crisis as a dilemma born of the need to settle the succession on a worthy heir is typical in his history plays; it merely gains heightened attention in *King John*. As Kenyon College's Professor of Political Science, Tim Spiekerman, has written, "the concept of 'legitimacy'…is the most salient theme of the Shakespeare history plays. At stake in these plays is the question not only of who will rule, but…who is *supposed* to rule…" (5).[6]

Succession and bastardy

By what other means in this history do we see Shakespeare's positioning of this play to subversive purpose in order to drive his audience's attention into the heart of this question about the succession? One might well begin to discover the answer by pursuing Shakespeare's curious and relentless focus on the issue that underlies the ferociously-argued series of claims and counterclaims in *King John*'s opening scenes that arise from so many of the characters with regard to the matter about which they all share a common preoccupation: bastardy and the rights attendant to bastards. For example, in the opening scene of Act Two, we hear a none-too-subtle suggestion from Constance that King John is, himself, a bastard (II.i.124-28)—an assertion for which, in Shakespeare's chronicle sources, there is not the tiniest shred of historical evidence, but which salient point Constance demonstrates, in raising the charge, that if the claim is true, bastardy obviously is not, has not, and cannot have been an insuperable barrier to the Crown, given that John, bastard or not, *is* the King of England.

But the claims of bastardy do not end with the assertion that England's Sovereign is a bastard, for in this same scene, we hear Eleanor declare that Constance's son, Arthur, another rival for the Crown, is a bastard, too (II.i.122-23)[7] —and all of these disputations follow hard upon the first act's extensive legal discourse on the rights of succession and prerogatives that belong to bastards in general, specifically as the rights of inheritance apply to the two fictional Faulconbridge brothers, one of whom, Shakespeare lets us know, is an unacknowledged *royal* bastard, the son, no less, of Richard Coeur-de-Lion, King Richard I. It's a point of no small matter inasmuch as Albert R. Braunmuller, Distinguished Professor of the Humanities at UCLA, underscores, in his Introduction to The Oxford Classics edition of *King John*, that "Richard Coeur-de-Lion's illegitimate son [the eldest son of an eldest son of the blood royal] gradually comes to seem the king's most promising successor" (62); indeed, says Professor David Bevington, "he is the play's greatest patriot" and is "instinctively royal" (702).

On this note, Kristian Smidt, a conventional Stratfordian reader and critic at the University of Oslo, expresses bafflement about Shakespeare's purposes in *King John*; Smidt quizzically asks his readers, "Why, especially [in this play] is there so much talk of bastardy?" (73). However, the question poses few problems for us when we recall Prof. Lily Campbell's point that we must interpret all this seemingly gratuitous and unhistorical action of the thirteenth century within the context of the Elizabethan present:

> Shakespeare…used history to teach politics to the present…[;] his purposes in choosing the subjects and incidents from history *as well as in his altering the historical fact* is ... made with current political situations in mind*…[E]ach of the Shakespeare histories serves a special purpose in elucidating a political problem of Elizabeth's day*" (125; emphasis mine).

Harold Bloom is in full agreement with Campbell; he acknowledges, for example, that whatever Shakespeare's history of *King John* may be construed to mean in the minds of audiences today, those interpretations *are totally meaningless* if our goal is to identify *Shakespeare's* purposes, particularly given that we know, in the words of Yale's Harold Bloom, that "John's peculiar interest for Shakespeare's audience was the king's ambiguous allusiveness to Queen Elizabeth's political dilemmas" (57).

But, if the issues of bastardy, legitimacy and rightful inheritance are central issues that Shakespeare, by his obsessive attention to them, wishes to advance, what can we deduce Shakespeare's purpose to be in telling us *what* he does about them, and how do we recognize the implications of these Shakespearean emphases for ourselves in our efforts to better interpret this play?

To begin with, we can recognize that, consistent with Sidney's doctrine and the observations of commentators that have followed centuries afterward, Shakespeare——given his sources and his disciplined reworking of those sources—is *not* about the business of mechanistically dramatizing established history or uncritically repeating its orthodox propositions. He is thoroughly content to throw official—"documented"—history's persons, events and speech from the reign of King John into all manner of seemingly-inexplicable confusion and disorder which he then creatively re-orders to serve novel narrative and argumentative purposes. As the annotator of *King John* published in the current edition of *The Riverside Shakespeare* observes, this play is a totally unreliable guide to the actual reign of King John; the play's "chronology is violently distorted" and "freely violated" (780, 788).

But the significance of Shakespeare's reworking of orthodox chronology does not end with the mere observation *that* he disorders it: as the late Richard Courtney, Professor at the University of Toronto's Graduate Centre for Drama, has expansively commented, *King John* is "a fascinating experiment in which Shakespeare freely mixes historical data with pure fiction in an *original* way" (125; emphasis mine). John Blanpied, of the University of Rochester, takes this one step farther on our journey to clarity by observing that Shakespeare's very act of disordering events in *King John* is emblematic of one of the play's central *themes* wherein Shakespeare emphasizes not only that in John's England "all is out of order" but that, "above all," in John's England, *"sequence* [itself] is undone" (112).

The conclusions derived by our appreciation and understanding of Shakespeare's transformative art are therefore not to be the subjective, impressionistic conclusions derived by readers who would have Shakespeare mean what they want him to mean by their dismissiveness of, or their refusal to practice, the biocritical method—the reasoned approach to the revelatory reading of texts so well defined by contemporary biocritical methodologists in their insistence on our attentiveness, in studying literature, to what Professor Jackson Benson of San Diego State University first called "the recognition of 'otherness'" (108). In fact, our conclusions about *King John*, properly derived by the guidance and tutelage of a master artist who is writing, after all, to be understood—not incomprehensible, even if his methods are, in part, opaque—are substantially reliant for their authority on our correct interpretation and appreciation of what it is that Shakespeare would have us understand by setting his reconfigured Angevin past against the Elizabethan present.

The Riverside Shakespeare's annotator, and many other commentators, have noted that a host of minor but abundant alterations to the historical record in *King John* signal, in small and sometimes inconsequential ways, the author's reworking of his sources to novel purposes; they have observed, for example, that Shakespeare's character of Lymoges, Duke of Austria, is a purely fictional construct. Indeed, Lymoges is a composite character that Shakespeare invented by first conflating two old enemies of Richard I and then transporting this new character to a future time.[8] The betrothal of the French Dauphin to Blanche of Castile and the arrival in England of the Cardinal envoy from the Vatican (to berate John for his refusal to install the papal nominee, Stephen Langdon, to the Archbishopric of Canterbury) are depicted by Shakespeare as virtually simultaneous occurrences when, in truth, they were separated by many years. Contrary to Shakespeare's declaration that Prince Arthur was taken to England as a prisoner following the French defeat at Angiers, we know that nothing of the kind transpired (Arthur was, indeed, taken prisoner by the English, but he was never removed to England from the continent).

Shakespeare also falsifies history by contriving a scene in which the citizens of Anjou, when asked to choose their king, refuse to do so (in fact, they rejected John and chose Arthur). Additionally, Shakespeare has Constance, Arthur's mother, and Eleanor, John's mother, die at almost the same time when, in fact, Constance died in 1201 and Eleanor in 1204; Shakespeare dismisses Holinshed's report that John died of an attack of what we, today, would describe as dysentery and substitutes for it the polemicist John Foxe's more spurious and characteristically anti-Catholic suggestion that the King was poisoned by a monk at Swinstead Abbey. And, of course, as all who are familiar with the play know, Shakespeare diminishes the stature of Arthur by transforming Holinshed's gallant and daring warrior into a pre-pubescent child, a mere babe, an almost helpless youth whose pitiful pleading for his sight and life form one of the more mawkish scenes in all of Shakespeare—a pre-Dickensian plunge into almost laughable sentimentality.

Moreover, apart from all that he distorts and omits from the chroniclers' accounts in composing his play,[9] Shakespeare declines to include and comment upon perhaps the most significant domestic event of John's tumultuous reign: the baronial revolt against John's authority that ultimately led, in 1215, to the submission of the King in Magna Carta. This conflict between John and the nobility is never broached by Shakespeare,[10] as indeed attention to most events in the actual reign of King John are subordinated by Shakespeare to his fixations on the conflict over John's legitimacy, the fate of the royal Bastard, and the politics of England's fate following the death of the sovereign. In this connection, Dartmouth's Peter Saccio perceptively comments that "as constitutional historians have seen more significance than contemporaries saw in the barons' challenge to John's authority at the end of the reign, so Shakespeare sees more significance than contemporaries saw in the contested succession" (206).

Significantly, too, in elevating and highlighting the issues that are in dispute over the succession, one might think that Shakespeare would surely include material recorded by historians that speak to the succession crisis in John's reign *as that issue had been recorded* in the various chronicle histories of John's reign that he consulted. But Shakespeare excludes Holinshed's important testimony that, during the reign of King John, William Longespée, 3rd Earl of Salisbury, was a bastard son of Henry II by Ida de Tosny, making him a half-brother to John and possessed, thereby, of a claim (however feeble [John, among other things, was older]) to the throne. However, instead of centering his attention on this real-life royal bastard, Salisbury, Shakespeare elects to *invent*, out of whole cloth, a bastard son of the King, one sprung from the loins of Richard Coeur-de-Lion, and he makes *him* the principal player and hero of his play rather than the *authentic* bastard son who appears in the play unattributed as a bastard.

And not only does Shakespeare cut *his* Bastard completely out of imaginary cloth and make him, an individual who never lived, the central character of his "history" play, but he makes him, astonishingly, the play's only repository of true, selfless love of country and the bearer of the regal dignity that John has betrayed and sold for private gain. Indeed, so prominent is this character of Shakespeare's imaginative conjuration that Jacqueline Trace, in her notable article, "Shakespeare's Bastard Faulconbridge: An

Early *Tudor* Hero" (emphasis mine), has said that the monumental achievement which Shakespeare's Bastard attains is nothing less than the "establish[ment of] himself in an arena of power politics as military genius, Protestant propagandist, and nationalist hero, exhibiting the qualities of military and national leadership of his natural father, Richard I, to become chief advocate of the divine right of kings" (66).

This royal bastard, a man invisible to history, is the only man, suggests Shakespeare, worthy to wear the Crown, but though Shakespeare makes it emphatically clear that the King knows who this deserving royal bastard is, he will do *nothing* to enable his succession! [11]

If, therefore, this play—a play that features a self-centered sovereign who will not elevate the one man of blood and merit to succeed him—is, as Professor Campbell and many scholars have suggested, a play that mirrors the *Elizabethan present* rather than the Angevin past—we might well ask ourselves what it is that Shakespeare may be attempting to say in this play about the politics of succession in his own day. The answer, in part, might explain why, perhaps significantly, and to the best of our knowledge, this play never saw print until the publication of the First Folio in 1623 and (apart from Meres' isolated and uncorroborated reference in *Palladis Tamia*), never saw any recorded public performance until 1737 when it was produced in Covent Garden by the Shakespeare Ladies' Club.

Bastards in Shakespeare

A play by Shakespeare that features a bastard pleading for his rights is not exactly novel in Shakespeare. We all know of Edmund's resentment of the exclusion he suffers due to his status as an unvalued bastard in *King Lear* ("Why bastard? Wherefore base? . . . Now, gods, stand up for bastards!" [I.ii.6,22]). Nor should we forget Thersites, that bastard master of wordplay, and his efforts to forge a bond of common cause with Margarelon, the bastard son of Priam, in *Troilus and Cressida* ("I am a bastard too,

I love bastards. I am bastard begot, bastard instructed, bastard in mind, bastard in valor, in everything illegitimate!" [V.vii.16-18]). We might also recall that *Troilus and Cressida* somehow escaped getting indexed in the First Folio and will remember that when it *was* published in folio, it had been stripped of its notorious earlier enigmatic preamble in Q that announced it was from "A Never writer, to an Ever reader," was identified as a play "never clapper-clawed with the palms of the vulgar . . . nor . . . sullied with the smoky breath of the multitude," had made its escape from "the grand possessors," predicted that "when he [the author] is gone" the world would "scramble" for the writer's other plays, and warned that when those plays would no longer be available, readers would see the establishment of what the writer of the prefatory epistle called "a new English Inquisition."

Moreover, no Oxfordian who is aware of the accusations of bastardy that were flung at Edward de Vere can miss the suggestive self-referential allusion to Oxford's acute sense of displacement, subordination and enforced silence in the fulminations of Don John, the bastard from *Much Ado About Nothing* when, in an angry lament like that of Sonnet 66 when the poet complains of being "tongue-tied by authority," the bastard half-brother of the Prince of Aragon roars: "I am trusted with a muzzle" —but promises "[i]f I had my mouth, I would bite...; in the meantime, let me be that I am, and seek not to alter me" (I.iii.32-33, 34-35, 36-37).

How similar Don John's outburst is to Edward de Vere's own enraged response to his father-in-law when he instructed Lord Burghley, in a letter of 26 April 1576, that he would no longer co-habit with Anne, a woman he never had wanted to marry (Haynes 45)—but would reserve saying *why* he would not do so for another time: "[U]ntil I can better satisfy or advertise myself of some mislikes . . . [w]hat they [my reasons] are – because some are not to be spoken of or written upon . . . – I will not deal withal. Some that otherwise discontented me I will not blaze or *publish* until it please me" (qtd in Fowler 248; emphasis mine).

Defiant, too, is Shakespeare's ahistorical bastard in *King*

John. He will not accept a patrimony that is not his, however lucrative, if it means he must forfeit his name. He turns aside any claim he could make to being the late Robert Faulconbridge's heir to, instead, affirm his royal blood, for he knows that although it would much enrich him in property to pose as the legitimate son of a man who was not his father, it would come at the cost of belying his true self. He takes pride in and celebrates his status as a prince in exile, a royal bastard whose lands have been given to another and who, accordingly, has to live without prospects—or at least without prospects if the Sovereign stubbornly fails to publicly proclaim him. He is proud of his royal blood though he carries an inferior title. He knows he is a prince, as does his king, though nothing, he knows, is likely to come of it. What is important for him, though, is the *truth*, for the truth of who he is does *not* change: "[B]lessed be the hour by night or day/ When I was got" (I.i.165-66), he exclaims; "I am I, howe'er I was begot!" (I.i.75).

After all, a *royal* rose is a *royal* rose, by whatever *name* that rose be known, and, indeed, the Bastard seems to know that should he bedeck himself with a rose, spectators just might intuit too much from it: ("[I]n mine ear," he declares, "I durst not stick a rose / Lest men should say, 'Look, where three farthings goes!" (I.i.143-44). Of course, to Shakespeare's audience, a three-farthing piece was a well-known coin of the realm, but this coin was *unknown* in King John's day. A three-farthing piece was a uniquely *Elizabethan* coin (minted only between 1561 and 1582), which, on one side, displayed the royal coat of arms and on the other, the Queen—with a Tudor Rose behind her head (Clayton).

Royal bastards in English history

It's hard to escape the conviction that discerning eyes and ears in an Elizabethan world would not see in Shakespeare's depiction of the royal Bastard in *King John* a figure worthy of the succession in their own era, for despite the irregularity of his birth, Shakespeare makes young Faulconbridge the bearer not only of royal blood but royal speech and regal purpose. No other character is so endowed with such gifts.[12] Barbara Hodgson attests to this in her observation that, in this play, "neither England's king nor its nobles . . . remain . . . 'true.' Only the Bastard, who speaks the phrase, retains that distinction" (31). G. R. Hibbard agrees: it is "the Bastard [who is] the enduring spirit of England" (143).

Every other active claimant for the throne, in contrast, is a posturer and a poseur, a figure of weakness or contempt—and all of them, given the indeterminate state of succession law, are of as much disputed legitimacy as the Bastard. Even King John, as we have observed, possesses the throne, as his mother attests, more by his "strong possession" than his "right" (I.i.40). John, too, to his disgrace, stands less for England than for himself, and he succumbs to vile compromise in his rule; he yields much, by concession, to schemers and parasites, solely to preserve his Crown.[13]

It is difficult, too, not to miss Shakespeare's implicit message to Elizabeth I in Faulconbridge; as Alison Findlay observes, in her study of the role of bastards on the Elizabethan stage, "Sir Richard's [Faulconbridge's] patriotism threatens to undermine *Elizabeth's* government" (208; emphasis mine), and Faulconbridge's own bastardy cannot but call to the Elizabethan audience's mind that bastardy, in itself, was no insuperable blight to one of royal blood, no barrier to the Crown. Elizabeth, after all, had been so stigmatized herself in 1536 by the Second Act of Succession, and yet this did not prevent her eventual coronation, even though her exclusion from the succession was fiercely pursued not only by her father and Parliament but by her half-brother and half-sister, and during her father's reign, heady work was underway to raise yet another half-brother of Elizabeth's, the bastard son of Henry VIII, Henry Fitzroy, to the Throne.

Prince Arthur—another claimant to the throne in *King John*—is depicted by Shakespeare as far less worthy than Faulconbridge to succeed but, interestingly, not because of his birth. For all his claim in blood, the boy is a weakling, "a 'powerless hand'" (Hodgson 31), an invitation to foreign domination of the land and therefore a danger to the State. Arthur, the son of John's elder deceased brother, Geoffrey, is, as Shakespeare depicts him, a frail, anemic child in the keep of a foreign enemy; for Shakespeare, he's less English than French and little more than a babe; he lacks gravitas and the wisdom to see that he is nothing more than a pawn in Philip of France's contest with John for rights in England.

Additionally, not *one* of John's many bastard sons appear in this play (and, by conservative estimate, John spawned at least *seven*).[14] Moreover, the real—the historically genuine—royal bastard of Richard Coeur-de-Lion also does not appear in this

Actor George Kemble as Faulconbridge

play—only this fictive substitute of Shakespeare's, Faulconbridge. Only Shakespeare's Bastard—the emblem of true majesty and noble purpose—speaks for the spirit of Coeur-de-Lion and becomes the visible spirit and voice of England in the play. "Now hear our English king," he thunders in Act V, "For thus his royalty doth speak in me" (V.ii.128-29). He alone is advanced by Shakespeare as the repository of England's hope (as A. R. Braunmuller attests, "our sense of closure depends upon the artistry and manipulation of Shakespeare and of his representative, the Bastard. Since the Bastard never existed . . . only his rhetoric, not his deeds, can conclude the play's historical action" [77]); he is a man who grows steadily in wisdom and virtue (much like Prince Hal, whose father wished him substituted for by a "changeling child in cradle clothes") through the overthrow of his indulgence in baser passions and personal ambition to the cultivation of personal and political maturity, high patriotic character and noble, selfless conviction.

James Calderwood, Emeritus Professor of English at the University of Washington, has pointed out that Faulconbridge's acquisition of command over his ambitious nature, by his transformation into an icon of the royal ideal, is exemplified when the Bastard cries out, "Withhold thine indignation mighty heavens / And tempt us not to bear above our power!" Calderwood notes that in making these remarks, the Bastard is speaking self-referentially, "acknowledging an impulse to kingship..." (100). This meditation on forging a forceful path and carving out his own way to the Crown, gives way, however, to selflessness and submission to patriotic duty as Faulconbridge matures in wisdom by dutifully taking command of affairs when no guiding hand in the kingdom can be found—and in doing so, he utters no hint that he need be anything other than a king in deed, though none in name. As he instructs Hubert,

> England now is left
> To tug and scramble, and to part by th'teeth
> The unowed interest of proud swelling state.
> Now for the bare-pick'd bone of majesty
> Doth dogged war bristle his angry crest,
> And snarleth in the gentle eyes of peace;
> Now powers from home and discontents at home
> Meet in one line; and vast confusion waits,
> As doth a raven on a sick-fall'n beast,
> The imminent decay of wrested pomp.
> Now happy he whose cloak and center can
> Hold out this tempest. Bear away that child,
> And follow me with speed. I'll to the King.
> A thousand businesses are brief in hand,
> And heaven itself doth frown upon the land.
>
> (IV.iii.145-59)

The speech well illustrates what Tim Spiekerman has pointed

out: "the Bastard makes no attempt to seize power for himself, as he surely could have" (53). Indeed, Shakespeare, here in Act IV— and most notably, as well, at the close of the play—takes pains to underscore the steadfastness of the Bastard's loyalty. Shakespeare's Bastard, therefore (as the writer would have us unambiguously understand), though a bearer of the blood royal, is no would-be usurper who would wrest his due from an unwilling hand, seize what is not offered, take what is not given; he is not "a dispossessed Machiavellian plotter" (Blanpied 101) but the patient bearer of unrewarded merit. What he lacks is not ability but *recognition* of what his labors for England promise, would but the Crown acknowledge him and make him royally capable of that promise.

Clearly, as Shakespeare develops this prince-who-is-invisible-to-history, this royal Bastard whose lofty deeds and character, in the words of Professor Michael Mannheim, "assum[e] importance which is utterly foreign to [those of the Bastard of] *T*[roublesome] *R*[aigne]" (*The Weak King* 141), the audience comes to see in young Faulconbridge a worthy youth, the best of commanders, a prince of the blood royal most deserving of the Crown. "[I]t becomes clear," as Richard Courtney declares, "that he would make a perfect king" (148). But what the audience also sees, with heart-wrenching disappointment, is the Crown's self-absorbed silence and refusal to bestow that recognition, a withheld conferral of royal authority that would make such perfect kingship possible.

To better impart the significance of the loss of this most promising end, it might not seem particularly surprising to us that Shakespeare chose the reign of King John to introduce to his audience his fictional character of the noble Bastard, for, as his audience likely would know, and as historians record, the consequence of John's reign was the near collapse of the State: domestic insurrection, threats of foreign invasion, and the alienation of many of England's possessions—losses that were not recovered under John's equally incompetent successor, Henry III, whose own misrule[15] added civil war and what John Gillingham rightly has called a "humiliating" failure in 1242 to win back England's lost territories in France (114) to the King's growing inventory of military misadventures. Who can miss the implication at which Shakespeare is pointing? Clearly, it is that England would have been better off had John made better provision for England after his death and been succeeded by a better man—in this case, by a bastard prince of the blood. And if this play, indeed, is less about the Angevin past and more about the Elizabethan present, what counsel—can we miss it?—is Shakespeare whispering to Elizabeth?

The audience for *King John*, lest we think otherwise, would also hardly be surprised to see a royal bastard so depicted on the stage; bastardy, after all, was no impediment to honour and certainly no impediment to succession. English history offered abundant examples of princes begot in less than perfect ways between the sheets (including the Conqueror himself), and many in Shakespeare's audience would not be unaware, as we noted earlier, that their Queen's father, Henry VIII, had sought to enable the succession of his own openly-acknowledged royal bastard, Henry Fitzroy (begot by the King upon Elizabeth Blount and raised in the household of Edward de Vere's paternal uncle, Henry Howard, the Earl of Surrey) until a so-called "legitimate" heir, by the King's third wife, Jane Seymour, was born in 1537. Indeed, at the time Fitzroy died, an act was working its way through Parliament to confirm the assent of the Commons to Henry's decision to put this bastard on the throne as Henry IX (Denny 85-86, 304, 322; Murphy 172-73, 246-47; Weir 387).

And not only in the Tudor era was the fact of royal bastardy a commonplace—not yet was it a status darkened by Victorian attitudes of shame and impropriety that substantially survive to this day. Edward IV, a near-immediate predecessor to Queen Elizabeth's grandfather, Henry VII, was notorious for fathering bastards. This fact, indeed, was the cornerstone of Richard of Gloucester's claim to the throne when, soon after Edward IV's death, it came to light that, in addition to the King's many other bastards, both the Prince of Wales and the Duke of York (better known to us as "the Princes in the Tower") were illegitimate children as well, sons to Edward by a bigamous marriage to Elizabeth Woodville (Lamb 67; Denny 67-8).

Chris Given-Wilson and Alice Curteis's book, *The Royal Bastards of Medieval England,* is but one of many texts that remind us English royal bastards were anything but rare. As they point out, "Forty-one illegitimate children of the English kings can be identified with near certainty. Including doubtful attributions, the figure is past the fifty mark. There must have been many more whose names have disappeared entirely…Henry I alone fathered at least twenty royal bastards, Henry II at least three and"—as we noted earlier—"King John at least seven" (17)—and *none* of those Johannine seven, as we have illustrated, figure in Shakespeare's play of the Angevin king within which the role of one particular royal bastard is nothing less than *central*! Hmm…

In the estimate of historians, all of the Tudor kings (apart from the boy king, Edward), likely were fathers of illegitimate children, as well. Sir Roland de Vieilleville, for example, for over four centuries, has been almost unanimously reputed by historians to be the bastard son of Henry VII (whose own father's legitimacy, it should be noted, was itself actively disputed, old Henry Tudor himself being but the descendent of Catherine de Valois and Owen ap Meredith ap Tudor, a groom in the royal stables); indeed, de Vieilleville's status as a bastard son of Henry VII is prominently attested today in works as significant as the *Dictionary of Welsh Biography.*

Royal bastards, however, like the Tudor bastards Roland de Vieilleville and Henry Fitzroy, were not only medieval commonplaces, and they certainly were not of negligible consequence; they often were highly regarded, respected, honoured and feared (Given-Wilson and Curteis 17; Ridley 41); controversy over them shaped the history of the English nation, and this was no secret to the courtiers and educated men who were the foundation of the Elizabethan State. Bastard sons of royalty regularly had been promoted in the past, supported by powerful statesmen and used for diplomatic ends; sometimes they were regarded by rival statesmen as grave threats. And Shakespeare—never given to steering the politically safe course in his plays—does not himself denigrate the royal bastard of this play; indeed, he gives him uncommon attention, often speaking to the injustice he suffers for lack of recognition and reward of merit. Kristian Smidt is but one of many modern critics who recognizes Shakespeare's ennoblement of his bastard hero in *King John* in his declaration that Faulconbridge "may not be 'true begot'...but he [is] certainly 'well begot'" (79). Even A. L. Rowse acknowledges "the nobility inherent in Shakespeare's portrait of Faulconbridge" (106), and in E. M. W. Tillyard's appraisal, Faulconbridge emerges as "one of Shakespeare's great versions of the regal type" (226).

Queen Elizabeth's children

During the reign of Elizabeth I, allegations in England and abroad that the Tudor Queen, like her father and grandfather before her, had herself spawned at least one (and perhaps several) illegitimate children—royal bastards—were widely rumored. Apart from the question of whether these rumors were true, it is noteworthy to consider that the fact of their advancement suggests that opponents of the Queen (herself a bastard, we recall, at least according to Catholic reckoning and the terms of her own father's will, as well as a couple of parliamentary decrees) clearly thought such reports might be regarded as plausible. Indeed, in the first half of her reign, rumors of the Queen's fecundity were openly subscribed to even by the Queen's loyalists in Parliament, and Ben Jonson himself asserted that Elizabeth was sexually intimate with a host of men,[16] though one might wonder how, absent some important connection at Court, *he* could have known.

Maybe most revealingly, we might look at the testimony offered by the author of *Leicester's Commonwealth* wherein the writer accused Robert Dudley of allowing the spread of rumors suggestive that he secretly had married the Queen. Moreover, declares the concealed writer, based upon what Dudley knew to be a widely-held (or at least widely-circulated) assumption—that the Queen had given birth to at least one (and perhaps as many as five) of his children—Dudley planned to foist one of his many illegitimate children on the realm as Sovereign if the Queen were to miscarry. This strategy was undertaken by the earl, declares the writer of *Leicester's Commonwealth*, in order that were Elizabeth suddenly to die, Dudley might "make legitimate to the Crown any one bastard of his own," and Dudley sought to accomplish this seizure of the throne for his heirs, the writer discloses, by contriving, in 1571, to replace, via an Act of Parliament, in Clause V of the Treasons Act of 1571, the words *lawful issue* with the words *natural issue* in order to broaden the definition of who, after the Queen's demise, could qualify as Elizabeth's heir (130). Under the circumstances, if Dudley was, in fact, the engine behind this device that Parliament enacted, one has to ask how Dudley and his allies could have hoped to prosper by such a transformation of the statute unless it *were* widely supposed and believed that the Queen, in fact, *had* borne a child of Leicester's and that with the assent of Parliament, that child could thereby, without question, be eligible to succeed to the throne on the occasion of Elizabeth's death.

Moreover, we know that several years before *Leicester's Commonwealth* was published, rumors were circulating within the kingdom and abroad that Elizabeth was the mother of many illegitimate children, the first of which, if any were true, may have been when she was brought to bed, as the result of having been sexually violated, in the presence of witnesses, by the ambitious and perverse Lord Admiral, Thomas Seymour.

Many, but not all, of the rumors about Elizabeth, as we might expect, were circulated and given credence by foreigners and Catholic enemies of the Queen. Carole Levin, Willa Cather Professor of History at the University of Nebraska, records, for example, an occasion in the 1560s when the Spanish ambassador reported that the Queen was rumored to be "pregnant and...going away to lie in." Levin also reminds us that an otherwise ostensibly loyal and non-Catholic subject in Ipswich, upon seeing the Queen in distressed condition, declared that Her Majesty "looked like one lately come out of childbed" [80-81]). Amongst Catholics, the Pope himself was sufficiently persuaded of reports that Elizabeth had given birth to a daughter that he thought negotiations for a Catholic marriage to this daughter might provide a means to draw England back to Catholic Christendom "without the hazards of war" (80).

The record of Protestant Englishmen who suggested that the Queen was no virgin is extensive (Levin 83-85). Francis Edderman of Chester is reputed to have declared around 1578 that the Queen was the mother of two children by Leicester (qtd in Chamberlin 184), and in 1581 Henry Hawkins maintained not only that Elizabeth had given birth to several children but declared that the Queen "never goethe [o]n progress but to be delivered" (PRO S.P. 12/148/157). Notably too, several years later, the testimony of Arthur Dudley in 1587 before Sir Francis Englefield established, to many people's satisfaction, that even if Arthur Dudley had not conclusively confirmed that he was a son of Leicester and the Queen, questions about his parentage were being raised by his revelations that some found difficult to account for by alternative explanation.[17]

This was an era in which, after all, like the Queen herself, intimacy was political and politics were intimate, so speculation about the camouflaged life of the Queen was pervasive and without end. Concealment, duplicity and mystery associated with the Queen defined the era itself. As Patricia Fumerton has written of the Queen's hiddenness, "This secrecy of Elizabeth's—this private, inward turning that simultaneously takes a public form like politics—characterizes not simply Elizabeth but the Elizabethan age for which she was the focus" (95).

Legitimacy, legitimacy

Against this background of an indeterminate succession, not only in *King John* but throughout the Shakespeare canon, we are confronted by "Shakespeare's persistent concern with questions of royal concern and usurpation" (Graff 145) and crises of legitimacy that surround irregular conception, birth, identity and the misplaced crowns that are central to the *agon* of Shakespearean drama. Indeed, the questions of who is legitimate and what makes a ruler legitimate in his authority rarely forsake Shakespeare's close attention, even when the context of the play is not England's past.

Legitimacy, legitimacy: Henry V, unrivalled warrior king and conqueror that he is, is obsessed by his *want* of it and fearful of the consequences of not having it: "Not to day, O Lord, / O not today, think not upon the fault / My father made in compassing the crown" (IV.i.294). Richard II anchors his demands for unquestioned loyalty and obedience to it—"Not all the water in the rough rude sea / Can wash the balm off from an anointed king / The breath of worldly men cannot depose / The deputy elected by the Lord…" (III.ii.57) – and then barters "the King's name" for mere survival and winds up getting neither. Shakespeare depicts Henry Bolingbroke actually confessing his illegitimacy and recounting to his son that, to gain the Crown, he had "stole[n] all courtesy from heaven / And dressed himself in such humility / That [he] did pluck allegiance from men's hearts" (*2 HIV* III.ii.50-2)—for which, as a consequence, Henry fears God will breed "revengement and a scourge for me"…and therein ratify his fears that he has been "mark'd / For the hot vengeance and the rod of heaven / To punish [his] mistreadings" (III.ii.8, 9-11).

The sins of adultery and bigamy by Edward IV nullify his heirs' hopes of advancement and the perpetuity of his line in *Richard III*; Edward's failure to discern and see aright lead to the destruction of his sons by the misshapen, club-footed abortion that is his brother, Richard; Claudius cannot maintain, especially in his own conscience, a legitimate hand on the throne due to his seizure of the Danish scepter by the crime of fratricide and refuses, in stubborn mindfulness of his sin, to repent his crime and abdicate, forsaking his incestuous marriage to his murdered brother's wife; Macbeth (married to a supremely willful queen who is ostensibly childless but who we know has suckled children at her breast

[I.vii.54-55]), cannot sustain his reign due to his commission of regicide, and he will take all Scotland to hell with him rather than renounce what he has conspired and murdered to achieve in servile obedience to a woman whose possession of him he cannot exorcise; Caesar, with an army at his back, cudgels the republic that had entrusted him with its defense and attempts to cloak himself in imperial power—but pays with his life, leaving the Republic dead and, like England under the Cecils, with the looming spectre of civil war hovering over the land; Saturninus accepts the empery of Rome as a gift of trust and sets about to no business faster than the betrayal of it—the sum of which leaves the capital a blood-soaked sewer—although the nameless royal bastard of that play, the son of Tamora and Aaron, escapes—but to where and what fate? Capulet and Montague, in combative contests for pre-eminence of a *name*, tyrannize over, rather than nurture, their offspring and so lose, first, their natural parental authority and then their children's lives; Lear forfeits legitimacy for himself and his heirs in the folly of his egoism, deaf to the authorial counsel of his wise fool; Richard III murders his way to power only to see that having obtained it, he can only, because of the means by which he has come by it, misuse and ultimately lose it.

King John's warning

So would be the outcome for England—captive to the legacy of a corrupt court and a declining monarch—in *King John,* were the fate of the realm left to such as King John; but in this play, Shakespeare suggests, that dread outcome for England need not be. Indeed, its fate might be altogether the opposite; if *King John* is a prophetic warning to Elizabethan England that the fate of a post-Elizabethan England need not be the fate of post-Johannine England, then England might yet find its way to regal greatness and dynastic continuity, not civil turmoil and foreign possession of the Crown. As Michael Mannheim has written of Shakespeare's optimistic tone in this otherwise tragic production, "Were it not for the Bastard, the play would end in a whimper. Instead, it ends with one of the most resolutely patriotic speeches in English drama" ("The Four Voices the Bastard"127).

And what is that defiant spirit of energetic, regal breath that the Bastard summons as though he already were a king? "This England never did, nor ever shall, / Lie at the proud foot of a conqueror, / But when it first did help to *wound itself*" (V.vii.112-15; emphasis mine). The Bastard, in the words of Irving Ribner, "at the supreme point of his rise, instead of seizing the throne for himself" (122) pledges, instead, in Shakespeare's words, "*true* subjection *ever*lastingly" (V.vii.105; emphasis mine). As the hero of the play, the Bastard, of course, gets the last word—and it's a word of hopeful promise—but it is a promise predicated on the recognition that *if* England would thrive and prosper, she must do her duty to those to whom that duty is owed: "…Nought shall make us rue, / If England to itself do rest but true" (V.vii.117-18). As Alison Findlay has observed in her book, *Illegitimate Power: Bastards in Renaissance Drama*, these closing words are significant, for "[b]y giving these words to a bastard, Shakespeare alerts the audience to a fissure at the center of power…" Faulconbridge's bastardy, ironically, therefore, "is a virtuous condition which isolates him from ruinous self-interest and allows him, as the bastard son of Coeur de Lion, to *relegitimise* the polity" (208-9; emphasis mine).

Who can miss in this, interpreted within an Elizabethan context, the suggestion that the Queen, in not placing a worthy Tudor heir, irrespective of his birth, before her realm and the world, is acting according to narrow self-interest rather than in the interest of the State—and, subsequently, if she would but establish an otherwise-unacknowledged Tudor successor as her heir, she, too, could "religitimise the polity" and reconsecrate England[18] to emerge from its desacralised state and, at last, "to itself…rest…true." [19]

Shakespeare, throughout the canon, shows us that *this* is the way for the re-sacralisation of the State to be achieved. And it's not a process of following mere succession mechanics. After all,

Guiderius and Arviragus succeed and "redeem the time" not only because they are true sons of the king but because princeliness inheres in their being and cannot be suppressed: "O noble strain! O worthiness of nature! Breed of greatness," Belarius says of the princes who know not—though Belarius knows (as do we)—who they truly are. "Cowards father cowards and base things sire base," he continues. "Nature hath meal and bran, contempt and grace. / I'm not their father, yet who this should be / Doth miracle itself, lov'd before me." Perdita, of course, is Leontes' and Herminone's lost daughter, but though displaced from her rightful due, her nobility does not perish into indignity merely because she is raised in rustic circumstances as a shepherdess; indeed, like the princeliness of Guiderius and Arviragus, Perdita's nobility is such that a prince like Florizel responds to it and cannot resist her innate grace.

For Shakespeare, such plays as these and *King John* attest that nobility of character endures even when it is buried by treachery, thrust aside by conspiracy, or denied. It is a quality of birth.[20] As such, it cannot be expunged. It is a sacred mark of anointing, an infallible sign of dereliction or imposture when that which ostensibly is regal bears no mark of it. None who "steal, grasp and usurp" in Shakespeare can make anything lasting by their thefts of that which does not belong to them. The quality, in Shakespeare's metaphysics, that protects nobility is a transcendent one, a sacred and mystical mark that summons those who recognize it to honor it, for not to do so is to dismiss nobility of its appointed task: the building up of the body of the kingdom that all parts of the realm might thrive because of it.

The Bastard must succeed

It therefore is not just a matter of simple justice that we recognize England's need of the heroic Bastard in *King John*. Though tempted, he forswears "commodity," the material gain and shallow advantage he might acquire were he to press to attain his own by force rather than receive it as a gift. As a prince of the realm, albeit unacknowledged, he cannot but live for the good of his kingdom and *must* forswear that which might but increase his worth in goods and land. England's despair over the future is, as the unacknowledged Bastard tell us, within England's power to cure, would that *she* should but choose to follow the course of *vere* —of truth—and do so: "This England never did, nor never shall / Lie at the proud foot of a conqueror, / But when it first did help to wound itself. / Now these her princes are come home again, / Come the three corners of the world in arms / And we shall shock them; nought shall make us rue, / If England to itself do rest but true" (V.vii.112-18). We feel the impending loss to the nation, the tragedy-in-the-making, the chaos in embryo, if this does not happen; the Bastard must succeed! As Harold Bloom has observed of the play's central argument and what it inspires in its hearers, "The Bastard [Faulconbridge] ought to be king, because nobody else in *King John* is at all kingly" (56).

Not even an orthodox scholar like Leah Scragg, in *Shakespeare's Alternative Tales,* can miss the point that the rhetoric in these plays confirms a sacerdotal character on princeliness as a mark of divine grace. It is an aristocratic theme that distinctively marks the royal sensibility of Shakespeare. Its presence in this play is all the more inexplicable if we are expected to believe that Shakespeare's philosophy flows from the pen of one to whom these qualities, and reverence for them, could hardly have been less: the grasping, litigious, acquisitive Will Shakspere whose avaricious practices and mercenary convictions will come to re-define the character and life of Britain in the early modern era, leading, as we see in our own day, to what would be the despair of Edward de Vere—the displacement of sacred government for authority groomed by a more modern, coarse, brutal instinct for power, manifest by bullying, obstructionism and the heedless pursuit of narrow class interests—acts of baseness that Shakespeare vilifies and scorns in dissemblers like *Henry the IV Part I's* Sir Richard Vernon, *Cymbeline's Jachimo* or Othello's *Iago*—vile, deceitful men who, devoid of grace, conspire to work by craftiness and guile rather than be guided by the codes of nobility, truth and honour. As Scragg sagely writes of King John's royal bastard predecessor in *Troublesome Raigne:*

> Philip has been brought from obscurity to prominence by some supernatural force...[for t]hroughout the turmoil into which Philip is plunged in the course of the play, it is his *lineage*...that the dramatist stresses. [H]e is the representative of an old order, and the associations that surround him serve to link him with the offspring of classical deities...rather than with the unfortunate products of more mundane, illicit unions. (42-43; emphasis mine)[21]

The prince's development, which Scragg attributes to "some supernatural force," is, in fact, for Shakespeare, simply the dramatic emblemization of *natura naturens*, a medieval principle that Virgil Whitaker, in his commentary on *King John* in *Shakespeare's Use of Learning*, identifies as the charism that "directs all things capable of growth or development toward fulfill[ment of] the purpose for which they were created" (142). It is aristocratic and feudal in its conception and constitution, and Whitaker admires Shakespeare's integration of this sophisticated, patrician metaphysics into his characterization of the Bastard—but he shrugs his shoulders in bafflement about how the butcher boy from Stratford acquired them. "These ideas are not in Shakespeare's source," Whitaker laments. "Wherever he got them, they reflect a considerably more learned kind of thought than is discernible in his earliest plays" (142).

King John imparts the dangerous suggestions that the sovereign, by compromise of conscience and silence to the truth, has consigned the nation to a course wherein commodity rather than integrity shall hold court, and honor can go a-begging while conniving ministers within her bounds set their sights on plundering England for the advancement of their own insignificant persons and properties. Is it any wonder, then, that the world didn't get a manuscript of this play until it had been politically sterilized by its assignation to a letterless provincial merchant— probably by the apparatchiks of that all-powerful censorial authority of Elizabethan-Stuart England—Oxford's ruthless brother-in-law, Robert Cecil—the Sonnets' "captain ill," that ogre of "limping sway" who presided over a corrupt and dissolute State and who Shakespeare, in Sonnet 66, complained "tongue-tied" truth and "disabled" his art?

Shakespeare's purpose

That Shakespeare's purpose was not the indifferent dramatization of the reign of King John is now, I think, to us all, indisputable. What he *was* composing, in effect, was an appeal for the preservation of the Tudor dynasty, and doing so, in substantial part, by crafting, from his many sources and his own personal vision, what Catherine Canino of the University of South Carolina has, I think, aptly labeled the Shakespeare histories: "a family history"—a history of England viewed through the dramatist's re-negotiated histories of the landed aristocracy, e.g., the Cliffords, the Stanleys, the de Veres. As Canino herself puts it:

> Shakespeare apparently realized the difference between a history perpetuated by a family and a history composed by an outsider, and he . . . invoked the aristocratic belief that family histories were safer loci for the preservation of an individual's personal identity and remembrance. . . . The genealogies of the nobility were more than a disparate collection of family stories that only affected a handful of wealthy and titled people. They were symbolic of the continuity of English society.

She continues, observing that

> [t]he monarchs and ruling families of England may change. The treatment and empowerment of the commons may change. The relationship and diplomacy between countries may change. The powers of Parliament and the monarchy may change. But the noble titles endure. Some of these titles had been in existence since the days of the Normans, . . . and they represented, in a unique way, not only the history but also the identity of England . . . . They were uniquely, enduringly, symbolically English . . . .

And why was all this of such great import to the late Elizabethan Shakespeare? Because

> [i]n the turbulent days of the 1590s, the only certainty was that
> England was about to be ruled by a new family, perhaps a
> family that did not derive its origins from the past and lands of
> England. That family could bring with it a new religion, new
> politics, and new alliances with new countries. It also most
> probably would bring with it a new history. The noble families
> of England . . . represented the only constant in English society.
> Perhaps that is what Shakespeare understood best when he
> wrote about them. (230-31)

Shakespeare, therefore, clearly had a strong political motive
in his writing, and what I think Professor Canino has contributed
to our better understanding of Shakespeare's purpose is her
identification of the method he strategically utilized in his art by
which his goals—"all one, ever the same"—were to be advanced.
Curious, one might think, in a man reputed by most Stratfordians
to be, unlike other writers of the era, a man of little or no formal
political education, experience, character or interest—and
especially curious, one might think, with respect to such a man's
vulnerability to arrest and prosecution that, were he the Stratford
man, Shakespeare surely would know that he was certain to face
were this play ever to set its daring foot on the floorboard of a
public stage.

In fact, for the great Stratfordian critic, E. A. J. Honigmann,
it's this very demonstration of Shakespeare's political *cajones* that
makes *King John* such an electrifying work, for Honigman is all
amazement at Shakespeare's astonishing political audacity in the
play; he trumpets, admiringly, that "Shakespeare's manipulation
of the historical fact brings out the similarities of the reigns of
John and Elizabeth excitingly, almost dangerously" (xxix); and
Harold Bloom, in full concurrence, adds that Shakespeare, in
writing *King John*, clearly knew that he needed cover and knew
the need to cloak his revelations in some measure of protective
ambiguity: "The parallels are certainly there between King John
and Queen Elizabeth I," Bloom observes, and, like Honigman, he
praises the playwright's bravery, compositional dexterity and
artful caution: "To compare, however implicitly, the ill-fated John
to Elizabeth was rather dangerous, and Shakespeare is too

circumspect to overwork the parallels" (57). Jonathan Bate, of Worcester College, Oxford, in his commentary on the daring and politically provocative character of Shakespeare's work, agrees, and he unhesitatingly affirms that "if things had gone just a little bit differently, Shakespeare could have been thrown in the Tower or even executed."

Shakespeare's obsession with the succession; his attention to royal bastards, displaced princes and changeling children; his preoccupation with incest; his tireless dedication to probing the question of legitimacy and loss of name; and, in *King John*, his re-assignation and/or diminution of all the historical characters of John's era while elevating a fictional figure (and a royal bastard, at that) to seemingly-unaccountable and exceptional prominence by bestowing on him the authorial voice—all suggest to us that in Shakespeare, as in Solzhenitsyn, we will only be able to discover the buried truths about a bygone regime (if those truths are to be found anywhere) in a literary revelation of truth that assuredly will *not* appear in official histories, government papers and documents created by bureaucrats determined to sanitize their secretive regimes' legacies. No, we must look to the authors of such as this play—not to the whitewashed and "politically correct" records of the Cecils and what the English stage historian Glynne Wickham has called their vast "machinery of censorship and control" (II.94)—to discern the true conditions of a kingdom where truth was maimed and suppressed by the evils of torture, corruption and official secrecy.[22]

Bloom and Jaffa instruct us of our single most needful duty in interpreting Shakespeare's works aright—in what is a foundational precept of biocritical practice: "Every rule of objectivity requires that an author first be understood as he understood himself; without that, the work is nothing but what we make of it" (10). For therein is the key—the key to opening the otherwise oft-perplexing world of Shakespeare to clearer understanding. Clarity is to be attained in first recognizing precisely that fact: that the author must be understood as he understood himself, and in so appreciating that, we thereby will understand that for Shakespeare, as for so many political writers, the personal *is* the political; the man, in his person and proclamation, are one. But we will never discover that until we pierce the illusion of the preposterous fraud that is the orthodox theory of Shakespeare authorship. We must find the man behind the mask, the face beneath the façade. And that means knowing, too, more than simply who he was— discovering meaning in Shakespeare has everything much more to do with discovering *what* he was.

The great Italian political writer, Ignazio Silone, declared, as he approached the end of his days, that "there is a secret in my life; it is written between the lines of my novels" (qtd in Pugliese 330). When, like Dante before Shakespeare and Silone after him, we affirm that, for great writers of genius and prophetic power, "the past has many uses, and one of them is to inspire the present . . . [via] an imaginary past" (Menand 94), *then* we will begin to fully appreciate and understand what Charles Beauclerk means when he says, "Get Shakespeare wrong and you get the Elizabethan Age wrong."

Conclusion

We now can see in *King John* a play directed not at the mob—the ale-swilling, bear-baiting, whore-chasing crowds who flocked to the public stage—but a dramatic plea in regal verse to the one who has the power to set England's course aright if she will but do her duty and do what she knows is right. To argue, as many Stratfordians do, that *King John,* along with the other history plays, was written by Shakespeare to admonish the mob and instruct the English public in its civic duty is to deny everything this play proclaims, for Stratfordians misread the plays not only by misidentifying the author but by misidentifying the audience as well. We can never lose sight of the fact that these works, as Fintan O'Toole reminds us, were "written by a man living in the first efficient police state, a writer whose two most important predecessors ha[d] recently met their deaths at the hands of the secret police..." (43) —written by a writer who had "explosive things to say about power, government and social justice in a viciously repressive state where free speech was a dangerous thing" (98) —written by a writer who, as Janet Clare has pointed out in her own excellent book on Elizabethan and Jacobean dramatic censorship, had to struggle to arm his message with potent substance while yet seeking refuge and protection in "strategies of evasion" (55).

No, in Shakespeare, what we behold is the author's preoccupation not so much with the unruly but with misrule; Shakespeare's accusatory finger in plays such as *King John* is not pointed at the *crowd*. It is pointed at the *Crown*. When the clouds of Stratfordian myth that obscure the Shakespeare plays' origins dissipate, the greater Shakespearean world will recognize this too. Then, not only will the world behold the true author in name, but it will see why *and for whom* Oxford became Shakespeare: it will see a man in the shadows, a prince like Hamlet in internal exile, an abandoned son like Edgar—the displaced heir in *King Lear* – pleading that he might be acknowledged his father's son, welcomed home from banishment and restored to his birthright by the parent who has forsaken him, hoping, like the Bastard of *King John*, that Royal Authority will see in him, its unacknowledged royal son, begging, in dramatic voice, in the words of Sonnet 66, to "behold desert a beggar born."

Endnotes

[1] Some Stratfordians, of course, agree with the common sense approach of the Oxfordians. For example, Allan Bloom and Harry Jaffa – aware of the intellectual foundation required for Shakespeare to become a deft and deeply-informed political writer – ask their colleagues who think Shakespeare was an untutored writer:

> Can one reasonably say that he [Shakespeare]…was ignorant of the essential facts of English history because he had never studied? This would be as much as to say that Jefferson, with no consideration of political principle, wrote the Declaration of Independence because he wanted to be well known and that its success is due to it being an excellent Fourth of July oration. (10)

Many others, unfortunately, seem to share the opinion of Stratfordian Harvey Scott who dismisses Shakespeare's formidable learning by attributing Shakespeare's knowledge not to rigorous study and immersion in a culture of deep erudition but to an evanescent quality of "genius"; indeed, Scott declares that Shakespeare and similar "men of genius do not date from schools of learning. Genius is a law unto itself" (83, 88-89).

[2] The doctrine is not just an ancient one, however. Truman Capote was but one of the most recent century's writers who subscribed to it; when Donald Windham, for example, challenged Capote to justify his interminable prevarication and tireless re-historicization of the past, Capote replied, "I remember things the way they should have been" [qtd in Windham 39]).

[3] Professor Campbell reminds us that "[t]he Elizabethan expected any work of history to act as a political mirror, to be concerned with *politics*" (16) and instructs us that if we would understand Shakespeare aright, we cannot assume an indifferent attitude on the part of the writer but must be aware of his polemical purpose (125). One might conclude that it would seem difficult for the informed reader to suppose otherwise, given that, as Catherine Canino points out, the chronicle sources of Shakespeare's plays were themselves hardly indifferent accounts of people, places and events; "the chronicles," in fact, as Canino reminds us, "were the best and most efficient vehicles for government propaganda" (20).

[4] All quotations of Shakespeare are taken from the 2nd edition of *The Riverside Shakespeare* (Boston: Houghton Mifflin, 1997).

[5] See, for example, comments from various textual scholars beginning with George Steevens' eighteenth-century surmise, in his edition of twenty of Shakespeare's plays, that "[t]he author seems to have been so thoroughly dissatisfied with this Play [*Troublesome Raigne*] as to have written it almost entirely anew, reserving only a few of the Lines and the Conduct of several Scenes" – emendations and edits that might account for the shift in focus from the pre-eminently anti-Catholic *Troublesome Raigne* to *King John* which, in the words of Leah Scragg, "places far greater emphasis upon the bastardy of Faulconbridge, exploiting the connotations that conveniently cluster around the figure of the illegitimate son" (43).

[6] As Albert Levi emphasizes of these struggles for the throne, Shakespeare "is primarily interested in the *condition* of kingship" (89; emphasis mine). For Shakespeare, he notes, "when . . . authority is in question, it is either because of some doubts concerning the legitimacy of the . . . right to rule or some demonstrated lack of that personal authority which is indispensable in leadership" (83).

[7] The charge made by Eleanor of Aquitaine, the Queen Mother, against Arthur in *King John* II.i.122,132, is an allegation apparently based on the fact that Arthur was born in 1187, many months (though not quite nine) after the death of his putative father, Geoffrey, which most historians suppose was in the summer of 1186, although the date and cause of death for Geoffrey have never been satisfactorily established to universal agreement.

[8] Ademar, the Viscount of Limoges, and Leopold, the Archduke of Austria, were adversaries of Richard Coueur-de-Lion, but Shakespeare conflates them in one non-historical character and anachronistically repositions them/him in *King John*, giving him/them the name of Lymoges, Duke of Austria.

[9] E. A. J. Honigmann's introductory notes to the Arden edition of *King John* survey several more Shakespearean distortions of the historical record and reference Shakespeare's compression of years into days (xxix-xxxii).

[10] It is unlikely that Edward de Vere, in *King John*, would want to forfeit sympathetic attention to his vicarious plea for recognition by recalling to the Queen's memory – and her adversaries – the English nobility's successful challenge to royal authority in Magna Carta. This omission would seem an especially prudent choice if, as seems clear from the text, Oxford wished to underscore that the Bastard is making a plea for recognition from the posture of a loyal subject and *not* as one challenging royal prerogative – so unlike Oxford's ancestor, Robert de Vere, 3rd Earl of Oxford, who, as one of the powerful magnates of thirteenth-century England and one of the chief architects of Magna Carta, *had* taken up fierce arms against the King and even offered the Crown of England to the French Dauphin (Warren 229; Anderson 39-40).

[11] It is worth pointing out that, at the time of John's reign (1199-1216), no pattern of succession had yet been firmly or uniformly confirmed in England, as the principle of primogeniture that came to govern the English royal succession in the later medieval era had yet to be established in law as the foundation of English practice; indeed, as both Ralph Turner and W. L. Warren note, conventions governing succession varied throughout the territories of the Angevin kings, and while blood relationship to a royal predecessor was necessary for advancing a claim, a candidate for the Crown at the end of the twelfth century needed *less* a lofty place in the royal birth order than the assent of the nobility to secure his investiture as Sovereign (Turner 164; Warren 48-49).

[12] As Kristian Smidt points out, "he has all the most memorable lines . . . , and only Constance approaches his level of poetic utterance"

(78). Julia C. Van de Water is of a similar mind in her assessment of the Bastard: "He is a veritable whirlwind of activity and eloquence . . . So it is no surprise to us to learn that in the ensuing battle it is Faulconbridge . . . alone who upholds the day" (143-44).

[13] In *A Chronicle of the Kings of England from the Time of the Romans' Government unto the Death of King James* (1643), Sir Richard Baker records that John "neither came to the crown by justice, nor held it with any honor, nor left it in peace" (qtd in Barton 50). Derelict in almost all of his royal practice, he made no provision for an heir until the final moments of his life (Appleby 271; Ramsay 501).

[14] John's sexual conduct was not only licentious but villainous. David Hilliam notes, for example, that "John was notoriously lecherous and lost support of many of his barons for raping their wives and daughters. He had at least seven or eight bastards" (215).

[15] As B. Wilkinson has pointed out, Henry III's "abilities were incommensurate with his ambition . . . He stooped to tricks and evasions, and more than once, by his failure to understand the changing world around him, built up an opposition as unanimous and formidable as that of his father's reign" (54).

[16] In a conversation with William Drummond of Hawthornden, Ben Jonson asserted intimate knowledge not only of the Queen's lasciviousness but an account for her lack of children in these trysts with his declaration that Elizabeth "had a membrane on her, which made her incapable of man, though for her delight she tried many" (qtd in Drummond 470).

[17] For more examples of charges made, both foreign and domestic, against the Queen's mythical virginity, see Frederick Chamberlin's *The Private Character of Queen Elizabeth*—especially chapter one, "The Seymour Affair. Scandal at Thirteen," and chapter eight, "The Direct Charges Against Elizabeth."

[18] It is worth reiterating that to the courtly, worldly reader and spectator of Shakespeare, no shame would be imputed to a bastard, per se, for no loss of honor would attend a man or woman of irregular birth. Indeed, as Donald Cory and R. E. L. Masters have pointed out in their compendium of incest literature in the Western tradition, siring a bastard would pale in comparison to other forms of sexual congress that would awaken religious horror in modern puritans, for Cory and Masters note that "among ancient peoples (and some modern ones), incestuous unions were reserved for occasions of sacred significance. On such occasions, incest was not merely tolerated, but might even be obligatory," as when the "incest of the gods would be paralleled by brother-sister marriages to their rulers" (4).

[19] For Shakespeare, the gift of nobility was a sacred dispensation that, when uncorrupted, reflected the divinity of its origin in the character of the recipient. In order to emblemize the contrast between those who had been marked for nurture of the realm and those who betrayed that sacred calling of stewardship for personal interest, Shakespeare gives over many of his plays to telegraph that anxiety to the Crown which, in his day, was in the process, under the Cecils, of commodifying its sacred charge to pursue what Charles Beauclerk has aptly called the "new opportunism" that the theoreticians and practitioners of sacrilege, realpolitik, proto-capitalist exploitation, empire-building and imperial expansion who surrounded the Queen were encouraging Elizabeth to embrace. As the Duke of Albany (and one of Lear's heirs to the Crown) warns: "That nature which contemns its origin / Cannot be bordered certain in itself. / She that herself will sliver and disbranch / From her material sap, perforce must wither, / And come to deadly use" (*King Lear* IV.ii.32-36).

[20] In contrast to such vampiric, opportunistic bloodletting of the realm in *King John* (witness Faulconbridge's florid expressions of grief at the death of Arthur wherein he mourns less the boy's death than the degradation and shame that have overspread a kingdom whose sacred head has conspired to kill its own [IV.iii.139-56]); behold the intensity of Shakespeare's conviction that nobility must strive to preserve its sacred purpose if England is to remain true to itself via Cymbeline, wherein we see that the princes, Guiderius and Arviragus, who have remained pure in their unasked-for exile from the corrupt court, are yet able to "redeem the time" not merely because they are true sons of the King but because the princely charism that inheres in their being is manifest in the unspoiled exercise of their gracious natures: "'Tis wonder / That an invisible instinct should frame them / To royalty unlearn'd, honor untaught" (IV.ii.176-78), Belarius declares. Like Sir Richard Faulconbridge, these boys, each also a worthy heir "lost" to the realm, vividly demonstrate Shakespeare's conviction that right rule, as opposed to misrule, adheres in nobility's original character and, when it is faithful to its purpose, does not degenerate by base subjection to the vile interests of would-be thieves and usurpers of the Crown like Cymbeline's new queen and her vain, arrogant, lust-driven son, Cloten.

[21] Scragg refers to the Bastard in *Troublesome Raigne*, but her description fully applies to the Bastard in *King John* as well.

[22] As Annabel Patterson has written, especially of the need for writers and dramatists of history to escape arrest and prosecution by suppressing the truth, openly lying, or writing – like Shakespeare – with the most circumspect care in the tyranny that was Elizabeth's England under the Cecils,

The importance of implied analogy, of all kinds, but especially between "this time" and episodes from past history, cannot be overstressed . . . . It was for this reason, among others, that the writing of history was specifically included in the province of official censorship by the Bishops Order of 1599. (55)

Works Cited

Anderson, Verily. *The de Veres of Castle Hedingham.* Lavenham: Terence Dalton, 1993.

Appleby, John T. *John, King of England.* New York: Knopf, 1959.

Barton, John. *The Hollow Crown: The Follies, Foibles and Faces of the Kings and Queens of England.* New York: Dial, 1971.

Bate, Jonathan. Commentary on *Richard II* in *Shakespeare Uncovered: The Stories Behind the Bard's Greatest Plays.* Narrated by Sir Derek Jacobi. Blakeway Productions, 2012.

Beauclerk, Charles Francis Topham de Vere. "The Psychology of *King Lear.*" Paper presented at the 9th Annual SASC (Shakespeare Authorship Studies Conference), Concordia University, Portland, Oregon, 9 April 2005.

Benson, Jackson J. "Steinbeck: A Defense of Biographical Criticism." *College Literature* 16 (1989): 107-16.

Bevington, David. Introduction to *The Life and Death of King John* in *The Collected Works of Shakespeare.* Ed. David Bevington. New York: Pearson Education, 2009. 700-02.

Blanpied, John W. *Time and the Artist in Shakespeare's English Histories.* Newark: U of Delaware, 1983.

Bloom, Alan with Harry V. Jaffa. *Shakespeare's Politics.* Chicago: U of Chicago, 1964.

Bloom, Harold. *Shakespeare: The Invention of the Human.* New York: Riverhead, 1998.

Braunmuller, A. R. Introduction. *The Oxford Shakespeare: King John.* Oxford: Oxford UP, 1989. 1-93.

Calderwood, James. "Commodity and Honour in *King John.*" *Shakespeare: The Histories: A Collection of Critical Essays.* Ed. Eugene Waith. Englewood Cliffs, New Jersey: Prentice-Hall, 1965. 95-105.

Campbell, Lily B. *Shakespeare's Histories: Mirrors of Elizabethan Policy.* San Marino: The Huntington Library, 1947.

Canino, Catherine Grace. *Shakespeare and the Nobility: The Negotiation of Lineage.* Cambridge: Cambridge UP, 2007.

Cervantes, Miguel de. *Don Quijote.* Ed. Diana de Armas Wilson. Trans. Burton Raffel. New York: Norton, 1999.

Chamberlin, Frederick. *The Private Character of Queen Elizabeth.* London: John Lane, 1922.

Clare, Janet. *"Art made tongue-tied by authority": Elizabethan and Jacobean Dramatic Censorship.* Manchester: Manchester UP, 1990.

Clayton, Tony. "Coins of England and Great Britain: 'Coins of the UK': 4 – Three Farthings." N.p., n.d., Web. http://www.coins-of-the-uk.co.uk/threq.html>.

Cory, Donald Webster and R. E. L. Masters. Introduction. *Violation of Taboo: Incest in the Great Literature of the Past and Present.* New York: Julian, 1963. 3-20.

Denny, Joanna. *Anne Boleyn: A New Life of England's Tragic Queen.* Cambridge, Massachusetts: Da Capo, 2006.

Drummond, William. "Conversations with William Drummond." *Ben Jonson: The Complete Poems.* Ed. George Parfitt. London: Penguin, 1975. 459-80.

Findlay, Alison. *Illegitimate Power: Bastards in Renaissance Drama.* Manchester: Manchester UP, 1994.

Fumerton, Patricia. " 'Sacred Arts': Elizabethan Miniatures and Sonnets." *Representing the English Renaissance.* Ed. Stephen Greenblatt. Berkeley: U of California, 1988. 93-133.

Gillingham, John. *The Angevin Empire.* London: Arnold, 2001.

Given-Wilson, Chris and Alice Curteis. *The Royal Bastards of Medieval England.* London: Routledge, 1984.

Graff, Gerald. *Beyond the Culture Wars: How Teaching the Conflicts Can Revitalize American Education.* New York: W. W. Norton, 1992.

Haynes, Alan. *Robert Cecil: Earl of Salisbury, 1563-1612: Servant of Two Sovereigns.* London: Peter Owen, 1989.

Hibbard, G. R. *The Making of Shakespeare's Dramatic Poetry.* Toronto: U of Toronto, 1981.

Hilliam, David. *Kings, Queens, Bones and Bastards.* Stroud, Gloucestershire: Sutton, 1998.

Hodgson, Barbara. *The End Crowns All: Closure and Contradiction in Shakespeare's History.* Princeton: Princeton UP, 1991.

Honigmann, E. A. J. Introduction. *King John* (The Arden Edition of the Works of William Shakespeare). London: Methuen, 1954. xi-lxxv.

Kott, Jan. *Shakespeare Our Contemporary.* Trans. Boleshaw Taborski. Garden City, NY: Doubleday, 1964.

Lamb, V. B. *The Betrayal of Richard III.* Stroud, Gloucestershire: Sutton, 1959.

Leicester's Commonwealth (1584). Ed. D.C. Peck. Athens, OH: Ohio UP, 1985.

Levi, Albert William. *Humanism and Politics: Studies in the Relationship of Power and Value in the Western Tradition.* Bloomington, IN: Indiana UP, 1969.

Levin, Carole. *The Heart and Stomach of a King: Elizabeth I and the Politics of Sex and Power.* Philadelphia: U of Pennsylvania, 1994.

Mannheim, Michael. "The Four Voices of the Bastard." *King John: New Perspectives.* Ed. Deborah T. Curren-Aquino. Newark, NJ: U of Delaware, 1989. 126-35.

---. *The Weak King Dilemma in the Shakespeare History Plays.* Syracuse: Syracuse UP, 1973.

Menand, Louis. "Seeing It Now: Walter Cronkite and the Legend of CBS News." *The New Yorker* (July 9 & 16, 2012): 86-94.

Murphy, Beverly A. *Bastard Prince: Henry VIII's Lost Son.* Stroud, Gloucestershire: Sutton, 2002.

O'Toole, Fintan. *Shakespeare is Hard, But So is Life: A Radical Guide to Shakespearean Tragedy.* London: Granta, 2002.

Patterson, Annabel. *Censorship and Interpretation: The Conditions of Writing and Reading in Early Modern England.* Madison: U of Wisconsin, 1984.

Public Record Office. Calendar of State Papers Domestic, Elizabeth I.

Pugliese, Stanislao G. *Bitter Spring: A Life of Ignazio Silone.* New York: Farrar, Straus and Giroux, 2009.

Ramsay, James H. *The Angevin Empire.* London: Swan Sonnenschein & Co., Ltd., 1903.

Reese, M. M. *The Cease of Majesty: A Study of Shakespeare's History Plays.* New York: St. Martin's, 1961.

Ribner, Irving. *The English History Play in the Age of Shakespeare.* New York: Octagon, 1979.

Ridley, Jasper. *Elizabeth I: The Shrewdness of Virtue.* New York: Viking, 1987.

Rowse, A. L. *The Elizabethan Renaissance: The Life of the Society.* London: Macmillan, 1971.

Saccio, Peter. *Shakespeare's English Kings: History, Chronicle and Drama.* Oxford: Oxford UP, 1977.

Sams, Eric. *The Real Shakespeare: Retrieving the Early Years, 1564 – 1594.* New Haven: Yale UP, 1995.

Scott, Harvey. *Shakespeare: Writings of Harvey W. Scott.* Cambridge, MA: The Riverside Press, 1928.

Scragg, Leah. *Shakespeare's Alternative Tales.* Harlow, Essex: Longman, 1996.

Shakespeare, William. *The Life and Death of King John* in *The Riverside Shakespeare.* 2nd ed. Gen Ed. G. Blakemore Evans. Boston: Houghton Mifflin, 1997. 809-40.

Sidney, Phillip. *Sir Phillip Sydney's Defence of Poesy and Observations on Poetry and Eloquence from The Discoveries of Ben Jonson.* London, 1787. 1-81.

Smidt, Kristian. *Unconformities in Shakespeare's History Plays.* Atlantic Highlands, NJ: Humanities Press, 1982.

Spiekerman, Tim. *Shakespeare's Political Realism.* Albany: State University of New York, 2001.

Steevens, George, ed. *Twenty of the Plays of Shakespeare.* 4 vols. London, 1766. I:10.

Tillyard, E. M. W. *Shakespeare's History Plays.* New York: Macmillan, 1946.

Trace, Jacqueline. "Shakespeare's Bastard Faulconbridge: An Early Tudor Hero." *Shakespeare Studies* 13 (1980): 59-69.

Turner, Ralph V. *King John: England's Evil King?* Stroud, Gloucestershire: Tempus, 2005.

Van de Water, J. C. "The Bastard in *King John.*" *Shakespeare Quarterly* 11.2 (Spring 1960): 137-46.

Vere, Edward de. "Oxford's London Letter of April 27, 1576 After Marital Rift." *Shakespeare Revealed in Oxford's Letters.* Ed. William Plumer Fowler. Portsmouth, NH: Peter E. Randall. 248-65.

Warren, W. L. *King John.* Berkeley: U of California, 1961.

Weir, Alison. *Henry VIII: The King and His Court.* New York: Ballantine, 2001.

Whitaker, Virgil K. *Shakespeare's Use of Learning: An Inquiry into the Growth of His Mind and Art.* San Marino: The Huntington Library, 1964.

Wickham, Glynne. *Early English Stages: 1576 – 1660.* 2 vols. New York: Columbia UP, 1963. Vol. II.

Wilkinson, B. *The Later Middle Ages in England: 1216-1485.* New York: David McKay, 1969.

Windham, Donald. *Lost Friendships: A Memoir of Truman Capote, Tennessee Williams, and Others.* New York: William Morrow, 1983.

Chapter 11

Identity Crisis

Charles Beauclerk

*This essay was originally published as Chapter 6 of the author's
2010 book,* Shakespeare's Lost Kingdom. *It is reprinted here
with the permission of the publisher, Grove Atlantic.*

The one word that explains the Shakespeare miracle is
unconsciousness.—Henry David Thoreau.

SHAKESPEARE'S THREEFOLD IMAGINATION

In *Shakespeare Identified*, Thomas Looney gave us a single
believable author, a human Shakespeare. In his hands the
works made sense as the poet's attempt to understand his
experiences by turning them over on the anvil of his imagination.
Looney could be said to have reunited Shakespeare with his
corpus—and thus with the history of his times—or at least to
have begun this heroic task. A vital part of the process is to see the
works as a single story, for despite their apparent diversity, the
tales Shakespeare dramatized have a strong thematic unity, bound
together as they are by the author's inner story. Even the genre
divisions of comedy, tragedy, history, and romance seem false.

Shakespeare's choice of plots for his plays was not arbitrary;
he chose them because they reflected themes that were crucial to

his life. All were taken from classical or medieval sources, which on the political level provided him with a vital tool, deniability. As Clare Asquith writes in her discussion of Shakespeare's sources for *Richard III*, "Like Hamlet who defends his political court play by claiming it is a harmless translation from the Italian, [Shakespeare] can point to an innocent precedent."[1] In other words, offensive material could be laid at the door of the source. Shakespeare did not wake up one morning and decide to write a play about honor because his last one had been about ambition; like all true writers, he wrote to heal the wounds to his soul, to remake the shattered world in which he found himself. Indeed, once one has noted the extraordinarily personal nature of his works, the author's soul journey emerges very clearly, from exuberant Renaissance prince (Berowne) to disillusioned courtier and political dissident (Hamlet) to social outcast (Timon) to visionary philosopher (Prospero). As for Shakespeare's motifs (which are the motive power of his works), they speak volumes about his own predicament: usurpation of royal right; the fall from grace; loss of power; loss of name; exile; disinheritance; banishment; the alienated courtier; the royal bastard; the concealed heir; the court fool who tells his truth in jest; the hidden man revealed; the lost man found; the poet-prince; the philosopher-king.

It is through an author's imagery and themes that one learns how ideas associate themselves in his mind, and gains an insight into the nature of his obsessions. As Caroline Spurgeon writes:

> Like the man who under stress of emotion will show no sign of it in eye or face, but reveal it in some muscular tension, the poet unwittingly lays bare his own innermost likes and dislikes, observations and interests, associations of thought, attitudes of mind and beliefs, in and through the images, the verbal pictures he draws to illuminate something quite different in the speech and thought of his characters.[2]

The key phrase here is "unwittingly lays bare," as the process of making images is largely unconscious, fashioned from the invisible components of the individual imagination, rather like an alphabet arising out of the unconscious of a new race. Some of the elements that go to make up an author's images are conscious, but many are unknown to him—are hidden or repressed—and constitute the material from which the formative myths of his life are woven. In this hinterland of the soul, where images hatch, we are very close to the heartbeat of motivation, of sensing why an author writes as he does.

Spurgeon points out that in drama, as opposed to more formal types of poetry, especially the Elizabethan drama, which was written "red-hot," the images poured forth in a surge of heightened feeling unimpeded by the conscious mind. This seems to have been particularly true in Shakespeare's case. Ben Jonson, for instance, wrote that Shakespeare "had an excellent phantasie, brave notions, and gentle expressions, *wherein he flow'd with that facility, that sometime it was necessary he should be stopp'd."* It is true, too, of all those fabulous talkers he created, including Hamlet, Romeo, Berowne, Benedick, Beatrice, Bottom, Falstaff, Philip the Bastard, Petruchio, Parolles, and Prince Hal.

The imagery and themes in Shakespeare's plays often operate as an undercurrent that goes against the tide of the primary or overt plot (the surface story), forming what might be described as an ulterior plot of their own, which gives depth and complexity to the characters' motives. This ulterior or subconscious plot is highly personal to the author and functions as a parallel drama within the play—a kind of soul drama in which the characters represent warring elements in the poet's being, of which he will be largely unaware. Nor are these characters in the least discreet; instead they resemble the players of whom Hamlet says, "[They] cannot keep counsel: they'll tell all."

In *Hamlet*, for example, the incest theme, of which very little overt mention is made during the play, branches out willy-nilly in Shakespeare's imagination (and far beyond his conscious intention) to penetrate the lives of Hamlet, Gertrude, Ophelia, Laertes, and even Polonius. In *A Midsummer Night's Dream* the royal marriage of Theseus and Hippolyta, together with the happy reconciliation of the four parted lovers, is undermined by a darker story, fraught with menace: the story of Bottom's lost kingdom, Bottom being an impolitic weaver of words, who enchants the fairy queen with his singing (poetry), but whose tongue must be tied in case he blabs. His "most rare" vision, which is beyond the wit of man to relate, is nothing as banal as the dream-like memory of an ass's head; it is the specter of the crown which the fairy queen's love for him seemed to portend. "Methought I was—and methought I had, but man is but a patch'd fool if he will offer to say what methought I had." As Caroline Spurgeon writes:

> It is noticeable how continually [Shakespeare] associates dreaming with kingship and flattery, so much so that one might almost deduce that he had often dreamed he was himself a king of men, surrounded by homage and sweet flattering words, and had awakened to find this but empty and vain imagining.[3]

The power of Shakespeare's ulterior plots bespeaks an intensely subjective art, a sort of literary narcissism, if that's not too strong a word. This subjectivity was noted by T. S. Eliot, who pronounced *Hamlet* an artistic failure on that score. He found that Hamlet's powerful emotions toward his mother, which dominate his actions, are "in excess of the facts [of the play] as they appear." In other words they have no objective foundation in the plot, or, in Eliot's special phrase, no "objective correlative." This is true. What Eliot didn't see, however, is that such excess of emotion is everywhere in Shakespeare and flows out beyond the confines of the plays; this is why his heroes are so disarmingly real and give the impression that they are speaking directly to us, over the heads of the other characters. King Lear's colossal unprovoked fury at Cordelia's honest profession of love has its origin outside the play, as does Timon's loathing of female sexuality: these emotions overwhelm the action, flooding the margins of Shakespeare's text and pulling us into his psychic flow.

Because there is no objective correlative for these overpowering emotions in the characters and plot of a given play, we must look instead to the life of the author himself (to what might be termed the *subjective* correlative). In *Hamlet*, the hero's suicidal despair, yoked as it is to his violent sense of disgust at the Queen, is likely to proceed from Shakespeare's own incestuous or quasi-incestuous relationship with his mother. And if his mother was the Virgin Queen, one can understand why he could not be more explicit (and why there is no objective correlative for Hamlet's horror of female sexuality); it would also explain his displaced rage toward Ophelia. Incest, it seems, is the cause of Hamlet's dissolving sense of identity and his inability to take his father's place on the throne.

The guardedness that Shakespeare necessarily exercised in his dealings with the state activated the unconscious to an extraordinary degree in his literary work, forcing hidden content into the light through the revelations of his characters. This happens most patently when characters are attempting to control their thoughts and hide their true feelings. For it is a truism that the more one tries to curb one's thoughts and speech, the more active the unconscious becomes in introjecting slips of the mind and tongue, which reflect the true feelings of the subject. Good examples in *Hamlet* are the speeches of Claudius in his lengthy conversation with the rebellious Laertes, in which the two plot to kill the prince. In his final speech before Gertrude enters, Claudius unwittingly describes the dynamics of the repressed thought: "If this should fail, / *And that our drift look through our bad performance,* / 'Twere better not essay'd." (Claudius cannot reconcile that he is both king and murderer.)

This same tide of feeling informs Shakespeare's humor, flowing through his works with wonderful indiscretion and filling the characters of his invention, as if the entire canon were one colossal Freudian slip. "Masters," cries Bottom to his fellow players, "I am to discourse wonders: but ask me not what; for if I tell you, I am not true Athenian. I will tell you everything, right as it fell out." Hamlet perhaps comes closest to describing the involuntary creativity of the unconscious mind when he says to Horatio:

And prais'd be rashness for it: let us know
Our indiscretion sometime serves us well
When our deep plots do pall.

(V.ii.7–9)

No character illustrates the power of Shakespeare's indiscretion better than Falstaff, who as king of misrule represents an essential function of Shakespeare's art. His priceless reply to Colevile of the Dale, one of the rebels at York, when Colevile kneels before him with the words "I think you are Sir John Falstaff," gives a perspective rather different from Hamlet's. "I have a whole school of tongues in this belly of mine," exclaims the fat knight, "and not a tongue of them but speaks any other word but my name. And I had but a belly of any indifferency, I were simply the most active fellow in Europe: my womb, my womb, my womb undoes me." This great teeming womb of Falstaff's is, of course, Shakespeare's almost monstrous creativity, which is his undoing both because of its wide-ranging indiscretion and because of its obsession with the author's identity (i.e., speaking his name). No wonder Jonson, in *Cynthia's Revels* (1601), satirized Shakespeare as Amorphus, a man "so made out of the mixture of shreds and forms, that himself is truly deformed."

All of this is to say that the unconscious supports and nurtures Shakespeare's text in a unique manner, which has much to do with the author's anonymity and frail sense of identity. The power of Shakespeare's art lies in its boundlessness; the fact that his characters transcend the roles they play in their allotted dramas, and engage us in the larger drama of the author's identity crisis. In this way, we partake of Shakespeare's mythic field of experience—his unconscious life. Indeed, the unconscious is an excellent metaphor for the concealed poet, because although it lies hidden, it uses its untold ingenuity to "break cover" and make itself known through arresting images and involuntary revelations, constantly balancing a character's assertions with their hidden antitheses. Its goal, as ever, is wholeness. In fact the unconscious *is* a concealed author or, in the words of D. H. Lawrence, a "secret agent," a carrier of ideas disowned by the individual or his society, or both. That Shakespeare himself was a concealed poet goes some way toward explaining why the unconscious mind was so active in his art.

Because the coordinates of Shakespeare's art lie in the unconscious, not in consistency of plot and character, he engages us more profoundly than any other writer. For this reason, too, his work is a gift to actors: their interpretive space is greatly expanded by all that is going on between the lines. The objective correlative in Shakespeare, the consciously contrived plot, takes second place to this vast unconscious intention, which is ultimately the remaking and assertion of the author's identity. It is the ulterior plot that fashions the hidden, poetic crown. As Richard II says, "Now is this golden crown like a deep well / That owes two buckets, filling one another, / The emptier ever dancing in the air, / The other down, unseen, and full of water."

There is another type of plot in Shakespeare's plays, between the primary and ulterior plots, which is an expression of the author's conscious attempt to tell the untold history of his time, and is very much the creation of Shakespeare the satirist, who, in disguising his portraits of court and government figures, carefully calculated how thin a coat of camouflage would protect him from the wrath of his victims. It was like playing a game of verbal cat and mouse. Through it, Shakespeare's verbal ingenuity was refined, making double meanings and hidden messages second nature. Even the names of characters contain clues as to their nonfictional identity. In the first quarto of *Hamlet*, for instance, the Polonius figure is called Corambis, meaning "double-hearted," a clear swipe at Lord Burghley's motto *Cor unum, via una* ("One heart, one way").

What might seem obscure or unmotivated to us may well have made more sense to Shakespeare's court audience and in particular to the queen, for they shared with the author a common field of experience that has been largely lost over time. Certain things did not need to be spelled out, such as private court feuds or who was sleeping with whom. Audiences would have picked up on the innuendo immediately, as when Hamlet holds up the portraits of his father and Claudius and asks Gertrude, "Have you eyes? / Could you on this fair mountain leave to feed / And batten on this moor?" One of Leicester's nicknames at court was "Gypsy," which, like "Moor," connoted dark looks. Equally, Hamlet's curious declaration to Claudius, "I eat the air, promise-crammed. You cannot feed capons so" is a gibe at Sir Christopher Hatton (cap-on = hat-on), one of Elizabeth's most richly rewarded favorites, for whom assurances of favor were never mere "promises."

The semi-royal prominence given to Laertes can seem puzzling to us, but Shakespeare's court audience would have understood the web of contemporary relationships that determined or reshaped those at Elsinore. With Elizabeth as Gertrude and her lover Robert Dudley, Earl of Leicester, as Claudius, it is not hard to see that Laertes, who is treated as a surrogate son by Claudius, stands for Leicester's step-son Robert Devereux, Earl of Essex. This identification makes sense of the mob's otherwise baffling cry of "Laertes shall be king, Laertes king!"—for such was the reaction of the London mob to the dashing Essex, who was rumored to be the bastard son of Elizabeth and Leicester. Claudius's earlier description of the disaffected Laertes, that he "keeps himself in clouds, / And wants not buzzers to infect his ear," is a brilliant evocation of the volatile and suggestible young earl. Finally, when Ophelia gives wildflowers to Laertes with the words, "You must wear your rue with a difference," she is punning on the name Devereux (rue with a difference = divers rue = dever-reux). Of course Laertes can have no possible claim to the throne, being the son of the king's chief minister, but if in Shakespeare's mind he is the Earl of Essex, such an anomaly becomes both natural and topical. Moreover, Shakespeare's own status and aspirations can be understood when one remembers Hamlet's expression of regret that "to Laertes I forgot myself; / For by the image of my cause I see / The portraiture of his."

One soon becomes adept at seeing both the primary and the secondary plots at once, or, in the words of Hermia in *A Midsummer Night's Dream*, seeing "with parted eye."

There are, then, three interlocking plots in any given Shakespeare play. The first or primary plot is the fictional foundation of the play and is determined largely by Shakespeare's sources. They provide him with a basic tale, which then acts as a stalking horse for the real story he wants to tell: the secondary plot. This plot is essentially topical satire based on the author's experiences of court life and could not have been told in an uncamouflaged form without endangering his life. It is in essence the story of his lost identity, with all its political ramifications. The interplay of the primary and secondary plots can lead to anomalies between what a character should plausibly be saying and what the author himself wants to say through that character. Thus, for instance, Hamlet's persistent complaints about his poverty and lack of status (he even goes so far as to refer to himself as a beggar) are contradicted by the facts of the plot; that is, they have no objective correlative. Hamlet is, according to Claudius, "the most immediate to our throne" and "has the voice of the King himself" for his succession in Denmark. There is no suggestion that he is being denied the perks and privileges pertaining to his elevated status. Yet for Shakespeare himself the feeling of dispossession is very strong. In comprehending these "rival" plots, we should bear in mind Puttenham's definition of allegory, from *The Art of English Poesie (1589)*, as those instances when "we speak one thing and think another, and that our words and meanings meet not."

The manner in which Shakespeare alters and modifies his sources is nearly always highly significant and is motivated by the demands of the secondary plot. In *Hamlet*, for instance, the Ghost, Polonius and his family, the play within the play, the prominence of Gertrude, and the death of Hamlet are all examples of material introduced by Shakespeare, and all serve his autobiographical designs.

The third or ulterior plot is the "soul story," a narrative created by the unconscious itself to give voice to the author's hidden interior life or mythic existence. This comprises the material that, according to Eliot, Shakespeare "could not drag to light." A good example is Shakespeare's treatment of Gertrude, or rather her treatment of him, for he evidently finds it difficult to keep her within the confines of the plot. Her general weakness as a character, for instance, is contradicted by the huge archetypal power—the king-killing, identity-annihilating power—with which Hamlet invests her. This is because Shakespeare's concept of Elizabeth has taken precedence over his portrayal of Gertrude, so that the demands of the plot are subjugated to his own psychic needs. The story of England, rather than Denmark, determines the inner logic of the play.

At the base of Shakespeare's portrayal of Gertrude, especially her extraordinary power over Hamlet's imagination, is the displaced theme of incest. When Hamlet confronts his mother in the closet scene, he pleads his dead father's virtues in the comparison of the two lockets (the one depicting old King Hamlet, the other the usurping brother, Claudius). His vehemence is such, however, that one gets the feeling he is pleading *his own* charms—that he is Claudius's competitor, not just for the throne, but for the hand of the queen, his mother. This hint of a sexual relationship between Hamlet and Gertrude is given by Polonius at the very opening of the scene with a series of unintentionally bawdy puns addressed to the Queen:

> A [i.e., Hamlet] will come straight. Look you lay home to him,
> Tell him his pranks have been too broad to bear with
> And that your Grace hath screen'd and stood between
> Much heat and him. I'll silence me even here.
> Pray you be round.
>
> (III.iv.1–5)

It is also made vivid by the explicit language Hamlet uses in describing his mother's licentiousness, both in soliloquy and to her face. The language is simply not consistent with a straightforward mother-son relationship, however strained. It is clear, too, that Hamlet has tormented himself a good deal with fantasies of his mother having sex with Claudius; he even associates the two of them making love with his mother's (imagined) betrayal of him. In this, he comes perilously close to casting himself in the role of jealous lover

"What shall I do?" pleads Gertrude, to which Hamlet replies:

> Not this, by no means, that I bid you do:
> Let the bloat King tempt you again to bed,
> Pinch wanton on your cheek, call you his mouse,
> And let him, for a pair of reechy kisses,
> Or paddling in your neck with his damn'd fingers,
> Make you to ravel all this matter out
> That I essentially am not in madness,
> But mad in craft.
>
> (III.iv.183–190)

The theme of incest emerges in Hamlet's first soliloquy in Act I, scene ii, and though the prince does his best to project his own uncomfortable feelings onto Claudius and Gertrude (who are brother- and sister-in-law), he cannot help expressing a sense of self-disgust so violent that it leads to thoughts of suicide. It is as if he himself has partaken of the incestuous relationship, and his body has been polluted as a result:

> O that this too too sullied flesh would melt,
> Thaw and resolve itself into a dew,
> Or that the Everlasting had not fix'd
> His canon 'gainst self-slaughter. O God! O God!
>
> (I.ii.129–132)

He cannot assuage his feelings by killing Claudius; such a course of action would only make things worse because he would in effect be replacing his stepfather as his mother's consort. *A little more than kin, and less than kind.*

The fact that commentators endlessly discuss Hamlet's motives, and those of Shakespeare's other protagonists, is surely evidence that we are dealing with the author's unconscious mind. This, as Thoreau pointed out, is the "miracle" of Shakespeare. We respond to him on a preconscious level—*between the lines*—almost as if we were co-creators, for the dynamic field in which his unconscious mind intersects with ours is intensely alive, making his work strongly akin to music.

Another wonderful example of the ulterior plot at work is Ophelia's death (half accident, half suicide), reported by Gertrude at the end of Act IV. This is a symbol-picture in little of Shakespeare's own fate. Ophelia is hanging her garlands of wildflowers on a willow when an envious sliver breaks, and she falls into the brook with her "weedy trophies." Taken together, the willow tree, sacred to the moon goddess and her priestesses (the nine Muses); the crown of flowers; the broken bough; the figure poised between land and water, all bespeak a striving toward some otherworldly kingship. It is an energy that Elizabeth and Shakespeare shared: she as a mythical virgin queen, he as a poet-king, both attempting to transcend the horror of their common background. Ultimately, Ophelia weaving her crown of flowers is Shakespeare composing his works in service to the moon goddess, who abandons him to the waters of the unconscious, which bear him up while he sings his songs (writes his poetry) before pulling him down to his death (anonymity). Ophelia's flowers floating on the water are a beautiful image for Shakespeare's poetry welling up from the unconscious, and the phrase "weedy trophies" suggests a laureate's wreath. If we are in any doubt about this fleeting identification of Ophelia with Shakespeare, Claudius's strange comment at the end of the graveyard scene should dispel it: "This grave [i.e., Ophelia's] shall have a living monument." This is the very image that Shakespeare uses in his Sonnets to assure the Fair Youth that he will live forever through the poet's works.

As Thomas Carlyle wrote in "The Hero as Poet" (1841), "There is more in Shakespeare's intellect than we have yet seen. It is what I call an unconscious intellect: there is more virtue in it than he himself is aware of. . . . Shakespeare's art is not artifice; the noblest worth of it is not there by plan or pre-contrivance. It grows up from the deeps of Nature."

More than anything else, perhaps, it is the intense suffering in the plays that goes to the heart of Shakespeare's reality. The deep psychic wounds that his characters bear are like shafts down into the soul of the poet. As no one consciously suffers, the expression of intense suffering in an author—whether Dickens, Dostoyevsky, Byron, or Shakespeare—is peculiarly revealing of the unconscious archetypes that shape the individual's life and thought. The suffering of Edgar in *King Lear* is a vivid case in point. There is no objective basis in the plot for Edgar's terrible suffering, least of all the agony he inflicts upon himself. This is a case of the author's emotional pain overwhelming the outer logic of the text with its own inner rationale. Without conscious intention on Shakespeare's part, it seems, Edgar is transformed from the curled darling of the court to the lacerated figure of Oedipus, the self-pierced pariah, half mad from grief. Yet in this no-man's-land of psychic disintegration a new language and, with it, a new mythology emerge into consciousness.

Tracing the roots of Shakespeare's pain brings us to an understanding of his identity, and his work. And when one realizes that Shakespeare's pain is real, the realization that Shakespeare himself is real cannot be far behind. It is a question of retrieving that vital connection between an author's characters and his soul life.

Just as it is an axiom of psychoanalysis that what we deny in ourselves drives our lives, so with Shakespeare what remains unsaid becomes the motive power of his corpus. Is it surprising that the works of an author who must remain hidden should be dominated by the theme of identity? And this excessive emotion, this field of potential: what is it but the mourning garment of a man who was forced to give up his identity and become nothing? And because Shakespeare's works have a hidden purpose, i.e., to reveal the author's identity and his claim to the throne, all his characters must in a sense *collude* in this undercover operation, helping to bear the burden of his secret. Each character, like its author, possesses a double identity.

Mistaken identity, concealed identity, loss of identity, enforced anonymity—all are crucial Shakespearean themes.

Though Shakespeare explores them to great effect for dramatic purposes, his very real disquiet about his own identity breaks through, often in the figure of the fool, who is beyond name and status, or by means of another outsider, the bastard. Even with a historical figure like Richard II, Shakespeare chooses—without any basis in fact—to present this troubled king as racked by an identity crisis: "I no, no I; for I must nothing be," laments Richard. *I know no I*: even his basic sense of self has dissolved. The emotion, however, is real. "Who is it that can tell me who I am?" cries Lear, whose preceding words—"Ha! waking? 'tis not so"—recall the final line of Sonnet 87, "In sleep a king, but waking no such matter."

Shakespeare's anxiety over his identity is dramatized by means of the fool, the bastard, and the king without a crown. They are the principal vehicles for his exploration of identity, and often merge. For instance, Philip, the royal bastard in *King John*, plays the fool, as do Hamlet, Lear, Edgar, and Richard II, all kings without crowns. Prince Hal, the heir to the throne, covers discretion with a coat of folly. Feste, the fool in *Twelfth Night*, assumes a quasi-royal status by describing himself as the "eldest son" of his mistress, Olivia, and calling her "madonna" to underscore the satire of the Virgin Queen. Another aspect of this same complex theme of the alienated man is the maverick prince or royal scapegrace, who rebels against the restraints of his birth, preferring the downright truths of his social inferiors to the finespun hypocrisy of the court.

The kingly fool finds its highest expression in Hamlet, yet it takes him by surprise, as it were, almost inhabiting him on the sly. When he is in his mother's closet, taking her to task for her promiscuity, he unleashes a volley of insulting remarks about Claudius, calling him "A king of shreds and patches." At that very moment the ghost of his father enters the room. The appearance of the ghost reminds us that Hamlet's princely identity is by now almost illusory, swallowed up as it is by his mother's incest. Thus Hamlet's insult rebounds on himself. He, not Claudius, is the royal fool or "king of shreds and patches," the truth teller believed by none. It is fascinating to note that, according to Charles Arundel, Oxford told "how God was fallen into a strange vein of crowning none but coxcombs [i.e., fools]."

Thersites, the Greek fool in *Troilus and Cressida*, is a bastard and not just any bastard, but the bastard son of "the mortal Venus," Helen of Troy—or so it is hinted. In a remarkable passage toward the end of the play, Thersites is encountered on the battlefield by Margarelon, the bastard son of Priam, who orders him to "turn and fight." When Thersites learns that his adversary is illegitimate, he responds with a mad insistence that recalls Edmund's obsessive repetition of the words "base" and "bastardy" in *King Lear*. "I am a bastard, too" he cries. "I love bastards. I am bastard begot, bastard instructed, bastard in mind, bastard in valour, in everything illegitimate. One bear will not bite another, and wherefore should one bastard? Take heed: the quarrel's most ominous to us—*if the son of a whore fight for a whore, he tempts judgement*. Farewell, bastard." This, I can't help feeling, was Shakespeare's predicament exactly: the son of a whore fighting for a whore. How was he to uphold Elizabeth's honor, and with it England's, if she was no better than a whore? As for bastardy, Shakespeare evinces an uncanny insight into the psychology of the bastard. Harold Bloom, referring to Edmund's dying words "The wheel is come full circle; I am here," writes: " 'I am here' reverberates with the dark undertone that . . . to have have been born a bastard was to start with a death wound."[4]

Identity in Shakespeare is closely linked to the idea of authority or power. The fool, the bastard, and the king without a crown are disempowered figures who have no place in society. On the surface their lack of identity engenders a lack of power, but what they lose in status they gain in self-awareness. Through exclusion and suffering they find a voice, and with it a deeper, more permanent identity. "And I am I, howe'er I was begot," cries Faulconbridge. They are figures who make it their business to speak out against the ills and injustices of society: Thersites, Faulconbridge, and Lear on the heath, all in their different ways, become the conscience of their nation.

They also serve as mouthpieces for the author, suggesting the sort of authority that Shakespeare recovered for himself. That is, the authority he renounced or was denied in the world of government and military affairs he recovered through authorship, and the theater. This became his chosen form of authority. Through it, using the alienated characters of his drama, he challenged the power of the politicians. Let them write the history of the age as they might, he would undermine their chronicles with the deeper truths of his art.

If there is a single leitmotif which directs the Shakespearean music, it is alienation. When Hamlet cries, "The time is out of joint," he is saying that he is out of sync with his age: he feels alienated from the social and political culture. Hamlet, Othello, Macbeth, King Lear, Edgar, Richard II, Richard III, Bertram, Jaques, Feste—all are misfits. Prospero on his island is perhaps the supreme metaphor in Shakespeare for this sense of alienation, which washes through the canon like a great tide of emotion. As Ted Hughes writes:

> Even more ominously than Goethe's Mephistopheles, or the vengeful, pitiless, lonely hatred behind Dante's *Inferno*, Shakespeare's misfit, in its elemental otherness and ferocity, suggests an almost pathological psychic alienation from the culture within which his plays triumphed, a radical estrangement that sits oddly with the traditional idea of the "gentle Shakespeare," the benign senior citizen of an English country town.[5]

SHAKESPEARE'S CORE MYTH

Every writer has a core myth or series of interlinking myths that sustain and nourish his work, even if he is considered a realist or naturalist: such a myth is the heart and destination of his work, the soil from which his images arise. Whatever he writes under the influence of this mythology—whether he knows it or not—becomes, in the words of Ted Hughes, "a subjective event of visionary intensity." The myth is like the author's own peculiar light, and whatever it touches it turns into itself or at least into its own frequency. According to Hughes, Sylvia Plath's work was shaped by a pair of interrelated myths—Phaeton and Icarus—both of which fed into and blossomed out of the early loss of her adored and inaccessible father. In his analysis of two closely allied poems, "Ariel" and "Sheep in Fog," Hughes shows how the Phaeton-Icarus myth, without being specifically mentioned, is at the very heart of Plath's later poetry, determining its catastrophic imagery. "Sheep in Fog," for instance, ends with Plath gazing at the "far fields" which "threaten / To let [her] through to a heaven / Starless and fatherless, a dark water"—like Icarus plunging away from his father toward the sea. As Hughes points out in the case of Plath, artists are hardly ever aware of the "working presence" of the myth while they are writing, even though the "mythic personality" is in control of selecting the imagery and directing the action of the poem or drama. In the end, it is the "blood-jet, autobiographical truth" that allows one to distinguish between a myth used consciously by a realist as literary ornament and "the mythic image as it appears in a truly mythic work." Shakespeare's core myth, which represents his essential autobiography, is so distinctive that it becomes an invaluable tool in determining his identity, especially as he used it for the first work published under his name. Hughes writes:

> Since Shakespeare only ever chose one mythic subject—Venus and Adonis—and since he chose it for his first and (considering *Lucrece* as an automatic sequel) only long poem, one can believe that [it constituted] an obsessive nexus of images to which he was drawn by irresistible fascination.[6]

Venus and Adonis, as Shakespeare tells it, is the tragic story of a beautiful youth who rejects the advances of the goddess and, pursuing his passion for hunting instead, is killed by a boar. In dying, he is transformed by the goddess into a flower.

Shakespeare's most fundamental change to the myth of Venus and Adonis is Adonis's rejection of Venus. In Ovid's *Metamorphoses* (Book X), and in all other variants of the myth, Adonis reciprocates the love of the goddess. Another striking Shakespearean divergence from the classical myth is the difference in age between Venus and the "tender boy" Adonis; in the earlier myths there is nothing to suggest that they are not contemporaries, but in Shakespeare's version Venus is presented as an experienced lover well past her youth.[7]

Indeed, although she boldly informs Adonis that she can still conceive, she is old enough to be his mother, and a good deal of maternal imagery is applied to her, as when she is likened to "a milch doe, whose swelling dugs do ache, / Hasting to feed her fawn, hid in some brake." Her fawn is Adonis, who bears the charge of the poem's son-sun images. Indeed, the very first lines of the poem clothe him in the mantle of the sun, which—like the flower that he becomes at the end of the narrative—is purple (i.e., royal):

> Even as the sun with purple-colour'd face
> Had ta'en his last leave of the weeping morn,
> Rose-cheek'd Adonis hied him to the chase.
> (lines 1–3)

If Adonis is the son of Venus in Shakespeare's personal mythology, then the youth's rejection of the goddess's love, which at times amounts to revulsion, is explained. There is a taboo here, which Adonis does not wish to transgress. After all, under normal circumstances, what young man would not give his right hand to make love to the goddess of love? For her part, although she pursues him as her sexual prey, Venus evinces a mother's concern and indulgence toward the pouting boy, and sees herself in him, his eyes being described as "two glasses where herself herself beheld." Another clue to the blood link between Venus and Adonis lies in the red and white imagery that Shakespeare applies to both characters, red and white being the colors of the Tudor rose. The boar, we are told, did not see—when he pierced Adonis with his tusk—"the beauteous livery that he wore." In other words, Adonis wore beauty's (i.e., Venus's) badge; he was of her house.

Several times during the course of the poem Venus is referred to as "queen," and there is no doubt that readers at court when the poem first came out would have identified the goddess, in her blazon of red and white, with the Tudor queen, Elizabeth.

Nor would they have been insensible to certain well-aimed gibes at the queen's character—for instance, her notorious indecision:

> A thousand spleens bear her a thousand ways,
> She treads the path that she untreads again;
> Her more than haste is mated with delays
> Like the proceedings of a drunken brain,
> Full of respects, yet naught at all respecting,
> In hand with all things, naught at all effecting.
>   (lines 907–912)

This is a very human Venus. Ovid in his account compares her to Diana, the virgin goddess of wild places, for she accompanies Adonis on the hunt, and this echo of Diana remains in Shakespeare's portrait of Venus. Indeed, it could be argued that much of Adonis's shocked revulsion at the goddess's behavior stems from the fact that, being a hunter, he had expected the love and protection of Diana, the patron deity of huntsmen, only to discover that Venus had usurped her place. This "double vision" is brought home to us at the end of the poem when Venus presides over the virgin birth of the purple flower from Adonis's blood, and, with the flower-child between her breasts, flies off to the island of Paphos, where she "means to immure herself and not be seen"—in other words, intends to hide the fact that she has given birth. The idea of the virgin queen giving birth incognito would not have been lost on Shakespeare's court readers, who would have interpreted the poem as the revelation of a dynastic secret. Certainly, when Venus addresses the purple flower, it is in terms of royal legitimacy: "Thou art the next of blood, and 'tis thy right." The curious language of Shakespeare's dedication of the poem to the Earl of Southampton bears out such an interpretation: "But if the first heir of my invention prove deformed, I shall be sorry it had so noble a godfather, and never after ear so barren a land, for fear it yield me still so bad a harvest."

Significantly, the boar also partakes of the red and white imagery, his "frothy mouth bepainted all with red, / Like milk and blood being mingled both together." As a heraldic animal, the boar is doubtless the badge of the author himself, as well as

215

representing the transgressive passion that engenders the tragedy not only of this poem, but of all Shakespeare's subsequent works. He is both totem and taboo. The boar is also a powerful symbol of the mother at her most rapacious (we still use the term "boar mother"): what in psychological terms we might call the "devouring mother." In the context of the poem, it becomes the incestuous mother, intent on ravishing her own child. The poem then becomes a shamanic dream or nightmare initiation, in which the dreamer or hero is transformed by the confrontation with the mother. One could almost rename the poem "The Rape of Adonis." Such a title certainly emphasizes how perfectly it mirrors its companion piece, *The Rape of Lucrece*.

But even before the boar-goddess moves to destroy the youth, her behavior as the lovestruck Venus is puzzling and strongly suggests a contemporary political context for the poem. The statement of her love is so extravagant as to put us on our guard. The lady, it seems, doth protest too much. Could it be a ruse of some sort, a means of accomplishing an ulterior end? From the start, it is clear that the goddess is kissing Adonis to prevent him from talking, fearful no doubt of what he might say:[8]

>   but soon she stops his lips,
> And kissing speaks, with lustful language broken,
> "If thou wilt chide, thy lips shall never open."

And:

> He saith she is immodest, blames her miss;
> What follows more, she murders with a kiss.
>   (lines 46–48, 53–54)

Just as Queen Titania orders her fairies "to tie up my love's tongue" and "bring him silently," so Venus, for some unstated reason, tries to gag her lover. Adonis's "mermaid's voice," which is the voice of the poet, expresses "melodious discord," i.e., harsh truths in sweet poetry. Nor is there any denial of the youth's mortal aim; he clearly has the ability to hit his target. We are reminded of Philip the Bastard in *King John* delivering "sweet, sweet, sweet poison for the age's tooth":

> Once more the ruby-colour'd portal open'd
> Which to his speech did honey passage yield,
> Like a red morn that ever yet betoken'd
> Wrack to the seaman, tempest to the field,
>   Sorrow to shepherds, woe unto the birds,
>   Gusts and foul flaws to herdmen and to herds.
>
> This ill presage advisedly she marketh:
> Even as the wind is hush'd before it raineth,
> Or as the wolf doth grin before he barketh,
> Or as the berry breaks before it staineth,
>   Or like the deadly bullet of a gun,
>   His meaning struck her ere his words begun.
>   (lines 451–462)

The relationship between Hamlet and his mother, Gertrude, who complains that his words "like daggers enter in [her] ears," springs to mind. This "most seeming-virtuous queen," as the Ghost calls her, refuses to face the truth of what she has done. Both Hamlet and Adonis stand for Shakespeare, the truth teller, whose words are his chief weapon. Both relationships share the undercurrent of incest.

The goddess's love, then, is revealed as a means of silencing the outspoken young man. And when he does manage to speak out, it is easy to understand Venus's discomfort, for Adonis accuses the goddess of love of not knowing what love is:

> Call it not love, for love to heaven is fled,
> Since sweating lust on earth usurp'd his name;
> Under whose simple semblance he hath fed
>
> Upon fresh beauty, blotting it with blame;
> Which the hot tyrant stains and soon bereaves,
> As caterpillars do the tender leaves.
>   (lines 793–798)

Thus Venus is using her sexual charms as a political tool, as Queen Elizabeth was notorious for doing. As for her motive for behaving in this manner, she is clearly anxious lest Adonis should reveal some indiscretion that might compromise her authority. If this is Elizabeth we're talking about and Adonis (Shakespeare) is her son, then it may be that she wishes to disguise her true relationship to him by courting him as a lover. After all, it was not politically expedient to have a disaffected royal bastard hovering in the wings. It may be that she held out the possibility of his becoming her consort instead of her son, thus conferring a quasi-royal status upon him through marriage. Either way, she is determined that he will not speak out. In the end, when she realizes that the headstrong youth will not be governed, she murders him in the form of the boar. In a reversal of normal male-female relations, it is Venus who penetrates Adonis (with her boar's tusk), suggesting an original model for Venus, who, although feminine by gender, possesses traditionally masculine attributes of power—for instance, the scepter of the monarch. The result of this piercing is "a purple flower" (or royal child), though in the imagery of the time "flower" also connotes a work of literature, especially poetry; thus this royal child becomes synonymous with the works of Shakespeare himself. In dying as the queen's son, Shakespeare becomes an artist.

The Rape of Lucrece tells the story of the rape and suicide of Lucrece, whose husband, Collatine, boasts of her chastity to his fellow officers while they are encamped near Ardea. Sextus Tarquinius, the king's son, inflamed with lust, leaves the camp and makes his way privately to the house of Lucrece, where, having enjoyed the lavish hospitality of his hostess, he rapes her, and flees into the night. Having summoned her husband and father, Lucrece stabs herself in their presence. The outcry following her death is such that "the Tarquins [are] all exiled, and the state government changed from kings to consuls."

It is, in other words, a poem about the desecration of an idol or divinity, resulting in the death of a virgin and the end of the monarchy. The predatory, sexual aspects of the goddess that were so evident in *Venus* appear at first sight to have been purified and purged in *Lucrece*, but they remain in muted form in the luscious sensual descriptions of the sleeping maid. There are also enough vestigial touches of an older myth for us to realize that Lucrece is the moon goddess, Diana. Her essential royalty or divinity appears in countless expressions and images. Collatine, for instance, boasts of her sovereignty; she is compared to the moon; and Tarquin's intended act is described as "treason."

Nor can it be without significance that Tarquin's lust is yoked with ambition for the throne; the many echoes of *Macbeth* in the poem serve to confirm this reading. As Tarquin gazes at Lucrece's breasts, Shakespeare writes:

> These worlds in Tarquin new ambition bred;
> Who like a foul usurper went about,
> From this fair throne to heave the owner out.
> (lines 411–413)

If we see the shadow of Queen Elizabeth behind the figure of Lucrece, then lust and ambition become inseparable. After all, with the Virgin Queen on the throne, how else could a man become king but through sexual conquest? Rape in this context was tantamount to staging a coup. Moreover, the piercing of the virgin's veil or exposure of the queen as a whore— symbolized by the rape of Lucrece—could lead to the end of Elizabeth's reign, even the end of monarchy itself.

There is a metaphorical rape at work here too, perpetrated by Shakespeare the iconoclast, who violates the queen's semidivine image through his works, puncturing the screen of illusion with the tusk of truth. Nor can Lucrece-Diana be entirely absolved from the sexual act of which she is the apparent victim. The expression of her shame, in contrast to the fugitive description of Tarquin's, rolls out for page after page, often carrying a tone of self-accusation, as if the breach of holy vow has been hers. She also betrays a curious concern—more suited perhaps to the psychology of Queen Elizabeth—with how future generations will regard her:

> Make me not object to the tell-tale day:
> The light will show character'd in my brow

The story of sweet chastity's decay,
The impious breach of holy wedlock vow;
Yea, the illiterate that know not how
To cipher what is writ in learned books,
Will quote my loathsome trespass in my looks.
(lines 806–812)

That Lucrece, like Venus, is intended on the level of political myth to stand for Elizabeth is confirmed by these lines in Henry Chettle's poem "England's Mourning Garment," written on the death of the queen in 1603:

Shepherd, remember our *Elizabeth*,
And sing her Rape, done by that *Tarquin*, Death.

After the rape, Tarquin is described as "a heavy convertite," for, like Actaeon, he has been transformed. He "faintly flies, sweating with guilty fear," like Ovid's Actaeon fleeing the goddess.[9] Nor is he able to utter his shame, skulking off without words. Thus we can understand Tarquin, like Actaeon, as the sacrificed king. It is through him that the kingdom is renewed, like the stag shedding and renewing its antlers.

If, as Ted Hughes suggested, one takes *The Rape of Lucrece* as an "automatic sequel" to *Venus and Adonis*, an interesting transformation occurs. Venus, who at the end of the previous poem flew off to Paphos, where she meant to "immure herself and not be seen," is transformed into the chaste and cloistered Lucrece; and the boar-pierced Adonis becomes "lust-breathed" Tarquin, who in destroying the chastity of "the silver moon," as Shakespeare describes Lucrece—i.e., in *deflowering* the goddess—brings down the monarchy. Thus Adonis becomes both the flower and the serpent under it.[10] The flower that the goddess presses to her bosom is beautiful but deadly, rather like the asp that Cleopatra nurses at her breast. Thus the Shakespearean hero-archetype embodies within himself both the redeemer (Adonis) and the destroyer (Tarquin), though in many plays these are split into two rival characters, such as Hamlet and Claudius or Edgar and Edmund. The heroine, on the other hand, embodies both Lucrece and Venus, the chaste and lustful projections of the great goddess.

The love dance or life-and-death struggle between the goddess and her son-consort, or the poet and his muse, is in essence a struggle for higher consciousness. The poet or divine son, while serving the goddess, attempts to free himself from her relentless and interminable cycle of life and death through transcendence. In poetic terms, this is often seen as an attempt on the goddess's life, a desire to destroy her.

The two poems, taken as one, can be seen as an allegory of Shakespeare's story as an artist. Adonis, symbolized by the sun god Apollo, is Shakespeare the lyric poet, transformed by his rape-death at the hands of the goddess into Tarquin, who, as a god of frenzy, is under the sway of Dionysus, patron deity of the theater, and so represents Shakespeare the dramatist. Shakespeare, it seems, is telling us what it was that transformed him from lyric poet to dramatist, namely the "death" he suffered at the hands of the mortal Venus. As with Hamlet, the theater becomes a means of asserting his royal right in defiance of the goddess. Politics and the removal of his own political status drive Shakespeare into the theater, or rather inspire him to create modern drama.

Through the poems Shakespeare reveals his secret story. "I am the son of the Goddess," he is saying, "and her amorous pursuit of me is at base a political ploy to disguise the fact that she is my mother. Despite her posturing she is not the Virgin Queen. Since our royal son—the purple flower—was born, I have been officially annihilated while she has 'immure[d] herself,' hiding behind the virgin veil of her mythology. This death at her hands has provoked me to challenge her power by means of the theater, the realm of Tarquin-Dionysus, and this in turn has served to confirm my status as royal outcast." The poignancy of his fate as a dissident writer is told in the beautiful thirty-line parable of poor Wat the hare (read "heir") in the middle of *Venus and Adonis*. This is Shakespeare, the royal heir, trying to stay one step ahead of the hunter (censor) by means of his literary skill:

And when thou hast on foot the purblind hare,
Mark the poor wretch, to overshoot his troubles,
How he outruns the wind, and with what care
He cranks and crosses with a thousand doubles;
The many musits through the which he goes
Are like a labyrinth to amaze his foes.

Sometime he runs among a flock of sheep,
To make the cunning hounds mistake their smell;
And sometime where earth-delving conies keep,
To stop the loud pursuers in their yell;
And sometime sorteth with a herd of deer:
Danger deviseth shifts, wit waits on fear.

(lines 679–690)

There is also a sense in which the two long poems can be read as myths of Catholicism and Puritanism, the two forces that pulled upon the conscience of the nation during the Elizabethan age and threatened the stability of the throne. (Eventually, during the Civil War, they would tear the country apart.) Elizabeth herself embodied this religious split in the psyche of Reformation England, the Virgin Queen being her Puritan projection—her Lucrece persona—and Venus, the mother of her people, her Catholic projection. It was this split in both mother and nation that Shakespeare attempted to heal through his art.

The example of William Reynolds, the very first reader on record of *Venus and Adonis*, who bought a copy hot off the presses in 1593, demonstrates that this dual perception of Elizabeth registered strongly in the national psyche. Reynolds not only equated Elizabeth with the Venus of Shakespeare's poem ("You are Venus herself," he wrote directly to the queen), but also was conscious of her projection as an otherworldly, Titania-like creature. As he wrote to the Privy Council in September of that year:

Also within these few days there is another book made of Venus and Adonis wherein the queen represents the person of Venus, which queen is in great love (forsooth) with Adonis, and greatly

222

desires to kiss him, and she woos him most entirely, telling him although she be old, yet she is lusty, fresh and moist, full of love and life . . . and she can trip it as lightly as a fairy nymph upon the sands and her footsteps not seen, and much ado with red and white.

Reynolds lived with his widowed mother in or near the Strand, and other letters he wrote reveal a man suffering from an acute Oedipus complex. Duncan-Jones describes "his intense devotion to her" as "Hamlet-like."[11] All Reynolds's negative thoughts toward his mother are repressed in his ecstatic panegyrics, being reserved instead for the queen, whom he accuses of neglect and wantonness. In other words, Elizabeth seems to fulfill the function of uncaring mother in Reynolds's mental-emotional world. Because he sees himself as Adonis in Shakespeare's poem, it is clear that Reynolds has made an intuitive connection between Venus and Adonis as mother and son. In one of his letters to Elizabeth, Reynolds accuses the queen of leading him on by means of her sexual charms, only to humiliate him, but he will not be cozened, "for I know what I do, and I understand what I write, neither will I be fed any longer with echoes nor appareled with shadows." Far from seeing her as the caring mother of her people, Reynolds paints her as wanton Venus, "trembling in her passion," a sex-crazed queen who will not scruple to hit upon her own son.

It is easy to dismiss Reynolds's rambling letters as the ravings of a madman, but the Privy Council took them sufficiently seriously to call him in for questioning; nor is his characterization of Lord Burghley as the robber of the realm wide of the mark. The importance of Reynolds lies in the fact that his Oedipus complex and frail sense of self—qualities shared by Shakespeare—allowed him to tune in to some of the deeper themes of the poem. Certainly Reynolds's technique, if it can be called that, of splitting his mother into two characters—the chaste, devoted mother living in the Strand, and the devouring, promiscuous mother living in the palace of Whitehall—is a signature of Shakespearean characterization.

The queen's suppression or "murder" of her son stimulated the poetic life of the times, as if she had fertilized the garden of

England's imagination by sacrificing the king. This king-sacrifice was a constant theme or leitmotif in Elizabeth's life and in the Elizabethan subconscious, and this is why we meet it so often in the literature.

The energy of the alienated son that Shakespeare's Adonis-Tarquin embodies is a powerful, if suppressed force, in the politics of the Elizabethan age, and one that has been overshadowed by the traditional historical archetypes of Elizabeth as mistress, Leicester as consort, and Burghley as father of the realm. Like the three Fates passing their one eye between them, these three dominant figures guarded the mysteries of government. There was, however, a powerful rogue energy crouching beneath the table of state like the proverbial tiger (long before the Earl of Essex burst onto the scene in the early 1590s), which manifested itself principally through the arts, in particular the court revels. This "fourth dimension" or son energy had an iconoclastic edge that challenged the political orthodoxy of the age. A kind of fourth estate, bearing heavily on the genesis of the public theater, it became the principal medium for challenging the government. Thus the struggle at the heart of Elizabethan government is realized as one of art versus politics, or truth versus propaganda, the truth being embodied in the figure of the hidden prince, whose task it was to fight the dragon of false rule. The dynamics become visible once we treat the works of Shakespeare as historical chronicles, not just as works of art. The English theater, as we know it today, grew out of the profound sense of alienation felt by the true heir and those who gathered about his standard.

This son energy, repressed on the political level, created severe tensions at the helm of state, for great efforts were required to keep it below decks. It drove the succession crisis, for instance, and intensified the culture of paranoia that had insinuated itself into every nook and cranny of the polity. It was positive, too, suddenly flaming upon the mast of state as a brightly pennoned patriotism. Ultimately, Elizabeth seemed to benefit from it, as she made sure she benefited from everything. Indeed, it is no exaggeration to say that the queen renewed and rejuvenated herself by swallowing this son energy, like some great Babylonian fish goddess swallowing the sun. It fed her cult of ever-youthful virginity, and kept all eyes focused firmly on her as the living goddess. This is beautifully and eerily depicted in the famous "Rainbow" portrait of the queen, painted around 1600 by Isaac Oliver, which puns on sun and son. Though Elizabeth was in her late sixties at the time, the portrait depicts an ageless, highly erotic figure, her gown covered in eyes and ears, and slits that look like mouths. Her left thumb and forefinger are inserted into the folds of the gown; this gesture, together with the large serpent on her left arm, suggests an androgynous and self-sufficing sexuality that can produce offspring without the agency of a male. There is no sun to be seen in the portrait, even symbolically, yet the queen grasps a phallic-looking rainbow in her right hand, above which appears the legend NON SINE SOLE IRIS, "No rainbow without the sun"—in other words, *No reign without the son.*

Endnotes

1 Clare Asquith, *Shadowplay,* Public Affairs, New York, 2005, p. 80.

2 *Shakespeare's Imagery,* Cambridge University Press, Cambridge, 1979, p. 4.

3 *Shakespeare's Imagery,* p. 190.

4 *Shakespeare: The Invention of the Human,* Riverhead, New York, 1998, p. 504.

5 *Shakespeare and the Goddess of Complete Being,* Faber and Faber, London, 1992, p. 504.

6 Ibid., pp. 39-40.

7 Or in the words of Professor Don Cameron Allen, "a forty-year-old countess with a taste for Chapel Royal altos."

8 I am indebted to Dr. Roger Stritmatter for this insight. See his "A Law Case in Verse: *Venus and Adonis* and the Authorship Question," *Tennessee Law Review,* Vol. 72, pp. 307-355.

9 Ovid, *Metamorphoses,* Book III, line 198.

10 Lady Macbeth, it will be remembered, says to her husband "look

like th'innocent flower, / But be the serpent under't." (I.v.65-66).

11 Katherine Duncan-Jones, "Much Ado with Red and White: The Earliest Readers of Shakespeare's *Venus and Adonis*," *RES New Series,* Vol. XLIV, No. 176, 1993, p. 482

Epilogue

Prospero's plea - "Set me free"

William Boyle

The purpose of an epilogue is to serve as further commentary on all that has just gone before. With that in mind, let this epilogue to *A Poet's Rage* then focus on the unifying theme of the book: understanding Shakespeare. And in my own Oxfordian journey towards understanding Shakespeare, there can be no better example than the epilogue of *The Tempest*.

The Tempest has had an interesting history in both Shakespeare studies and Shakespeare authorship studies. In the Oxfordian movement, for example, J. Thomas Looney wrote an epilogue to his own *Shakespeare Identified* in which he set forth his argument that *The Tempest* was not even written by Shakespeare. Within mainstream Shakespeare, studies a number of scholars have written that Shakespeare must have had co-authors, perhaps even First Folio editor Ben Jonson. The one thing that most seem to agree is that Prospero represents the author himself in some sort of farewell to the theater and/or to the world. This in itself is somewhat ironic since so much of the authorship debate is about to what extent the author Shakespeare is—or is not—embodied or represented by characters in his plays.

I must confess that I myself have had mixed feelings about this play for years, and it was certainly not a favorite. But in recent years I have come to a better understanding of it by way of a better understanding of its epilogue. My evolving understanding can be summed up by noting how much similarity there is between the epilogue and Sonnet 120. The importance of Sonnet 120 in the politics of succession/Essex Rebellion version of the Shakespeare story that this collection has focused on is discussed in my contribution to this book (Chapter 7, "Unveiling the Sonnets"). Without this political point of view of the Sonnets in hand it is doubtful that anyone had ever considered the sonnet and epilogue to have anything in common. It is just this sort of synergy between the plays and poems and the author that I believe can only occur when one is engaged in understanding Shakespeare through the authorship debate, and it doesn't happen all at once. It takes years.

It was also around this time, as my appreciation for *The Tempest* was increasing, that a new film adaption of the play came out—Julie Taymor's *The Tempest* (2010), with Helen Mirren playing the lead role as Prospera, a female sorceress. The first time I watched this film, I was particularly interested to see how the epilogue would be presented. So it was quite a shock to get to the end of the film and find it had no epilogue. It ended with Helen Mirren standing on a cliff, arms outstretched to the roiling ocean, speaking words from the last scene in the play. As the credits rolled, and I wondered why in the world Taymor had done this, I suddenly noticed that the words of the epilogue were a voiceover to the credits, being sung by Ariel and not spoken by Prospera.

So, just as I was coming to an understanding of *The Tempest* as a personal anguished statement from the author (similar to the voice of the poet in the Sonnets), I found myself experiencing a mainstream production that stood all this on its head, and not just with the gender swap of female for male, but with the complete discarding of the epilogue as possessed of any significance.

About a year later, the epilogue to *The Tempest* came up again. This time I was watching the PBS six-part series on understanding Shakespeare (*Shakespeare Uncovered*), first broadcast in 2012. The final play in the series was *The Tempest*, and the point of view taken throughout the episode was rather remarkable, at least for this Oxfordian. This was because the play was seen as special because the author himself was personally invested in it as Prospero. Over and over during the 45 minutes, the film returned to the theme that this, in the end, was all about Prospero and his personal stake in everything, and his heartache at retiring. Of course, the film couldn't quite explain who had betrayed him, let alone who he would be taking revenge on (those who had betrayed him?), or why he was a prisoner on an island. But it was all presented as very personal, very heartfelt. In the last 5-minute segment, narrator Trevor Nunn appears and turns to the camera while standing next to a bronze plaque on a huge boulder with the epilogue engraved upon it. He reads the final couplet ("As you from crimes would pardoned be / Let your indulgence set me free") and almost weeps, thus capping the episode's personal theme.

Well, needless to say, I was shocked—again. After 30 years as an Oxfordian fighting all these battles over whether the correct identity of the author matters and over whether the identity—and therefore the actual life lived—of the author has any bearing on understanding his verse, here I found myself looking at almost diametrically opposed interpretations of one play, and at just one passage in that one play. It leads straight to the key question we have been asking throughout this book: Is there a point of view about all this (the authorship) that is correct, or more correct than others? And following from that, is there a way to understand Shakespeare that is directly linked to having some good answers (or at least some reasonable theories) about who he is, how he lived, and what he was up to throughout his life and in his writing?

Well, I must say, yes there is. It goes right to the point Oxfordians have been making for decades, that having the right author in place *does matter*. Without knowing for sure who wrote the works—and within which historical context—interpretation can be little more than guesswork. And this really is the dirty little secret of most mainstream Shakespeare studies: anything can mean anything to anyone, and that's just how most folks like it. Shakespeare can be everyone's happy hunting ground, and who can ever say that any one interpretation is better than another? No one.

Unless, of course, you have in place a real author who led a real life about which enough is known that one can then start working the puzzle, moving pieces of the writing around to see how they align with pieces of an actual life lived (and, yes, filling in gaps with some theorizing). It is, after all, what is done with just about every other author in history. It's about time we did it with Shakespeare, and see what we can learn, or better yet, what we can understand.

I mentioned earlier that my recent fascination with *The Tempest* was centered on the realization that Sonnet 120 and the epilogue, when placed side by side (as they are at the end of this chapter, p. 233), were really the same author (The Poet, Prospero)

Prospero's Epilogue

saying the same thing ("Ransom me," "Set me free"). The moment of the epilogue occurs as if the entire play were a dream that has just ended—a dream of revenge in which everything turned out just fine: enemies punished but not hurt, apologies issued, property restored, even his own angry id (Caliban) taught a lesson, and his artistic spirit (Ariel) set free. And he, more sinned against than sinning, has forgiven everyone. It's all an "all's well that ends well" kind of moment. But then comes the epilogue.

Prospero literally walks out on stage and looks us all in the eye. He has been banished to this island, he reminds us, and *it is up to us* whether he returns to Naples or stays on the island (even though a moment ago we just saw him speaking (in the last lines of Act V) of returning to Naples ... but that was a dream ... it didn't happen). He begs for forgiveness, and ultimately, his own freedom. Take a look at these verses (side by side on the facing page), with key lines and words emphasized, and see what you think. There is something worth knowing here, something which can be understood once one is tuned into the correct author and the correct story.

For Oxfordians who see the authorship mystery as being the result of the author's life-long status as an outcast—i.e., the Prince Tudor theory's man who had to live the lie of his life-long involvement with the "Virgin" Queen Elizabeth and the succession politics of his time—the ending of *The Tempest* makes perfect sense. It is the author's disastrous crash landing and punishment emanating out of the Essex Rebellion, a punishment which has left him a prisoner stranded on an island, consigned to oblivion for eternity unless someone can save him.

And until someone does save him we will all be stuck with the Shakespeare authorship mystery, the notion that the greatest works in Western Literature were written by a man who not only couldn't have written them (for lack of education, access to court, and political protection), but more importantly *had no reason to write them*—a man who suffered nothing and sacrificed nothing. For Oxfordians, on the other hand, Oxford/Shakespeare/Prospero's ultimate fate—his punishment, his banishment—is the essence of the entire authorship mystery, and it is what he is often writing about in many of his late works (*The Tempest, The Sonnets, The Phoenix and Turtle, Hamlet*, etc.). It is probably the most severe punishment meted out to anyone in the entire Elizabethan era.

What Stratfordians cannot see in the ending of *The Tempest* (blinded as they are by the blank Stratford man and the non-story of his life) is that Prospero's plea is aimed straight at *them*, and all he asks for is *their* prayers and indulgence, for *their* mercy, for the chance, finally, to be "set free."

But they're not listening, because they have no idea who Prospero really is, let along what he's really talking about. But we hope that you, our readers, now do know who he is and do understand his situation, and that you will join us in helping to grant Prospero—once and for all and forever—the mercy and freedom and understanding that he craves … and deserves. Lord knows orthodoxy never will.

Sonnet 120

That you were once unkind befriends me now,
And for that sorrow which I then did feel
Needs <u>must I under my transgression bow,</u>
Unless my nerves were brass or hammer'd steel.
For if you were by my unkindness shaken
As I by yours, you've pass'd a hell of time,
And I, a tyrant, have no leisure taken
<u>To weigh how once I suffered in your crime.</u>
O, that our night of woe might have remember'd
My deepest sense, how hard true sorrow hits,
And soon to you, as you to me, then <u>tender'd</u>
The <u>humble salve which wounded bosoms fits</u>!
       But that <u>your trespass now becomes a fee;</u>
       Mine ransoms yours, and yours must <u>ransom me.</u>

Prospero's Epilogue

Now <u>my charms are all o'erthrown,</u>
And what strength I have's mine own,
Which is most faint. <u>Now, 'tis true,</u>
<u>I must be here confined by you,</u>
<u>Or sent to Naples</u>. <u>Let me not,</u>
Since I have my dukedom got
And pardoned the deceiver, <u>dwell</u>
<u>In this bare island by your spell,</u>
But <u>release me</u> from my bands
With the help of your good hands.
Gentle breath of yours my sails
Must fill, or else my project fails,
Which was to please. Now I want
Spirits to enforce, art to enchant,
And <u>my ending is despair,</u>
<u>Unless I be relieved by prayer,</u>
Which pierces so that it assaults
<u>Mercy</u> itself and <u>frees all faults.</u>
<u>As you from crimes would pardoned be,</u>
<u>Let your indulgence set me free.</u>

A Poet's Rage

Appendix A

The Prince Tudor Theory

Some of the following text has drawn upon the Wikipedia entry for "Prince Tudor," since much basic history is recorded there (names, dates, book titles, etc.). Most Baconian material has been omitted, except to note that they too had a theory involving illegitimate children of the Virgin Queen Elizabeth that explained why the Shakespeare authorship mystery had come to exist in the first place.

The simplest explanation of the Oxfordian version of the Prince Tudor theory is that it postulates that, 1) The Virgin Queen did have illegitimate children, 2) that such "bastard" children could be a factor in the succession upon the Queen's death if the powers that be approved and legitimized them, and 3) that Oxford himself (aka Shakespeare) and/or the 3rd Earl of Southampton (the Fair Youth in the Sonnets) were such children, placed in their respective households post-birth, being raised as the natural children of their adoptive parents. The single greatest point of controversy about all this is, of course, is that it takes us from a debate over who was Shakespeare into the question, "What is the truth about the legendary Virgin Queen of England?" and then finally into a much broader, more important question: "What is the truth of history itself? Who writes history?"

First, the key to understanding this controversial theory is to realize that its very existence is part of *a necessary, unavoidable step that eventually must be taken in the Shakespeare authorship debate*. It is a theory of motive, and at some point a theory of motive has to be put forth by anyone engaged in the authorship debate. Such a theory must attempt to explain not just how, but also why, the misattribution of the Shakespeare works to someone who could not possibly have written them came about. And as in any trial that has ever been held, if one doesn't have a theory of motive, one really doesn't have a case. So, if one is going to posit that the greatest works in Western literature were not written by the person put forward by history as the author, then one is obliged, sooner or later, to come up with not just an alternative author, but also with a story as to "what happened, and why?"

At the 1987 Moot Court trial on the Shakespeare authorship question Justice John Paul Stevens nicely summed up this need for a theory of the case that would explain everything:

> I would submit that, if their [Oxfordians'] thesis is sound, . . . one has to assume that the conspiracy—[and] *I would not hesitate to call it a conspiracy*, because there is nothing necessarily invidious about the desire to keep the true authorship secret . . . . [T]he strongest theory of the case requires an assumption, *for some reason we don't understand*, that the Queen and her Prime Minister decided, 'We want this man to be writing under a pseudonym.' . . . Of course *this thesis may be so improbable that it is not worth even thinking about*; but I would think that the Oxfordians really have not yet put together a *concise, coherent theory* that they are prepared to defend in all respects. (qtd in Boyle, "The 1987 Moot Court Trial" 7-8; emphasis added.)

Seeking out this "concise, coherent theory" is very different from the important and necessary work of doing archival research and making the detailed arguments about the basics facts of the authorship case: Shakespeare's education, his sources, his vast reading and knowledge, his unmistakable travels to Italy, etc. All this basic research is the forensic analysis of the historic period and all that happened in it, as best as can be discovered and understood. But if everything was known and in an archive somewhere, there would be no authorship debate. There would be no hint of any sort of hidden story behind the known "official" story.

So it is necessary, in the end, to seek out this hidden story as best we can. And should it be all that surprising that the "theorized" true story behind such a monumental fraud (as the Shakespeare authorship mystery truly is) would turn out to be a cover-up of one of the more incredible official lies/sex scandals in history? After all, that's what the Prince Tudor theory is—a theory that attempts to explain what is going on in Elizabethan England behind closed doors, and postulates —surprise, surprise!—that the big secret behind closed doors is a family sex scandal intertwined with a political scandal, in a society in which political power is based on family—and, in this case, a family which is headed up by a professional virgin. Which leads to this obvious question, here in the early years of the 21st century: "Why is anyone even shocked?"

The Prince TudorTheory – some background

The Prince Tudor theory (which is also known as the Tudor Rose theory, the Tudor Heir theory or the Southampton theory) is a variant of the Oxfordian theory of the Shakespeare authorship, which asserts that Edward de Vere, 17th Earl of Oxford, was the true author of the works published under the name of William Shakespeare. The Prince Tudor variant holds that Oxford and Queen Elizabeth I were lovers and had a child who was raised as Henry Wriothesley, 3rd Earl of Southampton. The theory followed earlier Baconian authorship arguments that Francis Bacon was Shakespeare and was also a son of the queen. A later version of the theory, known as "Prince Tudor II," postulates that Oxford was himself a son of the queen, and thus the father of his own half-brother.

The actual term "Prince Tudor" came from a 1973 book (Margaret Barsi-Greene's *I, Prince Tudor, wrote Shakespeare: an autobiography from his two ciphers in poetry and prose)* which purported to be an autobiography written by Bacon hidden within his other writings. In the 1990s Oxfordian Ron Hess then applied the term to Oxfordians who espoused the Tudor heir theory, and it has since become the name by which most people now refer to and debate the theory.

The simplest way to understand this theory is to see that it is a means by which to try to find what undoubtedly must be a hidden true history of the author known as "Shake-speare" in Elizabethan times. Further, the theory opens the way towards explaining how and why "Shake-speare" came to write his works, and, more to the point, why he wrote them the way he wrote them. For most people involved in the authorship debate there is a consensus that at some point the story of the Shakespeare works goes beyond the source material and into how much the works (especially the poems) are personal statements from the author.

Anyone who studies Shakespeare knows that he suddenly first appears on the scene in 1593, dedicating poems to the 3rd Earl of Southampton. Why? Why did the 17th Earl of Oxford dedicate two narrative poems *Venus and Adonis* (1593) and *Lucrece* (1594) to the 3rd Earl of Southampton under his newly adopted pen name at this time? Attempting to answer that question becomes a key towards understanding aspects of both these poems, and later, aspects of the plays.

Ultimately, however, the most compelling questions that need to be asked (and answered) about Oxford and Southampton surround *Shake-speares Sonnets*, the 154 numbered poems published in 1609. Indeed, it has been said that without the existence of the Sonnets the Prince Tudor theory itself would not exist. For once one accepts the prevailing view that Southampton is the younger man (the Fair Youth) being addressed by the Poet— and that real circumstances in both their lives is what is being discussed—an inevitable next step is to ask "What is their relationship?" And further, "What is being discussed?"

From there one soon arrives at the undeniable fact that royal language is directed towards the youth throughout the entire Sonnet sequence. If the Poet means what he says, then the reality of this language must be taken *not* metaphorically, but, rather, literally. For example, when Oxford writes to Southampton about "your true rights" (Sonnet 17), he uses a phrase similar to those in the Shakespeare history plays in reference to the rights of royalty. Another reference to Southampton as a prince occurs when Oxford addresses him as "my sovereign" (Sonnet 57).

Add to this view about the royal language the fact that there is only one putative Shakespeare who could possibly be old enough

to be Southampton's father—Oxford—and the result is a
"compelling" question about their relationship, neatly summed up
by Charlton Ogburn, Jr., in his 1995 pamphlet *The Man Who Was
Shakespeare*:

> We are left with a compelling question raised by the Sonnets. It is a
> question that is inescapable and one that traditional scholarship is
> resolved upon escaping at all costs .... How is it that the Poet of the
> Sonnets can—as he unmistakably does—address the fair youth as an
> adoring and deeply concerned father would address his son and as a
> subject would his liege-lord? (75)

The simple answer would appear to be that 1) Oxford is
Southampton's father, and 2) somehow a claim to the Crown of
England is involved in their relationship. Finally, in taking a
detailed look at the history of the last half of the 16th century it can
be seen that there are enough historical anomalies that anyone can
then see that a "family" theory about the Oxford-Shakespeare and
Southampton relationship is not all that unreasonable.

The time frame surrounding Southampton's official birth date
in October 1573 reveals that:

- Oxford had reached his majority (age twenty-one) at court
  in April 1571 and had continued in the highest favor of the
  Queen, to the point that in 1573 he was even rumored to
  be her lover. In June of 1574, soon after the date that
  Elizabeth would have given birth to a son by Oxford, he
  abruptly left England without authorization only to be
  brought back three weeks later. Despite his virtually
  treasonous actions, however, he remained in good graces
  with her Majesty.
- Meanwhile, at the Southampton household a boy was born
  on October 6, 1573—a boy who appears to have been
  conceived in adultery, at a time when the second Earl was
  still in the Tower of London under "close confinement."
  He was released at the beginning of May 1573, when his
  wife would have been four months pregnant; but he

remained under close watch of Elizabeth and Burghley, who had this Catholic family at their mercy from then on.

- If the Queen went on to bear a son by Oxford in May or June of 1574, there would have been no better place to eventually place the boy than in the Southampton household, after perhaps eighteen months in the care of a wet nurse. Several histories of the period refer to there being two sons in the household (the elder having died), and that Henry Wriothesley was the "second son."

- Later in the 1570s the Titchfield household of Henry Wriothesley, 2nd Earl of Southampton, erupted in marital turmoil. The earl accused his wife of adultery and banished her from the premises, forbidding her to see the boy. Control over the household was assumed by a mysterious figure, Thomas Dymocke, whom the second Earl prominently rewarded in his will prior to his untimely death at thirty-six in October 1581.

- Soon afterward the boy named Henry Wriothesley, third Earl of Southampton, to whom "Shakespeare" would dedicate his "love ... without end," arrived at Cecil House in London as a royal ward of Elizabeth under the guidance of her chief minister, William Cecil, Lord Burghley.

The Prince Tudor theory has created a deep division among Oxfordians for many years. Many regard it as an impediment to Oxford's recognition as Shakespeare. Prince Tudor theorists, on the other hand, maintain that their theory better explains Oxford's life and the reasons for his writing under a pen name.

To prove or disprove the theory

As the debate over this theory has raged on within the Oxfordian movement, a continuing flashpoint has been over whether the theory has been (or even can be) proved, while on the other hand much effort has been made to "disprove" it, followed by much debate over whether or not it has been "disproven."

Appendix A – The Prince Tudor Theory

It has been noted that J. Thomas Looney himself (founder of the Oxfordian movement with his 1920 book *Shakespeare Identified*) expressed his disapproval of the Prince Tudor theory right at the beginning of its development in the 1930s—in a letter from 1933, wherein he states that his followers Percy Allen and Bernard M. Ward were, "advancing certain views respecting Oxford and Queen Eliz. which appear to me extravagant & improbable, in no way strengthen Oxford's Shakespeare claims, and are likely to bring the whole cause into ridicule."

Just a few years later one of the early issues (April 1939) of the *Shakespeare Fellowship News-letter* in England carried a 29-page Supplement dedicated to a heated exchange on the pros and cons of whether the theory was plausible, whether postulating it in public was a good idea, and whether anyone should ever embrace it. And so the debate about this theory has gone on, decade after decade, right up until today—including the heated exchanges that have taken place among Oxfordians in the last few years over the inclusion of the theory in the 2011 movie *Anonymous*.

There are several things that should be stated right up front in any discussion of this theory. First, it is certainly true that the theory has still not been proven, and further, that maybe it never can be proven, in the strictest sense of the word. On the other hand all the various attempts to disprove it over the decades have really come up short of any real fatal blows. Chapter 2 ("Writing History") in this collection gives a good example of how this battle has been waged over just a few points of contention about what is or is not evidence.

Some other recent examples of these points of contention that have been debated about both key aspects of the theory ("Who are the real parents of Edward de Vere?" and "Who are the real parents of Henry Wriothesley?") include:

> 1548 … Did Elizabeth give birth to any baby in this year? There is actually now some agreement among Oxfordian that Elizabeth most likely did give birth, but the changeling (if it survived) may or may not have been Edward de Vere, placed in the de Vere household in 1550. Even some mainstream historians also agree that Princess

Elizabeth "may have" given birth at this time, but, again, no one has any idea what became of any baby born then.

1565 … When Margery Golding describes Edward de Vere as her "natural child," in a letter to Lord Burghley, is that the end of any possibility that he still might be the lost baby from 1548? This particular phrase, which seems to indicate that Golding is saying clearly that she gave birth to Edward, is the single most potent piece of evidence that, whatever happened to any baby born of Elizabeth in 1548, it cannot be Edward de Vere.

1573 … Who fathered the baby born on October 6th, 1573? There is some remarkable agreement that it is virtually impossible that the 2nd Earl of Southampton could be the real father, since he was in prison without conjugal visits at the time of conception. Who, then, was the father? In any event, since the 2nd Earl couldn't have been the father, this opens the door to the placement of some other baby in that household. It would also show that the letter written then (by the 2nd Earl), which would seem to imply that he is the father ("My wife was delivered of a goodly boy"), is open to interpretation. If the 2nd Earl could not be the father (given the fact of his imprisonment), that would explain the strange, distant tone of the letter which seems to fall short of enthusiasm over the birth of his son and heir. And as a final note, if this October 6th letter cannot be trusted as good evidence of who actually fathered the 3rd Earl, what does that say about Margery Golding's 1565 letter to Lord Burghley (above) and its words "natural child?"

The most accurate thing that may be said about the various attempts to strike a fatal blow against this theory is that they emanate more from "disapproval" of what the theory says about the Virgin Queen of England than about any actual "disproving" by way of the available evidence. And as this present volume attempts to demonstrate, in the end the explanatory power of this theory cannot be lightly dismissed.

History of the theory

Prince Tudor Part I
Southampton as an illegitimate child of the Queen

Early proponents (1930s-1940s)

During the first twenty years of the Oxfordian movement the Prince Tudor theory (then called the Southampton theory) was mainly advanced by Percy Allen and B. M. Ward in the 1930s. Ward did not develop the argument in his biography of Oxford, or in other published works; Allen, however, did. He published his initial views on Oxford and Shakespeare in 1932, developing the theory further in his 1934 book *Anne Cecil, Elizabeth & Oxford*.

Allen's theory was not well received by many Oxfordians, including Sigmund Freud, a supporter of Looney, who wrote to Allen to express his disapproval. Oxfordian Louis P. Bénézet pursued a version in 1937 that proposed Oxford as father of the younger man of the Sonnets, who was not Southampton, and excluded the queen as mother. As time went on, however, the Prince Tudor theory – based on the public dedications and the private sonnets – became solidified in its view that Southampton was the unacknowledged son of Oxford and Elizabeth.

Later proponents (1950s-1980s)

The theory was developed further by Dorothy and Charlton Ogburn in their biography of Edward De Vere, 17th Earl of Oxford, *This Star of England* (1952). They also adopted the view that Southampton was the hidden child of the queen and Oxford. They cited evidence from Shakespeare's plays and poetry that Oxford had drawn from his own life experiences to create the characters and events in the works attributed to "William Shakespeare."

The senior Ogburns proposed that after his concealed birth, Southampton was raised by parental surrogates. They asserted that the narrative poem *Venus and Adonis*, dedicated to Southampton, described the circumstances of his conception in the affair between Oxford (Adonis) and the queen (Venus). Southampton was also the "Fair Youth" of the Sonnets, of which the first seventeen (often called the "procreation sonnets") were written by Oxford to his natural (and royal) son, urging him to marry and produce an heir to continue his Tudor Rose bloodline. ("From fairest creatures we desire increase,/ That thereby beauty's *Rose* might never die" – Sonnet 1) Like Allen before them, the Ogburns rejected the supposition that the poet and the Fair Youth were homosexual lovers, stressing instead the fatherly tone of the sonnets addressing the younger man. *This Star of England* caused much controversy within the Oxfordian movement for decades, most especially because of this full-throated embrace and exposition of the Prince Tudor theory.

In 1984 the Ogburns' son, Charlton Ogburn, Jr. published the book that reignited the authorship debate, *The Mysterious William Shakespeare*. Ogburn was careful to steer clear of the Prince Tudor theory, except to mention its existence and that he took no position on it. Oxfordians at the time understood that this was a tactical decision to not let the controversy over his parents' book get in the way of explaining why the Stratford man could not be Shakespeare, and why Edward de Vere, 17th Earl of Oxford, most likely was. Given the explosion of new interest about Edward de Vere that Ogburn's book caused, this tactical decision can be seen in hindsight as a good one.

Current proponents (1990s to date)

The Prince Tudor theory was further expanded by Elisabeth Sears' *Shakespeare and the Tudor Rose* (1990, 2002) and Hank Whittemore's *The Monument* (2005). Sears explores how Elizabeth might have concealed one or more pregnancies, but decided to remain unmarried for political reasons. Whittemore believes the sonnets emphasize the royal blood of Henry Wriothesley, who was convicted of treason for participation in the

244

Essex Rebellion of 1601, but who otherwise might have been named as successor to his mother, Queen Elizabeth. This resurgence of interest in the theory speaks to the inevitability of one segment of the Oxfordian movement taking the final step towards a theory of motive.

The other interesting development during the 1990s was the entrance of Joseph Sobran into the authorship fray with his 1997 book *Alias Shakespeare*, which set forth the homosexual theory as being the underlying cause of how and why Oxford became Shakespeare, and also being the deep hidden secret that was being covered up. At the 1996 Shakespeare Oxford Society conference Sobran was on a panel with Oxfordians and Prince Tudor theory advocates Elisabeth Sears, Charles Boyle, and Roger Stritmatter to present his case for his take on the Sonnets and the homosexual theory. At the end of this panel a letter was read from Charlton Ogburn, Jr., in which he stated forthrightly that he was in favor of the Prince Tudor theory as the key explanation about the authorship mystery as a cover-up, and he rejected the homosexual theory.

Prince Tudor - Part II
Oxford as an illegitimate child of the Queen

A variation of the theory, known as Prince Tudor Theory Part II, advances the belief that Oxford was the son of Queen Elizabeth, born by November 1548 at Cheshunt, England. This theory asserts that Princess Elizabeth, then fourteen or fifteen years old, had a child by Admiral Thomas Seymour, a brother of the late Queen Jane, who had married Henry VIII's widow Catherine Parr; and that the child of this affair was secretly placed in the home of John de Vere, sixteenth Earl of Oxford, and raised as Edward de Vere, the future seventeenth Earl.

The known events of 1548 are reported in Chamberlains' *The Private Life and Character of Queen Elizabeth*, drawn from the surviving letters and interrogatories, and have been part of many histories of the period. A number of historians agree that, in all likelihood, a child was born to the teenage princess that year; what became of that child is another question.

The key argument about Oxford as the son of Elizabeth was first put forward in what is called the Freeman Manuscript, written by Walter Freeman and preserved within the archives of Farleigh Dickinson University in New Jersey. In 1990 the President of Fairleigh Dickinson at that time, Dr. Peter Sammartino, published a book (*The Man Who Was William Shakespeare*) on Oxford as Shakespeare in which he dedicated a whole section to Freeman's idea that Oxford was the hidden son of the queen. Later in the 1990s this hypothesis was pursued by Oxfordians Sandy Hochberg, Charles Boyle and Hank Whittemore (among others). It was often brought up and discussed privately throughout the 1990s, but was also discussed publicly at the 1996 Shakespeare Oxford Society conference by Charles Boyle during a panel discussion about the Prince Tudor theory. It was also mentioned in some publications from time to time.

Beginning in 1999, however, as Whittemore's breakthrough theory on the Sonnets was publicized in newsletters and discussed at conferences, the Prince Tudor Theory Part II became an open topic; and in the summer of 2000, when Whittemore was only a year into his six-year labors on the manuscript of *The Monument*, he posted a series of "chapters" on Oxford as the son of Elizabeth on the private online group known as Phaeton, supervised by Oxfordian researcher Nina Green, a fierce opponent of both Prince Tudor theories.

Author Paul Streitz, a subscriber to Phaeton during the Prince Tudor II discussions in the late 1990s and during 2000, published these ideas in his own 2001 book (*Oxford: Son of Queen Elizabeth I*); and now that the "Oxford as son" theory had been published, with increasing numbers of Oxfordians and others becoming aware of it, more controversy followed.

[This aspect of the Prince Tudor Theory is still not widely accepted among Oxfordians; most believe that the established date of birth for Oxford (April 12, 1550) is accurate. Thus Elizabeth (born September 7, 1533) would have been seventeen years older than Oxford.]

In 2010 Charles Beauclerk expanded on the implications of Oxford as the son of the Queen in his own book, *Shakespeare's Lost Kingdom*, a detailed examination of the entire Shakespeare Canon and the Shakespeare phenomenon which postulates that the deep psychology of the Shakespeare works is intimately bound up in Oxford's relationship with Queen Elizabeth. Without that relationship, Beauclerk effectively demonstrates, there would probably be no Shakespeare as we know him today. One of the chapters from this book ("Identity Crisis") is included in this collection (as Chapter 11).

Dramatization of the theory

The Prince Tudor II scenario also constituted part of the plot of the feature film *Anonymous* (2011), written by John Orloff, and was part of the controversy surrounding the film.

Following the basic scenario that had been laid out by Sears and Whittemore in their books on this subject, the film dramatizes the events leading to the Essex Rebellion aimed at removing Secretary Robert Cecil from his enormous power and hold over Queen Elizabeth. Against this background, flashbacks identify earlier episodes in de Vere's life. His literary genius is revealed in plays written for performance at court, but, seeing the power of popular theatre, he decides to make his earlier-written plays available for the public stage. Oxford is shown in the film using a front man, William Shakspere of Stratford, an actor – although Oxfordians are still far from consensus on whether the Stratford man acted as a front man during Oxford's own lifetime.

In the film, Oxford had been a lover of the queen and had fathered Southampton, who later becomes an ally of Essex. The latter's "rebellion" is an attempt to overthrow Oxford's longtime enemy, the hunchbacked Robert Cecil, not an attack on the queen. Oxford hopes to support Essex and Southampton by using his play *Richard III* to whip up anti-Cecil feeling (rather than *Richard II*, the play that was actually performed before the abortive rebellion).

He is outmaneuvered when Cecil discovers his plans; then the Secretary tells Oxford that the earl himself is a son of the queen. Essex and Southampton having been arrested and condemned, a devastated Oxford agrees to Elizabeth's demand that he remain anonymous as part of a bargain for saving their son from execution as a traitor.

In the DVD commentary on the film, Orloff reveals that he was unhappy with the scene in which Cecil asserts that Oxford is the queen's son. He had asked the director Roland Emmerich to remove it, but Emmerich insisted on retaining it.

Conclusion

The Prince Tudor theories open new windows on all the Shakespearean works—the poems, plays and sonnets. One immediate view is that Edward de Vere is always writing about Queen Elizabeth and the central issues of power and politics confronting her long, turbulent, fantastical reign, not the least of them being the succession to her on the throne. Suddenly this extraordinary monarch can be seen within an array of sharply drawn, memorable female characters—from Titania, Queen of the Fairies to Cleopatra, Queen of Egypt; from Olivia to Gertrude, from Rosalind to Silvia to Portia and Cressida; from Venus and Lucrece and even to the British kings Cymbeline and Richard II; and, too, in the most emotionally intimate way, the Dark Lady of the Sonnets.

But all immediate glimpses out of this newly opened window on the works will amount to just the start of the great Shakespearean revolution to come—the overturning of a pervasive false view of literature and history, along with its replacement by the truth. This shocking change will amount to the discovery of yet another New World, a mysterious landscape whose depth and breadth will be explored for the first time in more than four hundred years, drawing millions of pioneers in many fields through all the centuries ahead.

Let the revolution begin.

Works cited.

Allen, Percy. *The Life Story of Edward De Vere as "William Shakespeare".* London: Cecil Palmer, 1932.

Allen, Percy. *Anne Cecil, Elizabeth & Oxford.* New York: Archer, 1934.

Beauclerk, Charles. *Shakespeare's Lost Kingdom.* New York: Grove Atlantic, 2010.

Barsi-Greene, Margaret. *I, Prince Tudor, wrote Shakespeare.* Branden Books, 1973.

Emmerich, Roland et al. *Anonymous.* DVD, Sony Pictures Home Entertainment, 2012.

Looney, J. Thomas. *"Shakespeare" Identified as Edward de Vere, the 17th Earl of Oxford.* London: Cecil Palmer, 1920.

Ogburn, Dorothy and Charlton. *This Star of England.* New York: Coward-McCann, 1952.

Ogburn, Charlon Jr. *The Mysterious William Shakespeare.* McLean (VA): EPM Publications, 1984.

Paul, Christopher. "A new letter by J. T. Looney brought to light," *Shakespeare Oxford Newsletter*, vol. 43, no. 3.

Sammartino, Peter. *The Man Who Was William Shakespeare.* New York: Cornwall Books, 1990.

Sears, Elisabeth. *Shakespeare and the Tudor Rose.* Marshfield Hills (MA): Meadow Geese Press, 1990 & 2002.

Shapiro, James, *Contested Will: Who Wrote Shakespeare.* New York: Simon & Schuster, 2010.

Streitz, Paul. *Oxford: Son of Queen Elizabeth I.* Darien (CT): Oxford Institute Press, 2001.

Ward, B.M. *The Seventeenth Earl of Oxford, 1550–1604.* London: John Murray, 1928.

Whittemore, Hank. *The Monument.* Marshfield Hills (MA), Meadow Geese Press , 2005.

Appendix B

The Monument

In *The Monument* (2005), author-researcher Hank Whittemore sets forth his comprehensive theory to explain SHAKE-SPEARES SONNETS, the one hundred and fifty-four consecutively numbered poems printed in 1609. The Monument Theory holds that the Sonnets were written by Edward de Vere, 17th Earl of Oxford, to preserve for posterity "the living record" of Henry Wriothesley, 3rd Earl of Southampton, as his son by Queen Elizabeth and her rightful heir as King Henry IX of England.

Historical Context

In the broadest sense the theory represents a genuine breakthrough in the study of the Sonnets since, for the first time, it combines all the key elements that had been missing in previous attempts to decipher these seemingly enigmatic verses. The single greatest insight that Whittemore had was in seeing that the vast majority of the verses were triggered by the Essex Rebellion and its aftermath—specifically, the arrest and trial of both Essex and Southampton, the death sentences for both upon their conviction for treason, and the fact that while Essex was immediately executed, Southampton (the Fair Youth of the Sonnets) *was not*. Those triggering events thus date the composition of most of the Sonnets to the early 17th century, not the late 16th.

As Whittemore himself describes this insight in Chapter 5 of this book, he began by,

> …hypothesizing that the fair youth sonnets are in fact chronologically arranged from Sonnet 1 to Sonnet 126; and that they lead up to, and away from, Sonnet 107, when Southampton is released from the Tower in April 1603 after being "supposed as

forfeit to a confined doom."

That so-called "dating" sonnet (referring to its obvious allusions to topical events in the spring of 1603) involves not only the liberation of Southampton, but also the death of Elizabeth, the succession of James and the fall of the Tudor dynasty. If the other sonnets have no relationship to that enormously serious, political subject matter, then Sonnet 107 would be one huge anomaly within the series.

A simple question therefore became obvious. Given that Shakespeare is a masterful storyteller, and given that the high point of this story is Southampton getting *out of* the Tower, it stands to reason that he must have marked the time when Southampton went *into* the Tower. Otherwise there is no story at all, no suspense, and his liberation comes out of the blue, apropos of nothing.

Moving downward along the consecutively numbered verses from the high point of Sonnet 107, and following the allusions to legal matters and imprisonment as well as the dark language of suffering, I landed back at Sonnet 27 as marking that time on the night of February 8, 1601 when Southampton had entered the Tower expecting execution—when the author envisions him as *"a Jewel hung in ghastly night."* Then, moving forward or upward toward Sonnet 107 again, I tracked sonnets reflecting those crucial days after the failed Essex rebellion until the moment of Southampton's reprieve from execution in March 1601. And in that context it became clear that Oxford had made a deal with Robert Cecil to save the younger earl, a secret agreement that required complete severance of the relationship between himself and Southampton, which he recorded for posterity…:

From this followed numerous other insights that clarified more and more things about the Sonnets, and reinforced the idea that this was indeed the solution to the Sonnet mystery—for example, the realization that the abundance of legal language throughout the verses were references to *actual legal proceedings* (the trial, the death sentence, the reprieve for Southampton, and the aftermath of the whole affair) rather than legal metaphors for a love affair.

This realization then served to reinforce already existing ideas that the Poet—in addressing his beloved Fair Youth in language that expressed deep love for him and yet was also filled with allusions to royalty and royal status—must also be talking about something real. If the legal language was anchored in reality, and if the love and despair could be seen in the light of a real death sentence handed down to a loved one, then suddenly this royal language could also be seen as real, with the Poet indeed addressing someone who merited being called "my sovereign" (as in Sonnet 57).

Finally then, Whittemore realized that the Sonnets were—in fact must be—in authorial order, and therefore must have some sort of overall structure. From these insights he then got into the heart of the theory, which is that the entire Sonnet sequence is Oxford's "monument" of verse to the Fair Youth (as he says in Sonnets 81 and 107). The key to the structure is that the middle of the entire sequence comprises a "century" of one hundred numbered poems (a sequence of one hundred verses has ample precedent in sonnet collections of the 16th century). This centerpiece begins with Sonnet 27 on the night of 8 February 1601, when Southampton was arrested as a traitor deserving execution for co-leading the failed Essex rebellion; the sequence concludes with Sonnet 126, immediately following the funeral of Elizabeth on 28 April 1603, when her Tudor dynasty officially ended without her naming a successor.

The Monument Theory holds that Oxford is writing to and about Southampton as a father to his son who is also an unacknowledged royal prince. The "century" of Sonnets opens when Southampton has lost any realistic hope of gaining the crown; Oxford is recording his desperate attempt to save Henry Wriothesley's life and gain the promise of his ultimate release. To that end he enters into a bargain with the powerful Secretary Robert Cecil, agreeing to sever all ties to his royal son—who must never claim the throne—and to work behind the scenes helping Cecil engineer the succession of James VI of Scotland as King James I of England.

The Structure

The century of verse is divided into eighty sonnets (27-106) covering Southampton's prison years and twenty sonnets (107-126) from his liberation on 10 April 1603 to the envoy after Elizabeth's funeral. This design follows the exact same "eighty-twenty" structure found within Thomas Watson's sequence of one hundred consecutively numbered sonnets, entitled *Hekatompathia, or the Passionate Century of Love* (1582), which Watson dedicated to Oxford, his guide and patron.

Oxford's own "passionate century" of Shakespearean sonnets for Southampton contains ten "chapters" of ten sonnets apiece. In one chapter (Sonnets 77-86), traditionally known as the rival poet series, Oxford explains how he, "once gone, to all the world must die." That is, he must disappear behind the mask of "Shake-speare," the public pen name and persona that he adopted to support Southampton. Now that pseudonym has been turned against him to become, in effect, his rival. This ten-sonnet sequence amounts to Oxford's direct testimony that he was, in fact, the great author; and it adds further evidence that, according to the infamous deal with Cecil, his "name" would have to "be buried where my body is." (See Chapter 5)

The Monument theory views the century of Sonnets 27-126 as the *raison d'etre* for the entire sequence as published in 1609; and this crucial series of one hundred sonnets is positioned in between two equal sequences of twenty-six sonnets apiece. The opening sequence (Sonnets 1-26) numerically represents the first twenty-six years of Southampton's life until 1600, the year preceding his imprisonment. The sequence that follows the 100-verse centerpiece (Sonnets 127-152), traditionally known as the dark lady series, is actually written to Elizabeth during Southampton's confinement in the Tower until her Majesty's death in March 1603—a sustained outcry of emotional pain and fury over the queen's refusal to help their son and, finally, over her failure to name him (or anyone else) to succeed her. In Sonnet 152 at the end of this series, Oxford accuses Elizabeth of breaking "two oaths"—one to him, the other to their royal son.

The final pair of verses (Sonnets 153-154) comprises an epilogue that is actually the prologue. In these sonnets Oxford recalls the first and only royal visit to the City of Bath in western England, when Oxford accompanied Elizabeth and the court in August 1574—three or four months after she would have given birth to their son. Oxford calls him "Cupid" and "the boy" and "the little Love-God" who, upon his birth, was "sleeping by a Virgin hand disarmed" or cast aside by the so-called Virgin Queen.

The Double Image

The Monument presents a line-by-line analysis to show how Oxford uses words simultaneously producing two separate contexts—one fictional, the other nonfictional. The word "beauty," for example, refers to the quality that appears in the eye of the beholder; simultaneously, however, it also refers to Queen Elizabeth herself. By way of another example, all the legal words within the fictional context appear to be metaphors; but within the nonfictional context, the same words become specific and exact terminology of the law.

YOUNG WOMAN OR OLD LADY?

The double-image language is similar to a double-image picture, wherein every line is drawn in service of both images at once, such as the familiar line drawing that can be seen as either a young woman or an old lady. The picture itself never changes; whether we see one image or the other (or both at once) depends upon our own perception. Oxford describes this method at the center of the century, within No. 76, explaining that he uses "every word" (instead of every line) to create his own double image. By writing always about "all one, ever the same" (identifying Southampton and Elizabeth by their mottos), and restricting himself to them as his topic, he is then able to keep "dressing old words new" (exchanging one word for another to mean the same thing) to create an appearance of variety.

The two different narratives running in parallel have resulted in more than 400 years of confusion about the Shakespearean sonnets. Are they telling an imaginary tale or a true story? Is the author recording a romantic triangle? Or is it a poetical diary of personal and political matters of the most sensitive and volatile kind? The answer, according to the Monument Theory, is that Edward de Vere wove both images to preserve the dangerous secret history of England during his time, not to mention his authorship of the magnificent Shakespeare works, which the world otherwise would have never learned about.

Conclusion

Ultimately the Monument Theory describes and demonstrates the poetical sequence of the Sonnets as Oxford-Shakespeare's greatest single masterwork. This is Edward de Vere's *magnum opus*, which he initially wrote in the heat of the moment before carefully arranging and constructing its parts according to a deliberate design, producing a monument of verse with its virtually miraculous blend of complexity and elegance.

"And thou in this shalt find thy monument," he tells Southampton at the conclusion of Sonnet 107, marking his royal son's liberation from the Tower on April 10, 1603, "when tyrants' crests and tombs of brass are spent."

Following Sonnet 107 come nineteen sonnets corresponding with the nineteen days to the funeral procession for Elizabeth on April 28, 1603, the official end of the Tudor dynasty, marked by

Sonnet 125—followed by the farewell envoy from father to son, from an anguished and defiant father now crying to his boy of love, to his son of royal blood, in words and lines whose depths and meanings can begin to be fathomed only now:

126

O Thou my lovely Boy who in thy power
Dost hold time's fickle glass, his sickle hour:
Who hast by waning grown, and therein show'st
Thy lovers withering, as thy sweet self grow'st:
If Nature (sovereign mistress over wrack)
As thou goest onwards still will pluck thee back,
She keeps thee to this purpose, that her skill
May time disgrace and wretched minute kill.
Yet fear her O thou minion of her pleasure!
She may detain, but not still keep her treasure.
Her Audit (though delayed) answered must be,
And her Quietus is to render thee.
( )
( )

Here is surely one of Oxford's "great bases for eternity" to which he refers in the previous sonnet; and surely here is the base of his story, as if fulfilling Hamlet's dying plea to Horatio to "tell my story," with the final lines addressed to Southampton containing two empty parentheses—as if to say, again with the prince, "The rest is silence."